AS OTHERS SEE US

A STUDY OF PROGRESS IN THE UNITED STATES

BY

JOHN GRAHAM BROOKS

AUTHOR OF "THE SOCIAL UNREST"

New York

THE MACMILLAN COMPANY

1908

Norwood Press
J. S. Cushing Co. — Berwick & Smith Co.
Norwood, Mass., U.S.A.

DEDICATED

TO THE

RIGHT HON. JAMES BRYCE

CONTENTS

LIST OF ILLUSTRATIONS

AS OTHERS SEE US: A STUDY OF PROGRESS

CHAPTER I

THE PROBLEM OPENED

IT was an accident, but I shall always think of it as a happy one. In 1893, just starting upon a long lecture tour through the Middle West, I fell upon three volumes of Criticisms on our American Life and Institutions, "Travels in North America." They were written in 1827–1828 by a distinguished naval officer, Captain Basil Hall. They were in their time a classic in this literature of foreign observation. The mother of our veteran man of letters, T. W. Higginson, left an account of this traveller, who was introduced to her home by the historian Jared Sparks.

Later we hear that "everybody" is reading Captain Hall's book, losing their temper and wondering how he could accept so much hospitality and then go home to write three volumes of "abuse, stupidities, and slanders." I cannot imagine an American to-day reading those books with one flutter of fretful emotion. He was "honest as a Saxon"

and extremely painstaking. With hardy conscientiousness, he travelled several thousand miles, really
seeing most phases of life then observable in the
United States.

Quite two generations had passed between the
publication and my reading of these books. As the
author's letters of introduction opened all doors to
him, he saw much of what was best in the home
life of those days. An inveterate note-taker, he
made records of his observations upon our institutions, religion, manners, habits, politics, business,
and modes of life. Like most of the earlier English
visitors, he brought with him his own national
standard of well-doing, and to this test of propriety
he submitted every unhappy variation in our American behavior. By so far as it was not English, by
so far was it an object for correction and disapproval.
He visited Congress, where he was surprised and
offended because objectionable orators were not
forthwith coughed or groaned into silence, as was
the effective custom in the House of Commons.

He says: —

"I was much struck with one peculiarity in these debates,
— the absence of all cheering, coughing, or other methods
by which, in England, public bodies take the liberty of com-
municating to the person who is speaking a full knowledge
of the impression made upon the audience. In America
there is nothing to supply the endless variety of tones in which
the word 'Hear! Hear!' is uttered in the House of Commons, by which the member who is speaking ascertains, with
the utmost distinctness and precision, whether the House are

pleased or displeased with him, bored or delighted, or whether what he says is granted or denied — lessons eminently useful in the conduct of public debate."

In our own day we are not without agitation over spelling reform, but where among conservatives would one find a match for this doughty objector? The English Dictionary had to him a final sacredness which makes the slightest deviation an affront to the language. When he discovers a few new words, he cannot rest until he sets us right.

"Surely," he says, "such innovations are to be deprecated."

"I don't know that," replies the American. "If a word becomes universally current in America where English is spoken, why should it not take its station in the language?"

"Because," answers our critic, "*there are words enough in our language already and it only confuses matters and hurts the cause of letters to introduce such words.*" [1]

Another Englishman in our own day, far better instructed in linguistic matters than Basil Hall, shows us the change in literary tolerance. The latter declared his countrymen thought of the Americans as having received from England every good they possessed. It was rank impiety to take the slightest liberty with this inheritance.

He writes: —

"England taught the Americans all they have of speech

[1] Vol. I, p. 37.

or thought, hitherto. What thoughts they have not learned from England are foolish thoughts; what words they have not learned from England, unseemly words; the vile among them not being able even to be humorous parrots, but only obscene mocking-birds."

In the judgment of William Archer we now see how far we have left behind us this petty provincialism.

He writes: —

"New words are begotten by new conditions of life; and as American life is far more fertile of new conditions than ours, the tendency towards neologism cannot but be stronger in America than in England. America has enormously enriched the language, not only with new words, but (since the American mind is, on the whole, quicker and wittier than the English) with apt and luminous colloquial metaphors." [1]

There is scarcely a trait of our moral, intellectual, and institutional life that we cannot in the same way test by changes in the opinions of these critics who sit in judgment upon us.

Captain Hall came when the aristocratic traditions of property and religion were rapidly yielding to democratic forms and standards. This filled him with alarm. Every American aristocrat, together with all the lackey imitators of aristocracy, assured him that these democratic substitutes were the handwriting on the wall. The sun was about to set on the "great experiment."

This is the kind of alarm-signal which Hall selects to prove our on-coming calamities that are of most

[1] "America To-day"; William Archer, *Scribner's*, 1899, p. 218.

interest to us. He was sure, for instance, that both our manners and morals are in peril because we have no class among us to spend money with grace and distinction. He counted this among the highest of arts, "more difficult than the art of making it," — "the art of spending it like a gentleman." If we but had among us these models, free from the stain of making their own living, they could so spend income which others had earned as to set before the common people worthy and inspiring ideals. This "art of spending like a gentleman" may be taught like other arts. The Captain is confident that plain and honest folk in the United States would respond, if they could have in familiar circulation a goodly number of these models. Then they would show the most vulgar how to do it. Especially if one disburses unearned moneys, it may be done with a courtly abandon that cannot fail to impress the most stolid among the masses. He feels sure, too, that these artistic largesses would strengthen every bond of society as well as refine it. It would deepen the sense among the people that they were in the presence of superior persons, and this could not fail to quicken gratitude and sympathy even among the most lowly.

If there are any misgivings about this, you have only to look to the Mother Country, where a "permanent money-spending" gentry willingly serve as models with results so conspicuous as to silence all doubts.

That we should have given up flogging in the
army, struck him likewise as a peril to the Republic.
From careful inquiries, he finds what he feared —
that discipline is declining and, what one would not
have expected, " *the soldiers becoming discontented.*"
In spite of their writhings under the lash, they
really understood its beneficence. It was because
no profane hand had touched the custom of flogging
in the navy — thereby introducing discontent among
the flogged sailors — that the superiority of the navy
becomes clear to him.

It was a real perplexity to him that so many of
the common people behaved as if they were not inferiors. It was a kind of bluff that he had not before encountered.

An observed difference of manner in serving at
table calls out this comment : —

"At a place called the Little Falls, where we stopped to
dine, a pretty young woman, apparently the daughter of the
master of the house, also served us at dinner. When her
immediate attendance was not required, she sat down in the
window with her work, *exactly as if she had been one of the
party.* There was nothing, however, in the least degree forward or impudent in this; on the contrary, it was done quietly
and respectfully, though with perfect ease, and without the
least consciousness of its being contrary to European manners." [1]

That we should think of discarding primogeniture
and allow the property to pass equally to all the
children is another amazing blunder. How can a

[1] Vol. II, p. 3.

society survive in "the absence of all classification of ranks"? For the absence of ranks "prevents people becoming sufficiently well acquainted with one another to justify such intimacies."

The vast landed estates of the Livingstons on the Hudson were actually in danger of passing into the hands of Tom, Dick, and Harry. Where half a dozen landlords once lived, he finds to his dismay "as many hundreds may now be counted." [1] The fulness of the calamity can only be seen when its consequences are considered. It will not leave an income on which one may live like a gentleman without work.

In his anxiety for our welfare, he says: —

"The property of the parent, therefore, is generally divided equally amongst the children. This division, as may be supposed, seldom gives to each sufficient means to enable him to live independently of business; and consequently, the same course of money-making habits which belonged to the parents necessarily descends to the son. Or, supposing there be only one who succeeds to the fortune, in what way is he to spend it? Where, when, and with whom? How is he to find companionship? How expect sympathy from the great mass of all the people he mixes amongst, whose habits and tastes lie in totally different directions?" [1]

Captain Hall was here several years before England had done away with those rotten boroughs which enabled a few landlords to make all the laws of the land. Yet he was thrown into much heat by the suggestion that the House of Commons needed

[1] Vol. I, p. 307.

reforming in this respect. "I do not think," he says, "we could possibly make it better."[1] Birmingham at that time could send no representative to Parliament; yet this city, says Mr. Hall, "is in practice one of the best *represented* cities in the Empire."

So, too, our separation of Church and State is like throwing away "the fly-wheel in a great engine." Yet this intelligent gentleman had been in all parts of the world and was an honored guest and friend in the family of Sir Walter Scott, as we learn in Lockhart's Life.

The extracts given are not wholly just to him, as there is much good-will, innumerable shrewd comments on our manners and customs; and throughout, a certain obdurate purpose to learn the facts. In his final comments he even shows surprising humility. He discovers that his notes contain the most bewildering contradictions which reflect upon the finality of his observations. He adds: —

"For my part, I acknowledge fairly, that after some experience in the embarrassing science of travelling, I have often been so much out of humor with the people amongst whom I was wandering that I have most perversely derived pleasure from meeting things to find fault with; and very often, I am ashamed to say, when asking for information, have detected that my wish was rather to prove my original and prejudiced conceptions right, than to discover that I had previously done the people injustice."[2]

His serenity during the trip was often ruffled by

[1] Vol. I, p. 49.   [2] Vol. I, p. 167.

impudent inclination on the part of many Americans to disregard and even, in extreme cases, scoff at his good counsels. And thus, with much kindly feeling, we part from this guest and general adviser.

It was rather his strictures upon our minor vices, if they are minor: our much spitting, our unlovely voices, familiarities, curiosities, incessant national bragging, and undue sensitiveness to criticism that made me grateful to the author during those three months' journeying fifteen years ago. Reading his pages by bits in trains and in hotels, I was quickened to ask, what of these criticisms are still true about us? How far are we still the people described in those volumes? I had written four closely summarized pages of individual and institutional characteristics which Captain Hall thought he saw in us. With this list in hand, it was easier to note at least some great changes both in institutions and in our conduct as citizens and neighbors. With these observations for a background, one could take measurements. For example, like several other visitors in those days, Hall was struck repeatedly by the frigid isolation of men and women at social gatherings.

"I seldom observed anything in America but the most respectful and icy propriety upon all occasions when young people of different sexes were brought together. Positively I never once, during the whole period I was in that country, saw anything approaching, within many degrees, to what we should call a flirtation."

Again,

"The result of all my observations and inquiries is, that the women do not enjoy that station in society which has been allotted to them elsewhere; and consequently much of that important and habitual influence which, from the peculiarity of their nature, they alone can exercise over society in more fortunately arranged communities, seems to be lost."

All things are working, he thinks, to give the two sexes in the United States "such different classes of occupations, that they seldom act together; and this naturally prevents the growth of that intimate companionship, which nothing can establish but the habitual interchange of opinions and sentiments upon topics of common employment." [1]

Mrs. Trollope says she was at several balls "where everything was on the most liberal scale of expense, when the gentlemen sat down to supper in one room, while the ladies took theirs, standing, in another."

It was on this journey, that I first heard two university teachers with much experience in instructing men and women together, expressing alarm at coeducation. "It brings them," said one, "far too closely together, socially and educationally. The young fellow sees the girl at such close range and so constantly, that she loses the mystery and charm that are her best asset." I do not recall any argument based on the supposed lowering of educational standard because of coeducation. It was rather

[1] "Travels in the United States," Vol. II, pp. 150, 153. See also p. 157.

that academic and social intercourse had become too fraternal and intimate.[1]

Here, then, is a wide span between the icy disengagement of the sexes in 1827 and the present freedom of fellowship. If travellers in those days are to be believed, this condition has further illustration in the grotesque prudery of the women. To utter aloud in their presence the word shirt was an open insult. Mrs. Trollope does not state this more strongly than other writers when she says: —

"A young German gentleman of perfectly good manners, once came to me greatly chagrined at having offended one of the principal families in the neighborhood, by having pronounced the word corset before the ladies of it.

"I once mentioned to a young lady that I thought a picnic party would be very agreeable, and that I would propose it to some of our friends. She agreed that it would be delightful, but she added, 'I fear you will not succeed; we are not used to such sort of things here, and I know it is considered very indelicate for ladies and gentlemen to sit down together on the grass.'"[2]

When Powers's "Chanting Cherubs" were exhibited in Boston, it was necessary to drape their loins with linen, and a like treatment was accorded

[1] Von Polenz, in a recent book of admirable temper, speaks of the freedom of intercourse in its beautiful expression between the sexes. "Das Land der Zukunft," p. 231.

In 1904 a Frenchman writes, "I have nowhere seen a freer, happier, or more wholesome mingling of the sexes than in the United States."

[2] Vol. I, p. 192.

to an orang-outang which visited the city about the same time.[1]

It is a far journey from all this, to days when thousands of well-bred girls hasten, without parental resistance, to listen to plays of Bernard Shaw and to others freer still. Whether the change is approved or deplored, it is very great, and our critics furnish the personal perspective through which the change may be seen.

Returning home, I at once reread Dickens's "American Notes" and the parts of "Martin Chuzzlewit" which refer to the United States. I had forgotten the lively resentment roused by their first reading. What had happened that thirty years later the smart of his grossest caricatures had utterly disappeared? It was partly because one recognized so much truth in the picture. There were characteristics in our public and private life which richly deserved the kind of punishment which this great humorist administered. It is now plain history that we had many a promoter's scheme which the bunco-game of land sales in "Martin Chuzzlewit" scarcely exaggerates. Philadelphians wanted to put Dickens in a cell for telling such lies about their model prison. We now know that he told the truth; that he did a public service in calling attention to the essential barbarity of that boasted prison method. When he wrote "those benevolent gentle-

[1] McMaster's "History of the People of the United States," Vol. VI, p. 96.

men who carry it into execution, do not know what
they are doing," he was both seer and prophet.
We all learned, too, that Dickens, like Matthew
Arnold, was impartial. He was as pitiless in his
caricature of evils in England as of those in the
United States. Twenty-five years later (1868), he
came again to this country, noting the "gigantic
changes" — changes in the graces and amenities
of life, changes in the Press, etc., to which he adds,
"I have been received with unsurpassable politeness,
delicacy, sweet temper, hospitality, consideration."
The sting has gone from all his gibes, because we
are far enough away to measure both the critic and
the objects criticised.

For my journey on the following year, I took
Harriet Martineau's "Society in America," Hamilton's "Men and Manners in America," Mrs. Trollope's "Domestic Manners of the Americans."
The latter book I had long before read, but, as with
Dickens, the new reading was merely good fun.
To have as travelling companion a commentator
as penetrating as Harriet Martineau, had the quick
reward of added interest in one's fellow-passengers
on the train and in the happenings at hotels and
stations. Probably no one, except Mr. Bryce,
read more carefully in preparation for the trip than
this distinguished woman. There is no phase of
our life that her two volumes leave untouched. If
we add to these, the portions of her Autobiography
devoted to us, we have a cyclopædia of critical

observation on our institutions, religion, morals, politics, manners, voices, education, industrial and economic life, which is invaluable, if our purpose is to measure the ups and downs, the tendencies, changes, and progress in this country.

These authors finished, the interest excited proved so keen that for several years I rarely took a journey without putting into my bag one or more of these reviewers of American life and conduct. This has resulted in a collection of some seventy-five volumes, the titles of which are given at the end of these chapters.

It soon appeared that writers earlier than the Revolution (1776) dealt with a world so removed from our own, that the kind of comparison here aimed at was too difficult. Earlier than Brissot and Crèvecœur, I therefore do not go.

The list is extremely incomplete, even incoherent, and every reader will recall books of which no mention is made, as well as some books that are far better than many here used.

The list does, nevertheless, include most of those whose opinions we care to consider. To search out all the critics was no part of my purpose, neither to report all the opinions of those selected. The books are used solely to throw, if possible, a little light on social *movement* (whether forward or backward) in this country. For example, an Englishman as intelligent as Janson, living here thirteen years, comes to this conclusion about our government: —

Harriet Martineau

A malicious contemporary sketch of Harriet Martineau, emphasizing the
fact that she was a "Maiden Lady." From a rare cut presented
to the author by a daughter of the poet Longfellow.

"With all the lights of experience blazing before our eyes, it is impossible not to discern the futility of this form of government. It was weak and wicked in Athens. It was bad in Sparta, and worse in Rome. It has been tried in France, and has terminated in despotism. It was tried in England, and rejected with the utmost loathing and abhorrence. It is on trial here, and the issue will be civil war, desolation, and anarchy."

However haltingly it has gone with us, this lowering judgment is a landmark from which we derive encouragement.

If a statesman of the rank of Richard Cobden finds that no power on earth can prevent the swift triumph of free trade in this country; if he can tabulate all the reasons why liberty in trade will become as sacred to Americans as liberty in other spheres, that, too, is a landmark stimulating many reflections. Miss Martineau, as an economist, found sure evidence that labor and capital must in the nature of things live happily together under our institutions. She found entire absence of paupers and a state of bliss in the Lowell cotton mills.

Another has proof that "opportunity" together with "solitary confinement in our magnificent prisons" will cause the total disappearance of criminal classes and thus take off a great burden of expenditure.

The greatest of French critics tells us why our democracy will prevent the buying of votes. With what reflections would De Tocqueville now investigate Pennsylvania and Rhode Island or, indeed, most of our States?

These are samples of opinion two generations ago. Like landmarks, they fix and define the attention. A little later, we were assured that the days of the Republic were numbered because women were demanding "rights" which would turn into a license, "destructive of the very elements of social safety."

From such driven stakes, we may test movement and direction through the century. With specific exceptions, it is a story extremely chilling to the pessimist. It is, upon the whole, a story which gives the lie to a thousand dire prophecies that the people cannot learn self-government. It is above all a story that puts new vitality and interest into our home problems. It was an unexpected reward in reading these books to find a new charm in American life. Much that had seemed to me commonplace, dull, or trivial, was clothed with surprising interest. Why should this not be so?

We do not think it half intelligent to travel in Italy without our Burckhardt, Symonds, Taine, or other literature as interpreter. How many of us do this for our own country? There is no distinctive section of the United States that has not an illuminating literature. To pass along the trail of Andy Adams's "Log of a Cowboy" with that book in hand is to get three or four times as much pleasure out of the trip. The same service is done for other parts of the country by Thoreau, Cable, Fox, Craddock, Miss Jewett, Mrs. Deland, and a score of others.

I saw once three college girls on the boat plying between Richmond and Old Point Comfort. One was reading a novel by Daudet, the second was absorbed in the last story by Mrs. Humphry Ward, and the third by something quite as unrelated to the opportunities of the day. They were on their first trip upon this most interesting river in America. Not a sweeping curve of it that is not rich with memorable events. John Fiske's "Virginia and Her Neighbors" or one of James Rhodes' sterling volumes gives new and fascinating meaning to every mile of that day's journey. Think of a college girl passing Jamestown for the first time, dazed by a French novel! If romance were a necessity, one would think that the local color in stories, like those of Ellen Glasgow or Miss Johnson or Thomas Nelson Page, might meet the need.

In a still larger way, the best of these foreign critics arouse curiosity about problems and events which we so largely take for granted as to feel at most a sleepy interest in them. Even the superficial observations of the stranger, quick to notice all dissimilarity, arouse our home-consciousness in many ways. At the St. Louis Exposition, I saw a most intelligent and experienced American teacher thrown into a state of lively excitement by so simple a question as this. A German teacher asked: "In your Educational Exhibits, why do you display the work of the pupils so much, and the efficiency of the teachers so little? It looks as if you were trying to show them

c

off." "Well," he answered, "I never in my life thought of it before, but I think that is precisely what we do. Yes, we try to show them off too much." It was the contention of the German that far more should be made of the training and competence of the instructor; that this should be at the front rather than a display of the child. "We do not think one quite fit to teach in our German schools unless he is so solidly prepared and so far beyond his pupils as to be perfectly secure. If he has to show off the class, or to struggle with his subject in order to keep just ahead of those he teaches, the best result cannot possibly be reached."

With the merits of this observation, I am less concerned than with the effect upon the American teacher. He said, "The conversation with that German has paid me for coming to St. Louis, if I don't learn another thing."

About every phase of our life and institutions, this is what the outside observer may do for us.

An English writer does not overstate it when he says: "I read Bryce before I left home, and I read him again while here. The trip would have been worth the two hundred pounds it cost me if I had read nothing else. Bryce has added at least fourfold, both to the pleasure and profit."

It is almost an equal service that these books may render to us at home.

Before passing to the general account of these critics in the following chapter, one observation should be made. To criticise or to make merry over the peculiarities of foreign peoples has been from time immemorial one of the never failing sources of national gaiety. Every variety of personal and race difference becomes a natural target for ridicule or censure. An Englishman goes to live in a small French town in 1803. He writes home that "these barbarians make fun of me everywhere just because I am properly dressed and speak the language of a human being. They chatter like apes and dress like Punch and Judy." In spite of so much admiration, Voltaire sees the English, Shakespeare included, as essentially barbarians; while to the average Englishman of that time, the French were "half insane and half monkey." [1] This provincialism is not confined to the stay-at-homes or to the ignorant. It disturbs, as we shall see, the judgment of very wise men.

As one of our haunting perplexities will be in avoiding local standards of comparison, as our institutions and national behavior are brought to the bar, I shall make frequent reference to four critics who have nothing to do with the United States: Karl Hillebrand's "France and the French," Hamerton's "French and English," De Amicis' "Holland,"

---

[1] "Frenchmen," Coleridge said, "are like grains of gunpowder: each by itself smutty and contemptible, but mass them together and they are terrible indeed!" Johnson referred to Americans as "a race of convicts who ought to be thankful for anything we allow them short of hanging." He was "willing to love all mankind, *except an American.*"

and Taine's "Notes on England." These are
critics of so high a class; each with so much knowledge and so much cosmopolitan sympathy, that we
may by their help correct the narrowing tendency to
praise or condemn because our own village standards
are set at naught.

CHAPTER II

CONCERNING OUR CRITICS

IT would be better if four-fifths of the earlier
critical literature here dealt with could be expurgated.
We should thus be relieved from reading for the
fortieth time that we lack many things: courtly
behavior, a great literature, the ennobling ministries
of the fine arts, imposing ruins, and cathedrals.
We should be relieved of interminable commentary
on our bad roads, hotels, boarding-houses, rocking-
chairs, ice-water, hot bread, overheated rooms,
mountainous helps to ice-cream, and even Niagara.
A reasonable disclosure of these deficiencies en-
lightens and exhilarates, but there is a pitch of
reiteration beyond which hot bread and Niagara
alike become a surfeit. It was thus a pleasant
shock when H. G. Wells refused to admire Niagara.
He is the first to break the long monotony of approval.
The Falls may be said to be the only American
phenomenon in the praise of which all previous
critics agree. They pretty nearly agree about our
bragging and about the Capitol at Washington, but
with nothing like the unanimity with which they
approach Niagara. To all observers it is an instant

challenge to a literary flight. It seems as profane
to leave it undescribed as to pass it by altogether.
In recent years three objects have diverted attention
somewhat from the above list: the sky-scraper, the
observation-car, and the Statue of Liberty in New
York Harbor. To the visitor landing and departing,
this proud lady with her luminous torch "enlightening the world" is at once a symbol and an inspiration.
If he thinks well of us, the draped figure becomes
alive and radiant with hope. If he thinks ill of us,
the poor lady serves only for taunts and satire. So
conspicuous is she at the point of landing that ice-
water and rocking-chairs are in peril of being over-
looked by future travellers.

At whatever risk, I shall make slight use of all
these overworked objects. We shall not as a nation
stand or fall on our hot bread or even on our portentous helps to ice-cream or the majestic demeanor
of our hotel clerks. That in our thinly populated
days we should have had bad roads; that we should
be late in developing literature and the arts; that
the very immensity of our natural resources should
have hitherto chiefly absorbed our energies, putting
inventions, trade, and the dollar-mark much to the
front, are facts so easily accounted for that one
wonders why they should have called out so much
reproachful and condescending speculation.

As it is our purpose to get the best out of those
who come to study us, it is first necessary to ask who
our critic is, and, as far as possible, what motive

brought him. We have an English lecturer writing openly, "I really went out there [to the United States] for the express purpose of showing what a mess they are making of it." A very great person, socially, lived some months in Hoboken, New Jersey because he was a fugitive from English justice. He disliked us extremely and even had his fling at Hoboken as a place of residence. A tenderly nurtured gentleman with royal blood in him can be forgiven much under those circumstances. That Prince Talleyrand, after living his life among the most stirring events and brilliant company in Europe, should find us tiresome can be understood without much strain on the imagination. It is also satisfying that we have received our most abusive reproofs from men like Renan, Carlyle, and Ruskin, who never came to us. The poet-craftsman William Morris was also at one with them, until he was shown photographs of Richardson's architecture. This brought from him the exclamation, "Talent like that may save the States after all." To "Americanize" anything was, to Renan, the measure of its vulgarization.[1] All these safe-distance critics were urged to visit this country, but refused for the same reason that a famous American refused to go to Chicago, because — it was Chicago.

Many of those who came in the first half of the

[1] The French lecturer, M. Blouet (Max O'Rell), referring to Renan's fear that France would become "Americanized," replied, "May nothing worse happen to her!"

century are at pains to tell us about the motives that
brought them. In the main it was the desire to
study men and institutions developing under sup-
posedly democratic government.

Cut loose from England, what would happen with
power at last in the hands of the people! Nowhere
was curiosity about all this so keen as in France.
Prizes were there proposed for essays on this subject.
It was seen that Europe could not escape the influence of every democratic success in America. All
those who believed that the people should be saved
by their social superiors; that political and economic
blessings should be confined to the squire and his
relations, and common folk kept in their proper
stations, looked upon our independence as a threat
to the world's well-being.

The industrious Abbé Raynal had the good of
the universe much at heart. He concluded, in a
work ponderous with misinformation, that the discovery of America was a stark calamity. Another,
M. Genty,[1] showed in much detail why the happiness
of the race is put in jeopardy by our discoverer.
According to John Fiske, these timorous patricians
agreed in only one thing. One good and one only
must be accorded to the enterprise of Columbus —
quinine. That had resulted from the discovery, and
European fevers were checked. But the brave
Genty doubted if political and social fevers would
get any cooling from our shores. Even if commerce

---

[1] "L'influence de la Découverte de l'Amérique," 1789.

should swell, what result could follow but a plague of new wants to satisfy?

We get encouragement from only one of these prize writers. He had at least been to America, where he had served as general under Rochambeau. He had a noble enthusiasm for Franklin and Washington. This critic, the Marquis of Chastellux, was the author of that pen picture of Washington that has become so familiar but always pleasant to read again.

"His stature is noble and lofty, he is well made, and exactly proportioned; his physiognomy mild and agreeable, but such as to render it impossible to speak particularly of any of his features, so that in quitting him, you have only the recollection of a fine face. He has neither a grave nor a familiar air, his brow is sometimes marked with thought, but never with inquietude; in inspiring respect, he inspires confidence, and his smile is always the smile of benevolence."

He was also the author of other passages which prove him to have been a most philosophic observer. He thinks, as De Tocqueville did later, that we were fitted at least for stimulating vast material prosperity which might prove big with danger. This leads to the following reflection upon the inevitable coming of inequalities in a democracy due to great wealth among the favored few: —

"Now, wherever this inequality exists, the real force will invariably be on the side of property, so that if the influence in government be not proportioned to that property, there will always be a contrariety, a combat between the form of

government and its natural tendency; the right will be on
one side, and the power on the other; the balance then can
only exist between the two equally dangerous extremes of
aristocracy and anarchy. Besides, the ideal worth of men
must ever be comparative; an individual without property
is a discontented citizen, when the State is poor; place a rich
man near him, he dwindles into a clown. What will result
then, one day, from vesting the right of election in this class
of citizens? The source of civil broils, or corruption, perhaps
both at the same time."

He foresaw this danger from our politicians: [1] —

"The leaders rather seek to please than serve them [the
people]; obliged to gain their confidence before they merit it,
they are more inclined to flatter than instruct them, and fear-
ing to lose the favor they have acquired, they finish by becoming the slaves of the multitude whom they pretended to
govern."

As with the letters of Frederika Bremer and the
French Ambassador de Bacourt, Chastellux is all
the more valuable because, in making his notes, he
had no thought of publishing them.

But the importance of the motive will best be seen
through examples. Many of the first comers are
at no pains to conceal the purpose of their visit, or
what determined them to write a book about us.

The day of the reporter had not come, and there
was little fear of the press.

A good illustration of this is C. W. Janson's
"Stranger in America." He comes with a small

[1] "Travels in North America in 1780–1782," Chastellux, pp. 73,
131, 154.

fortune in search of investment.[1] Before he lands, he is nicknamed "the Grumbler." He says, "I am ready to confess that I put myself foremost in our struggle to redress grievances." In that character he lived more than ten years in the United States. His investments failed, and thus returning full of expansive aversion, he published his book in London in 1807. He is not only annoyed by our curiosities but lets it be known that he is annoyed. He avoids the hotel keepers because they are so "irksome." One of his first experiences was in knocking at the door of an acquaintance; Mr. Janson asked the domestic who opened to him, "Is your master at home?" "I have no master." "Don't you live here?" "I *stay* here." "And who are you then?" "Why, I am Mr. ....'s *help*. I'd have you know, *man*, that I'm no servant." [2]

In 1833 in his "Men and Manners in America," Hamilton shows his motive : —

"When I found the institutions and the experience of the United States quoted in the reformed Parliament as affording

[1] Vol. I, p. 83.

Janson copies from a paper in Salem, Mass., the following : —

"Died in Salem, James Verry, aged twelve, a promising youth, whose early death is supposed to have been brought on by excessive smoking."

The author claims to have seen this practice very generally among mere children. Several other writers note this excessive use of tobacco among the young.

[2] It is a pleasure to hear William Brown of Leeds, England, who was here four years, say plainly that he met no proud people, but only those in very humble circumstances. — "America," 1849.

safe precedent for British legislation, and learned that the drivelers who uttered such nonsense, instead of encountering merited derision, were listened to with patient approbation by men as ignorant as themselves, I certainly did feel that another work on America was yet wanted."

For nearly fifty years of the period here covered, it was a social advantage in England to print evidences against the United States. This may be seen in the tiptoe anxiety with which Buckingham beseeches His Majesty to look with favor on his fat volumes. It was obvious in Tom Moore, Dickens, and Mrs. Trollope.

In his "Diary"[1] Marryat writes: —

"Never was there such an opportunity of testing the merits of a republic, of ascertaining if such a form of government could be maintained — in fact, of proving whether an enlightened people could govern themselves."

When Harriet Martineau wrote her slashing review of his book, Marryat replied, "My object was to do injury to democracy." He desires that his opinions on democracy shall be "read by every tradesman and mechanic: pored over even by milliners' girls and boys behind the counter, and thumbed to pieces in every petty circulating library. I wrote the book with this object, and I wrote it accordingly."

This gifted writer, coming with so fixed a purpose, will, of course, find what he came for. After the same manner Thomas Brothers says, "My principal object was to convince you . . . that under what

[1] Vol. I, p. 132.

is called self-government there may be as much oppression, poverty, and worthlessness, as under any other form of government." He gives 254 closely printed pages in appendices, which are a solid collection of horrors and disgrace taken from the press.

What was the chief object of Mrs. Trollope? "To encourage her countrymen to hold fast by a constitution that insures all the blessings which flow from established habits and solid principles." "If they forego these, they will incur the fearful risks of breaking up their repose by introducing the jarring tumult and universal degradation which invariably follow the wild scheme of placing all the power of the State in the hands of the populace." Henceforth, in great abundance, this lady finds at every turn supporting evidence.

I do not claim that these predispositions destroy the value of the criticisms. They do, however, enable us, in making them an object of study, to classify and use them with more intelligence.

We have no difficulty with Francis Wyse and his three volumes when we know why he came. He wanted to warn all healthy Englishmen not to leave their country. English employers will certainly have to pay higher wages if this emigration continues; therefore, Americans are the least trustworthy of nations — they have a notorious and abominable disregard for truth and no regard for contracts.[1]

[1] "America: Its Realities and Resources," F. Wyse, 3 vols.

In this study of motives that merry poet, Tom Moore, is admirable as an example. His stinging lines against us stirred bitterness and rage in the hearts of thousands of Americans. It is a curious sort of American that cannot to-day read the rhymed squibs of this poet without any rankling. We were a fair target for some of those metered shafts. But more than this, we know about the poet just as we know about Mrs. Trollope. She was in the sorest stress for money. Her last resource for raising funds in Cincinnati had gone with her Bazaar. She must write a book about the Americans and about their manners from which she had suffered most. In a raw town of twenty thousand people, she had watched America from the windows of a second-class boarding-house. If her book was to sell, it must sell in England. Nine-tenths of the people who bought books at that time thought extremely ill of this country. With that class feeling constantly in mind, the disappointed woman wrote her volumes. Mr. Weller senior fully explains her and her kind, "An then let him come back and write a book about the 'Merrikins as'll pay all his expenses and more, if he blows 'em up enough."

It was not essentially different with the Irish poet. The son of a Dublin grocer, he goes up to London where he becomes at once the darling among fashionable diners out. "Where Tom sits no host feels insecure." The poet can entertain all companies. He comes to the United States in 1804, but loves best to dine with English officers, many of whose ships were then here. What do the poet's entertainers relish so much as merry verses and smart hits at the expense of the rustics on land? Over the rim of the champagne glass, or writing to Lady This or Lord That, he paints his word-pictures — a kind of rake's progress — solely for ears that delight in our disrepute.

When Lord John Russell says in his preface to Moore's letters, "the sight of democracy triumphant soon disgusted him," we know that the poet's conclusion was as much expected as it was pleasurable. He goes from Norfolk to Baltimore over roads that were "as barbarous as the inhabitants." He writes : —

"How often has it occurred to me that nothing can be more emblematic of the government of this country than its stages, filled with a motley mixture, all 'hail fellow well met,' driving through mud and filth, which bespatters them as they raise it, and risking an upset at every step. . . . As soon as I am away from them, both the stages and the government may have the same fate for what I care."

From Washington he writes to Lord Forbes that the days of Columbia are already numbered, for on her brow —

"The showy smile of young presumption plays,
    Her bloom is poison'd and her heart decays."

"Already has she pour'd her poison here
    O'er every charm that makes existence dear."

> "With honest scorn for that inglorious soul
>   Which creeps and winds beneath a mob's control,
>   Which courts the rabble's smile, the rabble's nod,
>   And makes like Egypt every beast a god."

> "Take Christians, Mohawks, democrats and all,
>   From the rude wigwam to the Congress hall, —
>   'Tis one dull chaos, one infertile strife
>   Betwixt half-polished and half-barbarous life."

These tuneful amenities contain the same opinions of us that we find in the private affectionate letters to his mother. He betrays thus no inconsistency.

Merely to state the social setting of this favorite minstrel and the time in which he wrote, should leave the most ardent patriot among us quite serene. There was even some excuse, as 1804 was the year when party scurrility and vindictiveness reached perhaps the lowest pitch in our history. The lampoons of Callender against Jefferson were of an incredible grossness that the present day would not for an instant tolerate. That the President was guilty of miscellaneous amours was the least of the charges. We may be certain that many a Federalist assured the poet that these libels were true. They knew Callender to be coarsely venal and a liar ; they called him so while he was their enemy. But now that, as turncoat, he attacked Jefferson, his coarsest blackguardism was welcome. The historian Morse says, "Every Federalist writer hastened to draw for his own use bucketful after bucketful from Callender's foul reservoir and the gossip about Jefferson's graceless debaucheries was sent into every household in the United States." The New England clergy took so active a hand in these defamations that Jefferson wrote: "From the clergy I expect no mercy. They crucified the Saviour, who preached that their Kingdom was not of the world: and all who practise on that precept must expect the extreme of their wrath." Josiah Quincy said Jefferson was a "transparent fraud" and his followers "ruffians." From Pickering, Cabot, Rufus King, Fisher Ames, and Griswold — the very light and leading of social respectability — the same ominous judgments may be quoted, while to the president of Yale College our government was in possession of "blockheads and knaves." These model citizens were at that moment freely circulating against Jefferson such bits of gossip as that "he had obtained his property by fraud and robbery; that in one instance he had defrauded and robbed a widow and fatherless children of an estate to which he was executor, of ten thousand pounds sterling," etc.

We are to-day justly sensitive against any insinuation that the high judiciary is corrupt, but in 1804 there was circulated in the press by a member of the Supreme Bench a charge that "the independence of the national judiciary is shaken to its foundations" and that "mobocracy" had us finally in its grip.

It is into this atmosphere that the Irish poet comes.

D

From the "best citizens" he hears night after night
more damaging criticism against our democracy
than any which he puts into verse. He is only trying
to find good rhymes for what well-to-do Americans
tell him about their government.

The essence of revolution is the passing of power
from one class to another. Federal control, with the
lingering intellectual feudalism still inhering in it,
was beginning to pass to the democrats at the opening of the nineteenth century. Nowhere among
these foreign critics is there such bitter censure as
our own "Society" was everywhere heaping upon
the new democracy. It was "as destitute of manners as it was of morals and religion." It had
"robbed life of decency and the future of hope."
These cheerful confidences were dinner table coin
from Philadelphia to Boston. An English visitor
in 1824 says: "These Americans are so merciless
in criticising their own government that nothing
is left over for the outsider."

These drawing-room aspersions were still at white
heat when Miss Martineau came thirty years later.
She was at first welcomed by very aristocratic
families "as the most distinguished woman that had
come to us." Of her reception she writes: —

"The first gentleman who greeted me on my arrival in
the United States, a few minutes after I had landed, informed me, without delay, that I had arrived at an unhappy
crisis; that the institutions of the country would be in ruin
before my return to England; that the levelling spirit was

desolating society; and that the United States were on the verge of a military despotism." [1]

Her own honest human sympathies protected her from this influence. But the average foreign critic had only to listen to such talk and then turn it to his own use. He is talking about us as those among us out of power were themselves talking.

When this is clear, there is little to resent. When we know that Sydney Smith had made a disastrous money investment in this country, we sympathize with his invective.

When Kipling first came, he was smarting against us because we had pirated his books. In this mood he found the first city in which he landed "inhabited by the insane"; the reporters were all like "rude children"; our speech was "a horror"; everybody was "wolfing" his food; and even our American enterprise was only "grotesque ferocity."

We can explain and account for many of our critics, leaving behind as little justifiable irritation on our part as in the case of Moore and Kipling. We object to a man like Thomas Ashe, because he was a plain liar, not because he finds fault with us. When Isaac Weld says our mosquitoes bite through the thickest boots, and a French author gets William Penn over here in the *Mayflower*, we are prepared to discount some of their confident generalizations. M. Moreau, as he closes a well-meant volume,[2]

---

[1] "Society in America," Vol. I, p. 98.
[2] " L'Envers des Etats-Unis."

relieves us generally of all difficulty in fixing his place among serious critics. Our road to ruin, according to him, is the drunkenness of our women. M. Moreau has just left us, so that his information startles us by its newness. Not only does the American woman drink, but she drinks like Falstaff. He sees the curse not merely as a cloud on our horizon, but as a heavy pall that threatens the very light of the nation's life. He compares the progressive deterioration to the rolling snowball, gathering weight and mass as it hurries to destruction. His words are strong. This plague among our women is an "atrocious evil," "a terrible menace." His climax of dismay at our impending doom culminates when he asks, "Are there exceptions?" As a friend of ours, he would fain believe that exceptions exist, yet the number of semi-sots is so great that he is in doubt. That the women drinkers "constitute a very strong majority" he is firmly convinced. He is moved to qualify his statement so far as to admit that it is rare to see the women "fall an inert mass" from intoxication, but in dangerous degrees they drink "so as to act unconsciously." [1]

This gentleman has seen a great deal of our life and met or corresponded with some of the ablest

---

[1] An Englishman writes that while the man in the United States consumes enormous quantities of liquor in the form of "coffee varnish" and "dead man's pallor," "if a woman took a glass of wine, they would send for the police."

Americans. I have tried to get the history of his dire prophecy of our downfall through woman's inebriety. In part at least it is this. There are a good many country clubs about our larger cities, frequented by lively young women who take great liberties with highballs and cocktails. They often order them with much bravado and with a kind of expansion that seems to fill the entire landscape. It is something from which one would like to look away, but its very singularity and extravagance hold the attention. The larger city has also a group of popular restaurants, patronized alike by the half-world and by those who feel far above it, but cannot be quite sure, except by close and constant inspection of their moral inferiors. Any and all of these much-haunted resorts would give a touring stranger just the opinion which Monsieur Moreau came to entertain. If he saw the most highly paced among our various smart sets, he might again draw sinister inferences about our future. But to draw large conclusions about national morals from these vagabond data is to lose one's head as a competent observer.

As far as possible serious critics alone will here claim our attention.

Among our visitors are the following: —

From France, Brissot de Warville; the Count de Ségur; the Dukes La Rochefoucauld-Liancourt and de Lausan; the Marquis of Chastellux; Chateaubriand; Lafayette; Volney (he of the Ruins); Prince Talleyrand; De Gasparin; a son of

Napoleon's favorite General Murat, who was here many years; De Tocqueville; Ampère; the Duke of Chartres (Louis Philippe); the Utopian Cabet; the economist Chevalier sent on a brief mission by Thiers but becoming so interested that he spent two years; the sociologist De Rousier; Professor Claudio Janet; the present Prime Minister Clemenceau; the publicist Carlier; the academician Paul Bourget; Madame Blanc (Th. Bentzon); Edmond de Nevers; Paul Adam; Abbé Klein; and Pastor Wagner.

From England have come Robert Owen; the Trollopes, mother and son; Harriet Martineau; Mrs. Jameson; Marryat; Dickens; Thackeray; Cobden; Fanny Kemble; Combe; and the redoubtable Cobbett; Sir Charles Lyell (four volumes); Tyndall; Huxley; Spencer; Frederic Harrison; Matthew Arnold; John Morley; Freeman, the historian; Kipling; Sir Robert Ball, the astronomer; James Bryce; and Joseph Chamberlain.

From Germany: F. J. Grund; J. I. Kohl; Weitling, the socialist; Professor von Raumer; Prince von Wied; F. Bodenstedt; Herr Grillenberger; Von Holst; Von Polenz; Karl Zimmermann; Professor Münsterberg; the historian Lamprecht; Fulda, the dramatist; and Professor Andreas Baumgarten.

In the way of approval, of censure, or of warning, these observers should have a various message from which a little open-mindedness and good-will on our part ought to pluck some profit.

CHAPTER III

WHO IS THE AMERICAN?

THE foreign students of this country have far less difficulty with our institutions, our government, our education, and general resources than with our more personal life. What has been done on this continent or left undone may be brought to judgment. But, Who is the American? He is the main object of inquiry.

Sometimes the question is, What kind of human being are they making in the United States? Again it is, What institutions are here being shaped by the American character? In both, it is the sort of man and woman in the making that is of fundamental interest to the inquirer. What, then, is the human product called the American?

The English historian Freeman used to speak of us as a lot of Englishmen who had strayed from home. We had taken with us a complete outfit of political and other traditions that we were working out under slightly different conditions. When he came here in 1883, he still said, "To me most certainly the United States did not seem a foreign country, it was simply England with a difference."

Something of this is in the thought of Matthew Arnold when he speaks of George Washington as if he were really an Englishman who was accidentally in America. We Americans should be made to understand that we had appropriated him far too exclusively. To understand Washington, we must learn to think of him as a good model of the English County Squire, — somewhat above the average of course, but a type very common and not in the least dazzling to the properly informed Englishman. Less than thirty years ago Bryce wrote, "The American people is the English people modified in some directions by the circumstances of its colonial life and its more popular government, but in essentials the same."

In 1795 Timothy Dwight was chosen president of Yale College. From that time until the publication of his "Travels" in four volumes, he journeyed some 14,000 miles in New England and New York, knowing that eastern country probably better than any other man. In his 477th letter he thus speaks of Boston: "The Bostonians, almost without exception, are derived from one country and a single stock. They are all descendants of Englishmen, and of course are all united by all the bonds of society: language, religion, government, manners, and interests." [1] Nearly half a century ago, Godley could speak of Boston as the best place for the stranger to see national characteristics "in their most unmixed and most developed state." [2]

[1] Dwight's "Travels," 1821, Vol. I, p. 506.
[2] "Letters from America," London, 1844, Vol. II, p. 136.

Boston was then puritan; to-day it is catholic.
It has nearly thirty nationalities. Yet until the Civil
War, we still had confident descriptions of the
American, as if he stood sufficiently apart and disen-
gaged from other peoples to admit of characterization. The Italians discovered us, throngs of French,
Dutch, and Germans very early made their homes
among us. There was yet enough in common, until
the middle of the last century, to make the question,
What is the American, at least intelligible. But
what meaning can it have to-day? New York is
already the chief Jewish city of the world. It will
very soon have a million Hebrews. They come with
qualities and traditions so diverse that their competition among themselves (as between German and
Russian Jews) is as relentless as it is against any
other class of the community.

Intelligent enough to leave petty gambling and
drunkenness to the Christians, they are appropriating
rapidly the very forms of property which give them
the strongest grip upon the destinies of the city.
Their capacity for work, their thrift, their family devotion, their temperance and consequent low death
rate, their sacrifices for education, their passion for
individualism, already modify our life, although in
our eighty-five millions they are a tiny fraction of a
million and a half. Christians have never hesitated
to classify and characterize the Jews as specifically
this or that. But as we know them better, the
characterization becomes blurred and uncertain.

How confidently we have repeated it! The Jew is
not a "producer." "He swaps and bargains and
exchanges, but he shuns the processes of producing
wealth." It is very slovenly reasoning to shut out
these trading activities from "production"; but
apart from this, the slightest observation would
correct this easy judgment. One of our great industries is the clothing trade, which in its entire
process is largely in the hands of Jews, as other
industries are in part on their purely "productive"
side.

I have asked a great many people what one
quality could surely be fixed upon the American.
I have a long list of answers, but the one that heads
the list in point of frequency is that the American,
above all other peoples, is "adaptable." It is of
course meant by this that the young American is
early thrown upon his own resources; that our society
has such mobility and range of opportunity as to
create the capacity for self-adjustment — of falling
upon the feet — in whatever part of the world one
alights.[1] But are we more "adaptable" than the
Jew? With centuries of savage hounding hither
and yon, what race ever had such occasion and
necessity to learn adaptability as this one? Is
there any delay in adjusting themselves to our

---

[1] Professor Leo S. Rowe, returning from long journeys among
the South American peoples, tells me that the American is handi-
capped there precisely because he is less "adaptable" than the
German.

economic and educational opportunities? If the Jew has a department store in a Southern city, he succeeds partly because he is so flexible in falling in with the peculiarities of blacks and whites alike. To say Miss or Mrs. to the colored purchaser is to get her trade. I hear it charged against the Jew that he will not stay upon a farm. As small farming has hitherto been done, this refusal of the Jew without capital is an assured sign of his intelligence. There is already indication that when farming is raised to its proper level; when science and good business methods are applied to it; when, in a word, it is commercialized and thoroughly worth doing, the Jew will be at the front in this work. To say that this people loves money, is sharp at a trade, has push, is aggressive, is merely to repeat what no end of foreigners have ascribed to Yankees generally. An Englishman who did business for several years in this country between 1840 and 1850, warns his countrymen against the Americans in these words, "Let him gain a foothold and before you are aware of it, you will find his hand laid upon all you possess, from your pocket handkerchief to the house that covers your head." [1] A friend, who has published a monograph on race questions, tells me there is one trait that he is sure is peculiar to Hebrews. Their aggressiveness has the unfailing trait of "intellectual impudence." *Frechheit* is a fair translation of this modified "impudence," and I have often heard in

[1] Brown's "America."

Germany that the truest mark of the Jew was this same Frechheit. But to what people under the sun would this name not be affixed, if they were as persistent and successful in playing the accepted competitive game as are the Jews? This labelling fares ill, even with a race so sharply outlined as the Hebrew.

What, then, shall be said of the American, now that nearly fifty nationalities are knitted into our national texture? In great areas of the Northwest one seems to be in Scandinavia, as large parts of several cities are like another Leipzig. We have "little Chinas" and "little Polands." In Lowell, Massachusetts, one may find himself in a Greece that is not even little. We have a hundred "little Italys" in our cities, and whole villages of them in the South and West, as in Worcester he may find himself in Armenia. As for Eastern and Southern Europeans, they are so in evidence in industries like iron and mining that an American laborer seems foreign and out of place. These piebald millions are now so interwoven with all that we are; at so many points we have been changed by their presence, that to silhouette the American becomes yearly more baffling.[1]

[1] "In nineteen of the Northern States of our Republic the number of the foreign-born and their immediate descendants exceeds the number of the native-born. In the largest cities the number is two-thirds, and even three-quarters. There are more Cohens than Smiths in the New York Directory. Two-thirds of the laborers in our factories are foreign-born or of foreign parentage. New England is no longer puritan but foreign." — "Aliens of Americans," by B. Grose, p. 236.

The early writers have no misgivings. In the following chapter we shall see above twenty confident traits set down to index the American off from other nationalities. Especially after the Civil War this confidence abates. The perplexities become too obvious. The railway facilities bring the visitor into contact with too many kinds of Americans. In 1889, I met a German correspondent who had been four times to the United States. He had done high-class work for what was then thought to be the ablest continental paper, the *Cologne Gazette*. He said he brought back from his first journey a clearly conceived image of the American. He was "sharp-visaged, nervous, lank, and restless." [1] After the second trip this group of adjectives was abandoned. He saw so many people who were not lank or nervous; so many who were rotund and leisurely, that he re-arranged his classification, but still with confidence. After the third trip he insisted that he could describe our countrymen, but not in *external* signs. He was driven to express them in terms of character. The American was resourceful, inventive, and supreme

[1] "The Yankee is a tall, gaunt, yellow-faced, hungry-looking dyspeptic. He is generally engaged in selling some very odd article, such as a button-hook and a cigarette-holder combined, or a pair of socks which change into an umbrella when you touch a hidden spring."

De Nevers, with many years' experience in the United States, sums up his conclusions as to our fundamental characteristics thus: "The love of gain, the spirit of practical achievement, curiosity, a rather supercilious exclusiveness and contempt for the foreigner." — "L'Ame Américaine," Vol. II, p. 94.

in the pursuit of material ends. "My fourth trip,"
he said, "has knocked out the final attempt with the
others. I have thrown them all over like a lot of
rubbish. I now don't know what the American is,
and I don't believe any one else knows." He still
thought we were more in a hurry than any other folk.
Beyond that, he was certain of no distinctive difference. On this remnant of confidence there is now a
very curious comment. So competent an observer
as Professor Münsterberg, eager to set German
opinion right on America, says we are not even in a
hurry. This conclusion has great surprises for us
and is worth quoting.

"It has often been observed, and especially remarked on by
German observers, that in spite of his extraordinary tension,
the American never overdoes. The workingman in the factory, for example, seldom perspires at his work. This comes
from a knowledge of how to work so as in the end to get out
of one's self the greatest possible amount.

"Very much the same may be said of the admirable way
in which the Americans make the most of their time. Superficial observers have often supposed the American to be
always in a hurry, whereas the opposite is the case. The man
who has to hurry has badly disposed of his time, and, therefore, has not the necessary amount to finish any one piece of
work. The American is never in a hurry." [1]

[1] More recently still, as good an observer as H. W. Horwill
finds us conspicuous for our careless, leisurely ways. He writes
in an English monthly that we can potter and dawdle as if life
were a continuous holiday. He has an array of evidence to make
good his point. Think of the time spent by thousands of smaller
business men in the innumerable "orders" and societies that fill our

Here is a conflict of opinion over a generalization that has been world-wide and is surely among our own beliefs about ourselves. This scholar who has been among us so many years now takes from us even this source of pride. If our preëminence as hustlers is to be put in question, what, pray, is left to us?

One writer, after journeys in Canada and Australia, first notes that the American can only be detected by his speech. He finds us so like the Australians that were it not for our "intonation," he should think himself in Victoria or New South Wales. He then travels some months through the West and South, concluding at last that "there are as many different *ways* of speaking in various parts of the United States as there are in England. I sometimes thought myself in Yorkshire, sometimes among London cockneys, and sometimes among the best bred people."

American "accent" (a word covering almost everything except accent) has played a great rôle

towns! Study our sports from racing to baseball at which vast multitudes are constantly seen! Even when we are hard-pushed and ought to hurry, he thinks us very awkward. An American who is in a hurry, he says, "will unhesitatingly take a car for two or three blocks rather than cover the same distance more quickly by walking, just as he will wait two or three minutes for an elevator to take him down a flight of ten steps, or will bring the resources of his typewriter to bear upon a postcard — which could be more speedily written by hand." The English workingmen brought here by Mr. Mosley were constantly expressing their surprise that they saw so little of this high pressure work.

in marking us off among the nations. Yet this traveller, when he comes to judge the people as a whole, is in despair. "I can," he says, "tell how they speak in any one of a dozen sections, but not how *the* American speaks."

Our trouble is scarcely less if we confine ourselves to the American woman or the American child. From Liancourt to Bryce, our women folk have proved a shining mark for flattering characterization, but the young girl and the child have had lampooning enough. Nor is there against a good deal of this criticism the slightest honest defence. That far too many of our children are grievously undisciplined, "lack reverence," are "loud and ill-mannered," registers the most obvious fact. Yet it is a partial one, not in the least inclusive of the American child.[1] Most of these travellers lived in hotels and boarding-houses. It was here that many of them took their impressions of youthful deportment.

---

[1] "And then the children — babies I should say, if I were speaking of English bairns of their age; but, seeing that they are Americans, I hardly dare to call them children. The actual age of these perfectly civilized and highly educated beings may be from three to four. One will often find five or six such seated at the long dinner table of the hotel, breakfasting and dining with their elders, and going through the ceremony with all the gravity and more than all the decorum of their grandfathers." — ANTHONY TROLLOPE.

Sixty years ago an English merchant who was "struck dumb" by the precocity of the American child, says he knew of one that ran away from home when only five months old. When caught, the child was master of the situation — "I heard they's going to call me Jotham and I jes' lit out."

The fidgety and noisy were of course most in evidence, and thus are etched into many an unlovely picture in this foreign literature. Writers like Thackeray and Miss Martineau, who see the child in our better homes, defend us most handsomely. Thackeray was charmed by the gay and playful familiarities between parent and child, much preferring it to the more formal relation which he recalls in England. Miss Martineau devotes a chapter to our children. She is careful to say that she finds everywhere "spoiled, pert, and selfish children." She sees that many are given too much rein and left without discipline. These exceptions do not, however, lessen her confidence that the freedom and familiarity are upon the whole a distinct gain for the child and for society. What moves her most to this conclusion is the general happiness of American children : —

"I have a strong suspicion that the faults of temper so prevalent where parental authority is strong and where children are made as insignificant as they can be made, and the excellence of temper in America, are attributable to the different management of childhood in the one article of freedom." [1]

Mental alertness she also thinks has surer development.

"If I had at home gone in among eighty or a hundred little people, between the ages of eight and sixteen, I should have extracted little more than 'Yes, ma'am,' and 'No, ma'am.' At Baltimore, a dozen boys and girls at a time crowded around

[1] Vol. III, p. 163, English Ed., "Society in America."

E

me, questioning, discussing, speculating in a way which enchanted me."

About the American woman there are the same cheerful generalizations. Many chapters are devoted to her. Early writers note her pruderies, her frigid reserve before miscellaneous gallantries, and her "lack of temperament." Ampère and Fanny Kemble are astonished at the extreme deference that men pay her, especially on the street and in all public places.[1] That a young girl can travel unattended from State to State, secure from insult or importunity, calls out admiring comment from critics of every nationality. Especially since the habit of travelling has developed with the railway, few things have more frequent mention than this serene young woman journeying alone and unalarmed where and when she will. In a severely critical lecture on the United States, I heard the historian Von Treitschke say to his class in Berlin, that even the enemies of America saw in this deference to the unprotected woman "a most hopeful sign of civilization." That she would be unsafe in Europe, he thought, marked, in this one respect, inferiority in the European social morals. Even if, at home and abroad, we have not

[1] De Tocqueville says: "It has often been remarked that in Europe a certain degree of contempt lurks even in the flattery which men lavish upon women; although a European frequently affects to be the slave of woman, it may be seen that he never sincerely thinks her his equal. In the United States, men seldom compliment women, but they daily show how much they esteem them." Vol. II, p. 260.

rather overworked this solitary young lady *en voyage*, she is too individual a phenomenon to be of much use to us.

Miss Faithful in her struggles to characterize our girls quotes the following:[1] —

"The most fascinating little despot in the world; an oasis of picturesque unreasonableness in a dreadful desert of common sense."

"Champagny — glittering, foamy, bubbly, sweet, dry, tart; in a word, fizzy! She has not the dreamy, magical, murmury loveableness of the Italian, but there is a cosmopolitan combination which makes her a most attractive coquette; a sort of social catechism — full of answer and question."

This does not wholly satisfy her, but her own conclusion is as tremulous in its uncertainty as the rest, save in its good-will, —

"Miss Alcott's Joes and Dolly Wards, Bret Harte's Miggles and M'liss, and Mr. James's Daisy Miller, — indeed, I feel more and more bewildered as I try to think which should be taken as strictly typical — save the one,

"So frankly free,
So tender and so good to see,
Because she is so sweet."

When writer after writer says America is "the Paradise for Women," we have a formula that submits to closer tests.

I was once on a Fall River boat with an English clergyman who had a passion for sociological statistics. He was so struck by the numbers of people

[1] "Three Visits to America," p. 316.

puffing at pipes, cigarettes, or cigars that he made
conscientious note of it, telling me that ninety per
cent of our people must be users of tobacco. This
appeared excessive, and I asked him where he got
his estimates. He said he had counted all the
people smoking and not smoking in the large space
into which we came from the wharf. He was much
shaken, when I told him that all his reckoning had
been made in the boat's smoking room.

America as the "Paradise for Women" is an
improvement on the statistical reflections of this
clergyman, but it too has to be challenged. As
compared to most of Europe, burdens are here
lighter and opportunities more open for women who
must work for a living. But there are some millions
of wives of wage-earning men and other millions
of farmers' wives. Is it quite a Paradise for them?
As in summer months, "There is nobody in town"
to leisurely city folk, so this Paradise is confined to a
relatively small section of the community. Even for
this limited portion, it is a "Paradise" that excites
reflections. To have the fewest responsibilities;
to have the children cared for by others; to have a
good bank-account and the consequent leisure to do
what one will, usually depicts this "Paradise." It
is especially and always to have a good deal of so-
called independence and freedom from the narrower
household cares. To have a husband willing to
slave while he furnishes the cash and is content to
stay behind if he is not wanted, always makes the

heaven of the American woman more complete in the eyes of these foreign naturalists.

It was left for a French scholar to say the final and triumphant word upon woman's real place in the United States. He finds the propelling force even of our material masteries in our women. In France and in Europe generally the woman must, he says, suit her expenditure to her husband's earnings. Be they small or great, this duty she meets. But the glory and distinction of the American woman; that which sets her apart as upon a pedestal from all her kind in other lands, is that she *makes her husband earn what she wishes to spend*. Petty obstacles like business rivals and trade conditions are not to be considered. What this exigent household queen wants, she must have and she *gets* it. It is not primarily the man, but the American woman who commands the business initiative. The root of all our commercial greatness is her ambition. Because her heart is set on those first necessities — the luxuries and superfluities — for that reason the railroads, stock-exchanges, mills, and mines are driven at white heat. It is man's business to work all the wonders of our business world in order that wifely expectations may not go unsatisfied. We thus get at the real origin of the much-noted American deference to woman. Fanny Kemble speaks for scores of these critics when she expresses her surprise that American men show such humility toward all women, even the humblest. The commonest ex-

planation of this attitude is the relative scarcity of
women during the three or four generations when
men were greatly in excess. To the average man
seeking a mate under these circumstances politeness
becomes his chief asset. I have heard a lady much
in the social world say that the manners of boys
varied according to the ratio of sexes at social enter-
tainments. "If the young men are few and the
girls many, the boys lose their grace and gallantry,
and most of them act like boors." This Frenchman
does much better. To him women evolve not only
as Queen and Dictator, but as the propelling force
behind all our commercial "initiative," "self-direc-
tion," invention, and other greatness. This torch-
bearer among the critics did not offer his explanation
as a compliment to our women. But never have
they received such flattery. It puts man as the
weaker vessel in his proper place. We can now
understand the document which Emily Faithful
reproduces from the early dawn of the "Woman's
Movement." She vouches for this speech in which
Mrs. Skinner, two generations ago, sets us right as
to man's place in the social order: —

"Miss President, feller wimmen, and male trash generally,
I am here to-day for the purpose of discussing woman's rights,
recussing her wrongs, and cussing the men.

"I believe sexes were created perfectly equal, with the
woman a little more equal than the man.

"I believe that the world to-day would be happier if man
never existed.

"As a success man is a failure, and I bless my stars my mother was a woman. (*Applause.*)

"I not only maintain those principles, but maintain a shiftless husband besides.

"They say man was created first — Well, s'pose he was. Ain't first experiments always failures?

"The only decent thing about man was a rib, and that went to make something better. (*Applause.*)

"And they throw into our faces about taking an apple. I'll bet five dollars that Adam boosted her up the tree, and only gave her the core.

"And what did he do when he was found out? True to his masculine instincts he sneaked behind Eve, and said, 'Twan't me; 'twas her,' and woman had to father everything, and mother it too.

"What we want is the ballot, and the ballot we're bound to have, if we have to let down our back hair, and swim in a sea of gore."

Another phase of this topic troubles our critics. Who is the "good," who is the "bad" American? To stiff conservatives, especially if they held the offices — the real American was always one who accepted rather slavishly the party platform. Carlier was thinking of our politics when he said, "The bad American is usually the best American." To show independence or to stand for some larger policy has ever brought out the reproach of being "un-American." We probably did not have five greater or more useful men in the half century that followed the Revolution than the reticent, educated, and resourceful young Swiss who landed here in 1790, Albert Gallatin. Though an aristocrat by birth,

with easy honors awaiting him at home, he turned
his back upon them because of republican sympathies that came to him like a religious conversion.
The word democrat has no nobler sense than
that which Gallatin put into every stroke of his great
public service in this country. Yet throughout his
most active career, he had to submit to this taunt of
being a bad American. Men with very proud names
were guilty of this ungenerous flouting. In our
own day another splendid figure suffered from the
same unhandsome conduct. Carl Schurz was show-
ered with honors whenever principle allowed him
to "stand pat," but at any brave departure he was
told that he was "no true American." When he
was fighting for some honor and humanity toward
the Indians; when he tried to temper some of the
blundering excesses of our reconstruction methods,
as well as during his long and heroic struggle for
the elementary decencies of Civil Service Reform,
Mr. Schurz had to meet this coarse upbraiding of
being un-American. He probably was never so
genuinely an American as when that term was most
hotly denied him, and this was as certainly true of
Gallatin. To fight for the next step that constitutes
progress should best define the American spirit.
It should be the essence of this spirit to expand the
conditions of political and social growth. Yet
those who have struck out most resolutely for this
enlargement have had to take the anathema — "no
true American."

The first speech I heard in Massachusetts in favor of the Australian ballot was attacked by a well-known jurist as being un-American and therefore to be condemned. In the West, during the stormy discussions over free silver and the gold standard, I attended many meetings. None of the peppery phrases so stuck in my mind as those that charged the friends of the "single standard" with being un-American. I can still see a trembling and scornful finger pointing at some of us who had asked questions. The speaker stirred all hearts by comparing the doubters to Judas. As he had bartered his soul, so had the gold men bartered theirs. "The soul of the true American has departed from them forever." Even at a meeting for the discussion of immigration, as good an American as I have ever known was angrily denied the name, because he steadfastly opposed plans for restricting immigrants.

There is nothing more hopeful at the present moment in our country than the spirit at work in our new forestry policy. It is, fundamentally, the same use of government powers to protect large and general interests, as against narrow and immediate private interests that have come into sharp conflict with public welfare. Yet I have heard the policy condemned with extreme venom because it was not the American way of doing things. The most dangerous kind of ignorance can hide behind this name. A New Hampshire farmer and dairyman, irritated by the standard of cleanliness which the

milk inspector submitted to him, burst out in reply,
"Yes, I've read a good deal in the agricultural
paper about this foolishness, but I'm an American
and I propose to stay on bein' an American." In
this sorry instance, to hold with sulky tenacity to
the beaten path becomes the definition of this proud
title. Few really illustrious names have wholly
escaped the epithet — un-American. Washington
and Hamilton lost all claim to it at the hands of the
Jeffersonian pamphleteers. Nor did Lincoln go
unscathed by Northern copperheads. When compelled to suspend habeas corpus in the heaviest
days of 1863, the hiss of un-Americanism was heard
on every hand. The most heroic moments in our
history are precisely those in which men have dared
to stand pluckily by some cause against which
popular fury had temporarily turned. Young
Quincy's defence of Captain Preston of "the Boston
Massacre" was a splendid bit of gallantry. The
frenzy against Preston in the community burned so
high that the elder Quincy wrote indignantly to his
son: "My God! Is it possible? I will not believe
it." The son answered that it was in his oath to aid
those charged with crime, the guilt of which was not
yet proved. To the angry reproach that his career
would be ruined, he answered: "I never harbored the
expectation, nor any great desire, that all men should
speak well of me. To inquire my duty and to do it,
is my aim." Months had not passed before it
became plain that an atrocious injustice would have

been committed to refuse this defence. Yet for moral intrepidity that adds lustre to those days and to all days, this young man was pronounced a bad and faithless American.

In the winter of 1882, when James Russell Lowell was our Minister to England, he had to face delicate matters growing out of the "Coercion Act" against Ireland. Two Secretaries of State (Evarts and Blaine) had successively paid tribute to Mr. Lowell's "sagacity, prudence, and fairness." Yet in and out of Congress the storm raged against him. At a great meeting in New York, "sickening sycophancy" and "Apostate to true Americanism" were among the pretty compliments paid to him.

As it has been in the past, so in the future this high test of moral courage will remain to try men's souls. Politics as well as religion tends to harden into institutional and dogmatic forms. To challenge these; to break the enclosing crust so far as to give way for the inner life and growth, will ask of men to the end of time this same hardihood. The best Americans have ever been and will continue to be those who, while standing for social stability and order, dare to stand also for the changes that widen into social progress.

CHAPTER IV

OUR TALENT FOR BRAGGING

I APPROACH this chapter with misgivings. When using the essential portions of it several times as a lecture, I have seen individuals leave the hall in a state of unmistakable displeasure. It was once given as the first of a series on the general subject with which these chapters deal. A protest was made to those having the lectures in charge that their continuance ought not to be permitted. As this was impracticable, a good many people took the question of continuing into their own hands and stayed away. It was maintained that "no true American would talk so about his country." As this lecture was immediately followed by one on the Sensitiveness of the American,[1] it brought a humorous confirmation which somewhat softened the asperities of the situation.

What was least tolerable to this wounded patriotism was an itemized comparison between some of our prancing Fourth of July oratory from eminent men and the broad caricatures of Dickens. In the

[1] Chapter VI.

"American Notes" and "Martin Chuzzlewit" our genius for self-laudation is travestied by this master with a free hand. Yet in our own oratorical zone, we can find the literary equivalents of Dickens's choicest specimens. One is honestly disconcerted as to which is the parody. When a senator can say at a banquet given by his constituents, that "America as a nation has now passed through the fiery furnace of doubt and obloquy, convincing the most ignorant of her foes and the most envious of her would-be rivals that our Republic stands at last as unstained in her matchless record as she is superior in all the higher attainments of a true moral and spiritual civilization," we think instinctively of the passages in "Martin Chuzzlewit." Does the most riotous burlesque of Dickens much outdo this senatorial outburst?

It is of course true that among nations we do not hold a monopoly of gasconade. It is very probable that the fête-day literature of other nations would furnish rodomontade equal to our best. That would only enlarge the geographical area of the plague. There are, moreover, so many ways of bragging. It may be stentorian and grandiloquent like that of Victor Hugo. It may be the sheer bluster of a Colonel Chick, "What is America *for* but to reform the world?" It may appear in the ineffable strut of the Prussian lieutenant, or in the unvoiced but unmistakable *assumption* of superiority that the world has very generally associated with the British.

This has often a most naïve and unabashed statement, as when Alexander Mackay says:[1] —

"England has her fixed position in the family of nations,
and at the head of civilization — a position which she has long
occupied, and from which it will be some time ere she is driven.
We care not, therefore, what the foreigner says or thinks of us.
He may look or express contempt as he walks our streets, or
frequents our public places. His praise cannot exalt, nor can
his contempt debase us, as a people."

This special form of bragging is attributed to us: —

"Other nations boast of what they are or have been, but
the true citizen of the United States exalts his head to the skies
in the contemplation of what the grandeur of his country is
going to be. Others claim respect and honor because of the
things done by a long line of ancestors; an American glories
in the achievements of a distant posterity.

"If an English traveller complains of their inns and hints
his dislike to sleeping four in a bed, he is first denounced as a
calumniator and then told to wait a hundred years and see
the superiority of American inns to British."[2]

Even that learned French publicist, M. Chevalier,
who is very friendly, cannot help warning us against

[1] "The Western World," p. 285.

Bryce says, "An impartially rigorous censor from some other
planet might say of the Americans that they are at this moment less
priggishly supercilious than the Germans, less restlessly pretentious
than the French, less pharisaically self-satisfied than the English."
— Vol. II, p. 635.

[2] This exact comment De Amicis makes on the people as he
journeys about Holland, "They are always talking of what they
are going to do and almost never of what they have done," but,
curiously enough, he interprets this in terms of humility. —
"La Hollande," p. 96.

Mrs. Trollope
Author of " The Domestic Manners of the Americans "

all illusions about the real thing in matters of national preëminence. He says: —

"It is because France is the heart of the world; the affairs of France interest all; the cause which she espouses is not that of a selfish ambition, but that of civilization. When France speaks, she is listened to, because she speaks not her own feelings merely, but those of the human race. When she acts, her example is followed, because she does what all desire to do." [1]

Another Frenchman is less considerate of our sensibilities when he says that "French civilization is so above and apart from that of all other peoples, that his countrymen need not shrink from encouraging a people like those in the United States in their ambition to imitate the glories of France." This has a loftiness with which Victor Hugo has made the world familiar.

It will lessen the smart, as we turn for our punishment, to remember these various eruptions of self-laudation.

That our special variety of braggadocio is extremely offensive to all sorts of foreigners, there is

---

[1] D'Almbert, in his " Flaneries," gives one special reason why the French should travel: Until they have looked in upon several nations lying in outer darkness, there is no way to measure the heights of French civilization. "Just cross the frontier and it at once begins to dawn upon us how unrivalled we stand in all the tests of moral and spiritual refinement. Our morals are *probes*, *élégantes et faciles*, and our character, chivalrous, loyal, and without selfishness. Yet, we must travel, travel, especially to the United States, only to see how wisely the good God has given the finest country to the best of nations — France."

not the slightest doubt. De Nevers thinks it rather odious to assume that the Almighty is especially and exclusively committed on the side of American prestige. Among his illustrations, he quotes our historian Bancroft, "The American democracy follows its ascending march, uniform, majestic as the laws of being, sure of itself as the decrees of Eternity." Another finds it extremely distasteful that the Americans, above all peoples, cannot leave home for another country without "carrying their whole national belongings with them."

"From the moment they set foot on foreign soil, they begin to compare things with what they left behind them. This is intelligent and unavoidable, but the American is never at rest until he has made as many benighted 'foreigners' as possible understand and *admit* that their civilization and ways of life are inferior. Hotels, railways, checking baggage, the size of farms, the telephone, the methods of despatching business, — one and all have to be 'rubbed into you,' to use their vernacular. Americans with any breeding, of course, do not do this, but it is the curse of the country that it has so vast an army constantly on the march that is never happy unless bragging about some superiority." [1]

This opinion represents the settled conviction of

[1] A well-known writer among our American women just returns from Europe with this appealing observation to her sisters during their stay abroad: "A little more repose, a little more appreciation of what is not American, a little more modesty about vaunting one's own in public, a little less criticism of other countries, a little more attention to the manner of expression and the timbre of voice — these are some of the things which would improve the American woman traveller, and yet leave her, as she should be, distinctly American."

all our earlier critics and of some recent ones from whatever country they come. They find in this aggressive self-complacency the least tolerable of our qualities. About no other one trait is the unanimity more complete. There would be some escape, if the charge were brought by this or that nationality from which we widely differed, or if it came from the over-critical and ill-disposed alone. It is the very gravity of the accusation, that it comes from those most friendly to us and from those who have studied us with most open minds. The early French writers were passionately on our side and against the aspersions of the English critics of America. Yet the most cordial of these are annoyed by the incessant exercise of this unhappy talent. None of the French brought a more generous and insistent sympathy than De Tocqueville. No one gave surer proofs of that sympathy than by the way in which he philosophizes upon and excuses crudities and annoyances necessarily incidental to travel and investigation seventy-five years ago in this country. Yet about our self-vaunting, he had this passage: —

"For the last fifty years, no pains have been spared to convince the people of the United States that they are the only religious, enlightened, and free people. They perceive that, for the present, their own democratic institutions prosper, whilst those of other countries fail; hence they conceive a high opinion of their inferiority, and are not very remote from believing themselves to be a distinct species of mankind." [1]

[1] "Democracy in America," Vol. I, p. 506.

Another passage indicates a type which we hope was limited

F

De Tocqueville's friend, the Academician Ampère, has far less insight, but through his long journey is so gallantly polite and so obstinately the gentleman in every mishap, that we quite fall in love with him. His good-will is exhaustless, but he suffers from hearing, day in and day out, that Europe is to be pitied for the lack of those perfections which blossom in the institutions and the character of Americans. "They are really very much hurt if you put these superiorities in question."

Abdy, who was here in 1833–1834, has many comments on this characteristic. He is led to examine our school books, giving from Hart's "Geographical Exercises" this sample: —

"Knowing that Asia," says the author, "is sunk in ignorance and gross superstition, the young reader will at once discover the cause of our moral superiority over the dull Asiatics, *as well as the great mass of more enlightened neighbors of the European part of the Eastern continent.* It need scarcely be repeated, that it is owing to the influence of the press shedding its rays of knowledge over the minds of a free people." [1]

and exceptional: "I have often remarked in the United States that it is not easy to make a man understand that his presence may be dispensed with; hints will not always suffice to shake him off. I contradict an American at every word he says, to show him that his conversation bores me: I preserve a dogged silence, and he thinks I am meditating deeply on the truths which he is uttering; at last, I rush from his company, and he supposes that some urgent business hurries me elsewhere. This man will never understand that he wearies me to death, unless I tell him so, and the only way to get rid of him is to make him my enemy for life." — Vol. II, p. 210.

[1] "Journal of a Residence and Tour in the United States."

Abdy has a theory that bragging is necessarily developed by the shifts of the demagogue in a democracy and "the adulation of the press." He quotes from the speech of President Van Buren before the New York Convention as follows: —

"It was the boast and the pride and the security of the American nation, that she had in her bosom a body of men who, for sobriety, integrity, industry, and patriotism, were unequalled by the cultivators of the earth in any part of the known world; nay, more, — to *compare* them with men of similar pursuits in other countries, was to degrade them."

This has its match in a quotation from Mrs. Trollope: [1] —

"Mr. Everett, in a recent Fourth of July oration, speaks thus: 'We are authorized to assert that the era of our independence dates the establishment of the only perfect organization of government.' Again, 'Our government is in its theory perfect, and in its operation it is perfect also. Thus we have solved the great problem in human affairs.'"

That we have not wholly recovered, is seen in a few lines from the reported speech recently given by one of our most honored governors. It was spoken in an Eastern State.

"In the depth and breadth of character, in the volume of hope and ambition, in the universality of knowledge, in reverence for law and order, in the beauty and sanctity of our homes, in sobriety, in the respect for the rights of others, in recognition of the duties of citizenship, and in the ease and honor with which we tread the myriad paths leading from rank to rank in life, our people surpass all their fellow-men."

[1] p. 163.

When Mr. Bryce was at work upon his first edition, he quoted the following passage from an address before a well-known literary association by one of our eminent citizens, who was speaking of the influence which the American principles of liberty, as embodied in the Declaration of Independence, were exciting in the world: —

"They have given political freedom to America and France, unity and nationality to Germany and Italy, emancipated the Russian serf, relieved Prussia and Hungary from feudal tenures, and *will in time free Great Britain and Ireland also.*" [1]

Thus the entire planet is saved by a few strokes of an American pen. Mr. Bryce evidently thinks this extravagant, for he adds: —

"I have often asked Americans wherein they consider their freedom superior to that of the English, but have never found them able to indicate a single point in which the individual man is worse off in England as regards either his private civil rights or his political rights or his general liberty of doing and thinking as he pleases."

I submit again that some of the above citations hold their own pretty evenly with the caricatures of Charles Dickens. If placed side by side and honestly compared, the reader will be much in doubt as to which is the burlesque. Most of these soaring eulogies are themselves caricatures. No such dizzy heights of cultural attainment have been yet reached by us. I was told that the final passage

[1] "American Commonwealth," Vol. II, p. 635.

quoted from the governor's speech received "enthusiastic applause from the entire audience." [1]

I have purposely omitted from this heart-searching the whole list of ill-tempered and grouty opinions from critics who too obviously did not like us. One of these says he came to stay a year, but had the misfortune to spend his first two weeks at the Chicago Exposition. On his first morning at the Fair, he hears an official say, "I guess this show will make them Europeans feel silly." "Why silly?" asks the visitor. "You don't suppose they ever saw anything like this, do you?" When the unhappy stranger disagrees, he is assured by the official that it only proves that foreigners can't even tell a big thing when they see it.

It was the habit of this observer to ask a great many questions, but he says he invariably got brag instead of information, until, unable to stand it further, he took a ticket for home, resolved never to set foot in this country again. This is petulance and need not much annoy us. Our wincing comes when wholly cordial and large-minded men like Richard Cobden have to speak of the "vulgar expression of our self-sufficiency," or when a man of

[1] There was a large gathering chiefly of leading business men, many of them university graduates. They were being gravely and unctuously assured that we "surpass all our fellow-men" — in what? In "sobriety," in "depth and breadth of character," "in the universality of knowledge," "in reverence for law and order," "in respect for the rights of others," "in recognition of the duties of citizenship," etc. This cosmic preëminence is not here measured

science full of gentle courtesies like Sir Charles
Lyell turns aside from men and occasions in order
to avoid "what one can stand now and then, but
not everywhere and all the time." It is this type
of man who often asks why we should have this
ungracious habit. Why should it be so conspicuous?
Is it from a permanent disease of "congenital eminence"? Is it because the people of the United
States began by accepting a theory of equality
which they soon saw could not possibly be applied
to actual life? Emerson thought the lack of virtues
could be detected in any man who loudly talked about
them. Is it because at heart the inhabitants of the
States really doubt their greatness that they so
clamorously insist upon it? Is it because they
themselves see such a gap between their formulated
democratic ideals and their actual practices that
they "put on an extra strut of self-assertion before
strangers"? Another tries to find out "whether the
Yankees brag among themselves as they do before
strangers." He finds the evidence on this point very
perplexing. On the one hand, he is assured that
the natives have an inexhaustible delight in abusing
their own country and its institutions, and will even
entertain a foreigner with tales of political and other
self-abasement beyond any pitch of defamation that
the most bitter outsider ever conceived.[1] Against

by business and commercial tests, to which we have been much
accustomed. It is measured by the very highest spiritual values
that human beings attain in this world.

[1] There is much truth in a remark of Mr. Bryce to the effect

this he is told that Americans are bored by this national habit more even than are strangers. Two "men of distinction" (probably both from the East) tell him that as you travel West, the note of bragga-docio steadily rises until you reach the Pacific coast, where it would be deafening if your approach were not so gradual, as the big trees in the Yosemite are dwarfed because, on the route thither, you see so many larger and larger trees that the giant pines do not finally much surprise you. But this inquirer agrees that the "riot of self-flattery does culminate in the far West," its commonest form being that everything, from scenery to general culture, is the sublimest or the biggest in the universe. He notes down some forty objects or achievements that are indisputably "the finest in the entire world." G. W. Steevens writes of his own discipline in these words : —

"'I am now, Sir, about to show you my creamery. It is not yet finished, but when it is I anticipate that it will be the most complete and the best appointed,' — I shuddered, for I knew instinctively what was coming — 'in the world.' Shall I ever escape this tyranny of the biggest thing in the world?" [1]

that, worse still than any bragging is the habit of an occasional American of finding delight before strangers in decrying his own country.

[1] "Land of the Dollar," p. 167.

Professor Lamprecht recently writes, "Denver boasts of more buildings costing over $200,000 to erect than any other city of its age and size in America." After seeing so many largest and most imposing sublimities, he adds, "Ich habe sogar — the purest water in the world — getrunken." — "Americana," p. 68.

Kipling, on his first journey, says he was told the Palmer House in Chicago was "the finest hotel in the finest city of God Almighty's earth."

Another amazed visitor, who admits the facts
about our boastings, tries to defend us on the theory
that a great deal of it is a form of American humor.
He takes a passage from the novelist Marryat, who
reports as follows: —

"I was once talking with an American about Webster's
dictionary and he observed, 'Well now, Sir, I understand it's
the only one used in the Court of St. James by the king and
princesses and that, by royal order.'"

There is in this instance some inherent suggestion
of whimsical indulgence on the part of this defender
of the Yankee dictionary, but the well meant thesis
that our vaunting is largely jocular has, alas, very
scant truth in it.[1]   But the entire elimination of this
element leaves a quite terrifying amount of strident
vaporing still to account for.   When Emerson said
the American eagle was a good deal of a peacock,
and Lowell, as ambassador, groans "that so many
of my countrymen will allow the European to take
nothing for granted about the greatness of America,"
they are both telling the truth.

Nor can it be allowed to pass that this glorifying
is in any way exclusive of the West.   There just
comes to hand an official document of the Jamestown Exposition from which, among many, I take

---

[1] When some American deep-divers gave a public exhibition and
one of them, before slipping into the water, called out, "We can
dive deeper and stay under longer and come up *drier* than any
divers in the world," the classification becomes easy.

these sentences, "greatest military spectacle the world has ever seen," "grandest naval rendezvous in history," "greatest gathering of warships in the history of the world," "the largest military parade ground in the world," "the greatest military and naval parade ever witnessed," "the greatest display of gorgeous military uniform," and "the greatest military and naval celebration ever attempted in any age by any nation." This is an Eastern and not a Western product, and much more Atlantic rhetoric with the same resounding note could be reproduced. Foreigners both at the Chicago and the St. Louis Fairs, only on the edge of the West, found that "the world" standard was no longer adequate, so the "universe" had replaced it. On a very recent visit an English bishop was delighted with one of our less conspicuous Eastern colleges. He smilingly told its president that it was very restful to find a school that was not in endowment, in rapid growth, in distinction of alumni, or in some other way "the biggest in the country." The bishop reports that he noticed instantly the look of surprise and protest as his host replied, "But we do cover more *space* than any college in the United States." "From this time on," says the bishop, "I avoided all occasions of bringing this extraordinary endowment into play."

In considering later (Chapter VI) the asserted supersensitiveness of the American people, a little light may be thrown on the origin of this self-magnifying by the reaction on national habits of that

long border life incident to the slow extension of
our population toward the Pacific coast. It was a
life in which the individual was so thrown upon his
own resources, as to call out every extreme of self-
assertion and independence. Successes were determined by his own conscious achievement rather
than by social coöperation. Given several generations in which this border life advances so rapidly
and with such signal triumphs over the most redoubtable external difficulties, and these extremes of
self-confidence are not unnatural. It is not alone
the duration of this border life with its reactions,
but, even more, its rapidity and its sense of mastery
and overcoming that have left so powerful an
impress upon the mind and character.[1]

Yet the origins of the blemish are not nearly so
important as the main fact that we have as a nation
sorely overdone this business of calling attention to
our eminence. I have tried on several occasions to
trap a Japanese into some chance exercise of this
gift. It has never met with the least success. At
a small gathering in New York, at which four Japanese of distinction were present, an American officer
asked if the Japanese would take Port Arthur.
With the same modesty, amounting almost to self-
effacement, in which he had spoken of the entire

[1] An obvious comment on this theory is that we are by no means
alone among nations in having a long "border life." If other
peoples (as in Australia) had this experience without the excess of
brag, the theory is inadequate.

war, this reply came: "We do not know. The Russians fight with so much spirit and die so well! but still we hope in a few months we shall get possession of it." Only in this tone could they be induced to speak of a single incident of their great struggle.

Later a Japanese official was congratulated upon their great naval victory by one of our own admirals. "Yes," was the reply, "we think in Japan that our future tasks will be less difficult." [1]

Remembering the degree of exultation which followed Manila and Santiago, what vocabulary would have served us had the Russian fleet gone to pieces before our own ships? If Dewey's fleet was so easily made to overtop Nelson at Trafalgar, what heroic fellowship would have been found worthy of an American Togo! And yet whatever revelries of self-admiration we may still yield to under unwonted excitement, nothing is clearer than the slow abatement of our boasting. More and more it has to be done with indirection and restraint. This toning down has come as we have grown more securely conscious of a national strength about which there is no question. The quoted bluster from political speeches in the first half of the last century would be far more likely to meet with derision before any average American audience at the present

---

[1] De Amicis says for the Dutch that in all their towns he never heard a trace of national braggadocio — *personne ne laisse percer l'ombre de vanité nationale.* — "La Hollande," p. 95.

time. It was a part of the change which Dickens noted, even in the quarter of a century that separated his two visits to this country.

There is truth in Bryce's words: "Fifty or even forty years ago, the conceit of this people was a byword. It was not only self-conscious but obtrusive and aggressive. . . . But American conceit has been steadily declining as the country has grown older, more aware of its strength, more respected by other countries." These are reassuring words. They are, moreover, true to the extent that we are more easily and quickly ashamed of bluster than we were in the days when we had plenty of shrewd suspicion about our failings, but did not like to have them specified and posted by an outsider. In such improvement as there has been, let us rejoice, but not forget that the talent still requires a great deal of careful watching.

CHAPTER V

SOME OTHER PECULIARITIES

IF there was an excess of emphasis in the last chapter upon a single alleged characteristic, it is because foreign comment on our boastfulness has itself such emphasis and unanimity. Upon no other one thing is there entire agreement. That we are sordid in our love of money is asserted by a majority of these onlookers, yet some of our ablest censors, as we shall see, now come gallantly to our defence against this charge. That our manners are pretty bad is very commonly said, but this, too, is denied by at least a few first-rate foreign judges. The variations in opinion are found about every peculiarity noted in this chapter. Some will have it that our democracy is full of envy; others, as Professor Münsterberg, deny this. The "American voice" excites almost universal dislike, yet it has here and there a defender. But through the century, so far as I could learn, not a single voice is heard to defend us against the charge that our gift for bragging has no international competitor.

Our frailties, queernesses, peculiarities, distinctions, make a rather portentous showing. To begin

in lighter vein and with external characteristics,
we can be spotted in any part of the world by the
way our elbows rest upon the table. This trait vexed
a French *savant* until he discovered our habit of
eating corn from the cob. If for some exceptional
reason this sign fail, we may be known by our manner
of eating soup. We are the only people who fill
the spoon by first moving it *away from the body*.
This lacks something of the simplicity of the corn-on-
the-cob theory.[1] It also, as I have proved by investigation, excites incredulity among many Americans who assert that since they could be trusted with
soup, the spoon has been filled by moving it *toward*
the body. The amount of gold displayed in the
teeth is another safe token. As we have the best
"fire brigades" because of the frequency of our fires,
so we have the best dentists because our teeth are
bad. A Frenchman hears that girls in the United
States are often married with no other dowry than
the gold "mined into their teeth." In any European
crowd we may be known by our "inability to keep
still" or by a "certain facial pallor." As we are
studied in our own habitat, there is great "monotony"
or "lack of variety" in our lives and ideals; rooted
suspicion toward people and things we do not
understand; lack of thoroughness in our habits and

---

[1] One budding naturalist among our visitors is delighted to
find in Anthony Trollope an account of the American squash. It
was often served to him, but he "had no conception of its origin."
Now he learns that it is the "pulp of the pumpkin."

undertakings; slight capacity for pleasure for its own sake; we are "very silent"; we are the most sensitive of peoples under criticism; we are lawless, especially about everything that touches our business interests; we put up supinely with small injustices against which other nations kick. Especially the French endow us with a miraculous instinct for creating all forms of associational activity. M. de Tocqueville writes: [1] —

"In no country in the world has the principle of association been more successfully used, or applied to a greater multitude of objects, than in America. Besides the permanent associations, which are established by law, under the names of townships, cities, and counties, a vast number of others are formed and maintained by the agency of private individuals."

Chevalier says: —

"The Yankee type exhibits little variety; all Yankees seem to be cast in the same mould; it was, therefore, very easy for them to organize a system of liberty for themselves, that is, to construct a frame, within which they should have the necessary freedom of motion."

Then, of his own French people he writes: —

"As for us, who resemble each other in nothing, except in differing from everybody else." [2]

[1] "Democracy in America," p. 242.

Dr. A. S. Crapsey, for twenty-eight years active as a clergyman in Rochester, N.Y., in speaking of "the hundreds of orders and associations" in that community, says, "They are so fundamentally a part of our social life that our civilization would fall to pieces without them."

[2] Chevalier was a man of the world and a wise one, but these quoted words offer so genuine a bit of obtuseness and provincial-

These modern writers, from De Rousier and
Professor Vigoroux to the last book of Paul Adam,
continue to note this quality. M. Adam is so struck
by it that he speaks of it as more peculiarly our distinction than the aggressive individualism which most
writers identify with our character and society.

If our political and social pretensions as expressed
in our Declaration and patriotic literature are serious, we must be said to exhibit a most unexpected
aptitude for snobbery. Both De Tocqueville and
Laboulaye find amusement in the desire of Americans
to have it known as soon as possible that they are
probably descended from certain distinguished
English families. On this point a great deal of
embarrassing evidence is given from the behavior
of many Americans in Europe, from the agility
with which purchasable titles are clutched at in
marriage, and from the amazing extension of societies ready to furnish heraldic blazonry (for a
consideration) to all comers.[1] Harriet Martineau

ism that they deserve comment. The Eastern traveller, Palgrave,
says that practically the whole East in his time honestly thought
all Europeans alike. They in the East were, of course, profoundly
different one from another, but to the inhabitants of Bagdad or
Mosool, there was not the slightest difference between a Frenchman, an Englishman, and a German, nor could they be made to
understand the most obvious distinctions. Hamerton says that to
the average Frenchman the English are pretty much alike. "Each
nation is aware that there is now, and always has been in past
times, an infinite variety of character within its own border, but it
fails to imagine that a like variety can exist in a foreign country."

[1] One spectator, scoffing at our pretence of equality, says, "The

A Scene at a Campmeeting

Illustration by Cruikshank in "The Playfair Papers," published in 1841

has much to say about snobbishness in the older cities. Boston was even more intolerable to her than it was to H. G. Wells. As she had taken our pretensions to equality seriously, she expresses her first surprise to find that the most interesting people are so sharply separated by social barriers. In Philadelphia she makes inquiries about the cultivated superiorities, and is told "that the mutual ignorance was from fathers of the Arch Street ladies having made their fortunes, while the Chestnut Street ladies owed theirs to their grandfathers. Another, who was amused at a new fashion of curtseying just introduced, declared it was from the Arch Street ladies rising twice on their toes before curtseying, while the Chestnut Street ladies rose thrice. I was sure of only one thing in the matter, — that it was a pity that the parties should lose the pleasure of admiring each other, for no better reasons than these: and none better were apparent." [1]

Among our "grands traits," De Nevers insists that a supercilious exclusiveness (*l'exclusivisme dédaigneux*) is to be found. He says that between three and four thousand American families, with hungry credulity, have traced their ancestry to those who have occupied thrones somewhere in Europe. It is this writer who attributes to us a unique development of "altruistic vanity" which is *un pro-*

Americans seem to have no notion that Nature went into the business before the Declaration of Independence."

[1] "Society in America," Vol. I, p. 173.

ç

duct absoluement Américain. This amiability is illustrated by the generous and free distribution of titles which encourage the "ambitions and the good nature of the community." It was Marryat, I think, who met "in the United States chiefly colonels and captains who had never been in any army, but owed their dignity to the good-will of their neighbors." The rebuke of Mr. Bryce is conveyed with such literary skill that one must italicize a part of it. He speaks of our "enthusiasm for anything that can be called genius with an *over-readiness to discover it.*"

Again, one of our primary passions is "to overdo things." If we take on any new habit, like the tipping of waiters and attendants, we are not content to exercise it with the least restraint. It must be carried into all forms of demoralizing excess. An Englishman is taken to one of the more fashionable New York clubs on several occasions. He says that his American hosts in no instance gave less than a dollar tip to the cabman.[1] "What," he asks, "can you expect of a system that gives as a tip three times as much as my *fare* from the station to my club in London ever costs me?"

---

[1] This seemed to me extravagant both as a tip and a story. I have, however, verified it. A gentleman frequently at one of these clubs tells me: "I have several times gone there to dine with two fellows whom no one would call rich. I have repeatedly seen a crisp dollar bill given as a tip. I supposed it was the fare, until I found out, in this instance, that the cabs were paid for at the club."

Our "pitiless hospitality" is another phase of this "genius for overdoing." That the Yankees are tuft-hunters can be seen in "this inability to let any kind of celebrity alone a *minute*." They will drive him to death if they can get some glory out of it. Frederika Bremer has many complaints of this. She writes: "And that is the way they kill strangers in this country. They have no mercy on the poor lion, who must make a show and whisk his tail about as long as there is any life left in him. One must really be downright obstinate and stern, if one would be at peace here. And I feel as if I should become so. It is said that Spurzheim was regularly killed with kindness by the Bostonians."

This "impulse to excess" has many dangerous illustrations. "When the passion has vented itself, interest dies out," as in our "prolific and insane passing of laws." "For every conceivable evil, real or imagined, the Yankee must have a law, but when it is passed, he goes about his business as if nothing more were required." The result being that "nowhere is there such a bewildering mass of unenforced and forgotten laws as in America."

Among civilized folk, we have the least agreeable speaking voice; we have a passion for exaggeration and bigness apart from quality and excellence. This latter shows itself not only externally (as in our advertising and our press methods) but in our tastes and habits of thought.

Perhaps not unconnected with this is another

observation that is often expressed by foreign students about our educational institutions. It is admitted that we have specific schools of the highest rank in administrative efficiency, but that the visiting student is surprised by nothing so much as the larger number that have elaborate up-to-date external equipment and housing with feeble and ineffective teaching. An English educator, after seeing our schools during a five months' trip, says, "There are no better schools in the world than a few I could name, but in many others with imposing and costly plants, the teaching is so poor that your public appears to trust the magnificence of the plant rather than the capacity of the teachers."

To continue our discipline, we have an extraordinary optimism, especially where there seems to be no justification for it; we are also "fatalists," accepting grimly or cheerfully all sorts of defeats when once the issue is decided; we are "the only people to whom hotels and travelling are ends in themselves." This is a part of our surplus (or morbid) energy and love of change, which excites many comments. Our curiosity is very highly developed; we have little "love of locality." We have unusual powers of adaptability to new and sudden emergencies; we are "most intellectually tolerant," have "great good nature," [1] "unlimited push," "inven-

[1] Sir Arthur Helps puts these words into the mouth of his lawyer, "I think you cannot help being struck by their good nature, even when they [the Americans] commence blowing their tiresome national trumpet." — "Essays on Organization," p. 208.

tion," "energy," "versatility," and a widespread "whimsical humor."

It is very painful to find that other nations do not think us the wittiest folk in the universe, but "a certain generally diffused humor" is readily granted to us. We are known, finally, by one other ugly distinction which gives us easy and sinister precedence among civilized folk of all the world. Side by side with lordly hospitalities for all the embodied enlightenments, we show a mania to foster and support multitudes of impostors. Mr. Muirhead's words were, "the home of the charlatan and the quack." Why, it is asked, should a people so priding itself on its practical good sense open its arms to every religious and medical charlatan on earth? One visitor tries to make a record of all the obvious quacks in a small city of twenty thousand. Palmists, clairvoyants, fortune-tellers, soothsayers, astrologers, innumerable healers, magicians, exorcists, he finds in such numbers that he is sure "the Americans don't know themselves what a pest of vampires and parasites they harbor." More dangerous than this swarm of necromancers, however, is the patent medicine fiend. Here our passion for humbug is exercised at terrible cost. This investigator gives up his task of counting the quacks, but says he now understands why we are "a headachy and dyspeptic people." "It is a nation of nervously disturbed people." A French engineer, four years in the West, thinks the Americans are not to be feared by competing nations, because they will lose their prestige and strength through the quack doctor.

De Nevers, also, connects our ill health with "the colossal use of drugs."

One writer thinks the palmists and sorcerers generally are welcomed and maintained as we welcome vaudeville or any source of fun. We get amusement enough out of them to justify the expense, but are not really fooled by them. The quack doctor and patent medicine man are not thus accounted for. They are like a "permanent devastating plague." "Why should this most beschooled and newspapered nation in the world freely exhaust itself by fostering this army of leeches?" One gives a long list of advertisements of which the following is an illustration: —

"Great Clairvoyant! Mme. Stuart; THE SEVENTH DAUGHTER OF THE SEVENTH DAUGHTER, has read cards since 11 years of age, — life revealed, past, present, future, — ladies or gents, 50c."

Here is the full and redoubtable catalogue of our peculiarities, both in terms of weakness and of strength, as gathered from this literary annotation on our institutions and behavior. It is a medley of vigors and incompletenesses, of many offences and some sturdy excellences.

There are innumerable variations given to these supposed characteristics, but for the most part they analyze into the more general ones here given. Between several of these, as we have seen, any real distinction is difficult to maintain. For example, if there is a "fatalistic" quality in our character, it is not something inherently different and apart from our "indiscriminate optimism," or even from our "general good nature." If we are careless and indifferent about common social wrongs and grievances, this is not distinct from our "tolerance." "Adaptability" is a part of our "love of change." If we have "a passion for bigness," that becomes a general term for other minor shortcomings like our "lack of tact," our "importunate hospitality" and "lack of restraint." Some of these require no comment, as they are merely human and race frailties, not in the least peculiar to our geography. With only a portion, even of the truthful strictures, can we deal. But first: Toward the main charges, what attitude are we to take? Shall we greedily accept the flattering ascriptions, but bristle with testy denial at the unflattering ones? This would too easily justify our critics. Smugly to take the praise and show affront at the blame, would prove that one damaging criticism is true: that "the American cannot stand criticism"; that "unless you coddle him, he sulks and won't play." One writer in 1840, examining our prisons, says: "I found I could not criticise with the slightest freedom. Unless I had plenty of compliments, I could not even get the information I wanted. If I put it all on with a trowel, I could get any question answered." We shall see later what a mass of evidence there is on this point. The only proof that we have outgrown this childishness must be in our present readiness to face the censure as gayly as the approbation.

Another form of that early oversensitiveness is to boast fussily that we don't in the least *care* what foreigners think of us. This only adds stupidity to childishness.

To be intellectually hospitable to these critics is not in the least to admit their infallibility. Much less does it admit that criticisms once true are still true. Some of them that were meant as a stigma or weakness are virtues in the making. "Yankee curiosity" has received much abuse, but it is one of the most hopeful signs of growing intelligence. Several of our more recent visitors express surprise that this prying curiosity of which they had read or heard so much is nowhere to be found except as an exceptional phenomenon. So, too, with the charge of "suspicion." That we are exceptional in this has probably no shred of truth so far as it is meant to stand for a national characteristic. For-eigners far oftener note an extreme openness and frankness of mind which even become objects of criticism. Suspicion is a product of social or class conditions, or it is the merely human expression of timidities and doubts when inexperienced folk are placed in wholly new and unwonted surroundings. One of the critics explains that he never saw this suspicion in Americans in their own country, but observed it only when he saw them in Europe.

Even such a count against us as that we are the "happy hunting-ground of all extant quackeries," that we "are the only nation of rank that fosters and protects all forms of charlatanism," raises an issue that is not to be dismissed as if it were a final judgment.

There are specific forms of commercialized humbug that are definitely known to be such by the simplest tests and common experience. Against these no scathing can be too severe. But our critics include in their condemnation far more than these. There is the assumption of some existing religious, educational, scientific, moral, or political standard, from which any departure is a depravity. Yet much of the world's new truth is constantly breaking in upon us through those that at the time *are called* cranks and impostors. What would become of religion, science, medicine, politics, art, and education, social reforms, if in each the strictly orthodox contingent were allowed to define and dispose of heresies; if to those various orthodoxies were given sole power to decide the activities and the destinies of those groping and experimenting on life's frontier? There is none to whom the race has more cause for gratitude than the long list of those who were the erratic and ostracized of their day. The accusation against the English, that they suffer still because they cannot bear with eccentricity, is as late as John Stuart Mill. Tolerance has its dangers, but a straitened conventionalism has perils greater still.

Again, a French writer complains that we are cold and unresponsive. That is what the Latin race would ascribe to all northern races. De Amicis knew Holland well, and that is his criticism against the Dutch. That all northern peoples are more indifferent to pleasure for its own sake, is true from the Latin point of view.

Still other of these traits are explained by the character of the period of development. They would be as true of other nations when the corresponding stage was reached. Given our facilities for constant travel, and they, too, will be "restless" and "incessantly on the go," and apparently have "slight attachment to the home."

"Lack of thoroughness," in the sense meant, was inevitable and even justifiable in the early decades of the last century, when the criticism was oftenest made. Americans have, says one, "an absurd lack of thoroughness." It will be remembered that words like "absurd" and "ridiculous" are usually applied by us to objects and happenings, the real meaning or explanation of which we do not understand. The "absurdity" is properly in our own lack of comprehension.

For example, our "flimsy wooden houses" have excited a great deal of emotional rhetoric. They were almost the first objects noted by Dickens. They seemed "to have no root." They looked as if they "could be taken up piecemeal like a child's toy," and crammed into a little box.[1] Another says

[1] "American Notes," Vol. I, p. 23.

they are "as absurd as they are dangerous and wasteful." A stately English scholar said while lecturing here: "Your wooden houses, I can't understand. Why don't you put up something in stone and brick that will be solid at the end of three hundred years, as we do in England?" An American, to whom the question was put, answered: "It is because we don't want that kind of a house. Changes, improvements, new comforts of all sorts come so fast, that we don't want a house to last too long. This house is what I want, but not what my children will want. Even I want to make some structural change every ten years. I can now do it without being ruined, as I could not in one of your three-century dwellings." "Bless my heart," replied the Englishman, "I never thought of that. You want houses that will easily take on improvements as they come, and be free to build a new and better one every generation, if you want to." I heard the Englishman say later, as he was commenting on the above conversation, "It is really extraordinary how stupid most of us are in not trying to discover why people do things in different ways, before we set up as judges." This bit of obvious wisdom applies quite as well to a good many of the "characteristics" which here occupy us.

There are, however, some of these strictures that are not to be explained away or even to be internationalized. Stretch the margin of exceptions widely as we may, the "American voice" in many parts of

the country and among a considerable portion of
the population is so sadly deficient in resonance and
pleasing quality that no ardor of patriotism can save
our pride about it. That the great mass of us do
not set ourselves — like the English, for example —
stoutly against recognized evils and nuisances of
the commoner sort is incontestable. Herbert Spencer
saw in this one of our chief weaknesses. It is again
and again asked, Why should a people of such un-
doubted vitality and assertion have this failing?
Chevalier says: "They eat what is placed before
them, without ever allowing themselves to make
any remark about it. They stop at the pleasure of
the driver and the captain, without showing the least
symptom of impatience; they allow themselves to
be overturned and their ribs to be broken by the one,
without uttering a complaint or a reproach; the
discipline is even more complete than in the camp."

A British critic calls this "the little-understood
stoicism of the Yankee" in contrast to which, he
says that "if an Englishman finds his chop slightly
burnt, he barks at everybody in sight."

That Americans in the presence of great and
impending evils show extraordinary mettle has often
enough been said at home and abroad. Even the
English found us sufficiently lively as kickers in 1776
and 1812. The sacrifices for an idea North and South
in the Civil War mark the first profound change of
tone in foreign criticism. John Bright could say,
"A nation that can suffer like that for its principles

has answered all critics that are capable of understanding ideals." But these are the great events. It is conceded that these stir us to real unselfishness and intrepidity. The criticism concerns those lesser evils and injustices which continue to afflict most communities, and which Mr. Lowell thought likely to continue because of "the divine patience of my fellow-countrymen." The illustrations of this lethargy are troublesome from their very number.

I choose three very simple instances from New England communities that are often spoken of as exceptional, so far as educational opportunity and general well-being are concerned. In the first one, serious political evils had developed during the last twenty years, largely in connection with carelessly bestowed franchises. From this root came treacherous politics and slovenliness in the care of the city streets and sanitation. After some ten years of this, I heard the following comment from the one citizen who, by common consent, was foremost in public spirit. He said, "No effort that we can make seems really to move the mass of our best citizens at all. Some of them will come to a meeting and talk manfully, but when it comes to giving their time and continuous work, even one evening in the week, they fall down. The college graduate as a class, and men from whom you would expect most, are about as good as so many dead men. They usually say they are too busy, but I find a large part of them using up four or five times as many hours as this public service would require, at golf, at their clubs, or at the card table. Enough men play poker every day from four o'clock till dinner, to set these things right in six months."

The second instance is a much-schooled community in which harassing juvenile misdemeanors, among other things, have long been such a plague as to excite much discussion. The Captain of Police, who had special experience with these offenders, said in my hearing: "You needn't blame the kids; the trouble is in the public, but especially in the educated and well-to-do people. There are just two in this town who have sand enough to take any real trouble after they make complaint. Those two will go to court and see it through, but the rest of the citizens just grumble, but can't be made to do anything about it."

When these facts were brought out at a public meeting in the third town, a sociological professor made the reply: "We thought all the time you were talking about us. Several of our citizens have given up raising fruit and flowers, because there seems to be no way in which stealing and destruction can be prevented. One of my acquaintances cut down his fruit trees, although he never would take the trouble to appear in court against the offender, even when the petty thief had been caught. He gave as a reason that he always imagined a distracted mother would appear and make such a fuss for her boy that he couldn't stand it." This professor enriched the discussion by adding that the reason why our domestic service is so bad is that almost all mistresses are too cowardly to tell the truth. When the servant leaves, and the mistress gives a "recommendation," she tells the most atrocious fibs about the girl's real faults, and then excuses herself on the ground that she "really can't hurt the girl's prospects." This coincides with one of Mrs. Bacon's conclusions about the servant question, that little is to be hoped for. "Until women can offer honesty in their written references, and supply full details to written questions, they have no right to complain of bad service from bureaus or employees." [1]

It is this hesitation to face unpleasant facts rather than to be disagreeable and pugnacious about them, after the genius of our English cousins, that calls out the criticism. James Muirhead says, "Americans invented the slang word 'kicker,' but so far as I could see, their vocabulary is here miles ahead of their practice; they dream noble deeds, but do not do them; Englishmen 'kick' much better, without having a name for it." [2] I have never found an American who denied this criticism after he had fairly considered it. One remembers little spurts of protest now and then. Indignant letters are sent to the press to complain of late trains, crowded trollies, or soft-coal smoke. Yet the

---

[1] *American Magazine*, February, 1907, p. 360.
[2] "The Land of Contrasts," p. 801.

difference between our general acquiescence, and the English habit of quick and lusty resistance to minor evils, has no exaggeration in Herbert Spencer's comment. A humorous illustration of the English habit is shown me by Mr. Muirhead in the English "Who's Who" for 1904. Mr. Ashton gives, as one of his recreations, writing letters to the press on various subjects; of these, over 550 call attention to neglect of graves of noteworthy people.

In one of our smaller cities, the overchoked condition of the street-cars called out a protest in the press. The local trolley magnate was incensed by this lack of consideration on the part of the public. He said the company couldn't do any better, adding, "The seats only pay our expenses: *the straps give us our dividends.*" As long as we submit to rank affronts of that character, we deserve what we get.

For the degree of truth there is in the criticism, what reasons can be given? Is it a part of our "miscellaneous good nature" or of our "fatalism"? Is it that our "gift of tolerance," which Klein notes, includes things evil as well as good? The extemporized reason is usually that we are "too busy with our own affairs." I have even heard it said that we have too much "humor" to be fussy about ordinary evils. A sociological teacher in one of our colleges states it thus: "The truth is, our individual relation to the whole pest of lesser injustices and evils is so slight and so indirect, that anything an individual can do strikes him as ridiculous. I am

CAPTAIN BASIL HALL
Author of "Travels in North America"

asked, for instance, to join the protestants against 'city noises.' They are an infernal nuisance, but when I think of any conceivable thing I can do to check the nuisance, the incongruity makes me smile." That we do not like to make ourselves conspicuous or disagreeable accounts, I think, for more of this easy acquiescence than surplus of humor.

It is not unlikely that one deeper reason why the English are blunt and abrupt about their rights, is because class lines are so much more sharply drawn there. Within these limits, one is likely to develop the habit of demanding his dues. He insists upon his prerogatives all the more because they are more narrowly defined. When an English writer [1] says, "We are not nearly so much afraid of one another in England as you are in the States," he expresses this truth. In a democracy every one at least hopes to get on and up. This ascent depends not upon the favor of a class, but upon the good-will of the whole. This social whole has to be conciliated. It must be conciliated in both directions — at the top and at the bottom. To make one's self conspicuous and disagreeable, is to arouse enmities that block one's way.

This is in part what De Tocqueville means in one of his few severities, "I know of no country in which there is so little independence of mind and real freedom of discussion as in America." Professor Münsterberg evidently thinks Germany has more "inner freedom"; and even adds, "If I consider

---

[1] Jowett, Book VIII, p. 588.

H

the outer forms of life, I do not hesitate to maintain that Germany is even in that respect freer than the United States."[1] An honored citizen of Maine has given it as the worst feature of their constitutional prohibition that "it paralyzes the intellectual independence of our politicians." He named three men prominent as statesmen. "I know personally that every one of them heartily disbelieves in that liquor legislation, but they will not imperil their careers by saying so in public." That this "saving subserviency" will be found in every nation of the world is, of course, true. That it is more necessarily prevalent in a large and loose democracy is what these criticisms imply.

As other of these imputed characteristics are to have further consideration under topics which they serve to illustrate, the next chapter will be devoted to a peculiarity that is a kind of tap-root from which others spring; namely, the extreme sensitiveness of the American people under criticism.

[1] "American Traits," p. 33.

CHAPTER VI

AMERICAN SENSITIVENESS

ONE of our critics reports that he meant to make a third trip to the United States, but that he suffered so much from the perpetual inquiry, "How do you like America?" "How do you like our city or town?" that he concluded to stay at home.

The fame of Frederika Bremer gave her universal welcome among us in the middle of the last century. Her two volumes [1] are full of appreciation, but she is "vexed to distraction" by insistent personal questioning, of which this is one example : —

"At the hotel at Buffalo I was again tormented by some new acquaintance with the old, tiresome questions, 'How do you like America?' 'How do you like the States?' 'Does Buffalo look according to your expectations?' To which latter question I replied that I had not expected anything from Buffalo." [2]

This plague of questioning assumed many forms and became a sore trial to her. She thought as she went South she might be free from it. But there, too, it haunted her.

[1] "Homes of the New World," two volumes, Harpers, 1853.
[2] "Homes of the New World," Vol. I, p. 596.

"You are asked, for example, —
'Will you have butter?'
'Yes, I thank you.'
'Will you take fish or meat? chicken or turkey?'
'Chicken, if you please.'
'Have you any choice?   The breast or a wing?'
Then comes, 'Will you have pickles?'
'No, I thank you.'
A pause and calm ensues for two minutes. But then
somebody to your left discovers that you have no pickles, and
pickles come to you from the left. 'May I help you to
pickles?'
   'No, I thank you.'
After a few minutes more somebody on the right sees
that you have no pickles, and hastens to offer you the bottle.
'Will you not take pickles?'
   You then begin an interesting conversation with your next
neighbor; and, just as you are about to ask some question of
importance, a person opposite you observes that you are not
eating pickles, and the pickle-bottle comes to you across the
table." [1]

If we are to believe several other visiting celebrities,
the question, "How do you like us?" begins before
landing, never fails at the dock, and continues until
the poor victim is under shelter in his native land.
If the traveller has a turn for philosophizing, he is
sure to ask why the American has this itching desire
to know what every foreigner thinks about his town
or country. One maintains that "familiarity with
half the world" never elicited this inquiry in any
other country. An American who had spent much

[1] "Homes of the New World," Vol. I, p. 334.

of his life in Europe told me he never remembered once being asked, " How do you like Italy, or England, or Germany?" Bryce says in his Introduction, "In England one does not inquire from foreigners, nor even from Americans, their views on the English laws and government; nor does the Englishman on the continent find Frenchmen or Germans or Italians anxious to have his judgment on their politics." G. W. Steevens[1] thinks that while personally we are "entirely free from self-consciousness," our *national* self-consciousness is extreme in its development. We are "uneasy unless we know what the observer is thinking." Buckminster notes in 1838[2] that "the first citizen of Pennsylvania, Nicholas Biddle," in an address delivered at Princeton College, used these words, "When some unhappy traveller ventures to smile at follies which we do not see or dare not acknowledge, instead of disregarding it or being amused by it, we resent it as an indignity to our sovereign perfections." This differs little from Mrs. Trollope: —

"If I say to an American that the country he lives in is a fine one, 'Ay,' he replies, 'there is not its equal in the world.' If I applaud the freedom which its inhabitants enjoy, he answers, 'Freedom is a fine thing, but few nations are worthy to enjoy it.' If I remark the purity of morals which distinguishes the United States, 'I can imagine,' he says, 'that a stranger who has witnessed the corruption that prevails in other nations, should be astonished at the difference.' At

[1] "Land of the Dollar," p. 315.
[2] "Travels in America," Vol. II, p. 45.

length, I leave him to the contemplation of himself; but he returns to the charge, and does not desist till he has got me to repeat all I have just been saying. It is impossible to conceive a more troublesome or more garrulous patriotism; it wearies even those who are disposed to respect it." [1]

Alfred Bunn, an English lecturer, writes: [2] —

"Such an unhappily sensitive community surely never existed in the world; and the vengeance with which they visit people for saying they don't admire or like them, would be really terrible if the said people were but as mortally afraid of abuse as they seemed to be. I would not advise either Mrs. Trollope, Basil Hall, or Captain Hamilton, ever to set their feet upon this ground again, unless they are ambitious of being stoned to death."

M. de Tocqueville says: [3] —

"Nothing is more embarrassing, in the ordinary intercourse of life, than this irritable patriotism of the Americans. A stranger may be well inclined to praise many of the institutions of their country, but he begs permission to blame some things in it, — a permission which is inexorably refused."

It is a different phase of this same feeling to which Mr. Howells refers when he asks why it is that we Americans insist, when abroad, in being appreciated "in the lump." Why must the poor alien show a fondness for the whole nation? This is a form of sublimated patriotism which we do not practise at home. We do not ourselves like Americans "in the lump." After our tastes and sympathies we

[1] Vol. II, p. 275.
[2] "Old England and New England," 1853, pp. 190–191.
[3] "Democracy in America," p. 311.

have affections and likings for individuals. We do not dote on the totals in the census.

A lecturer, recently here from Cambridge, England, said of this characteristic: "We Englishmen don't care a rap whether England is liked or disliked as a nation. We like some human beings here and there. Some Americans quite win our hearts, just as some Englishmen do. But I won't love the whole of America any more than I love the whole pack of my own countrymen." This is clearly what we all act upon in our ordinary relations. In spite of "Triple" or any other alliances, no nation loves another nation, no race loves another race. Can we even say that the South loves the North, or the North the South? Does the East love the West, or the West the East? Does Chicago love St. Louis, Cleveland grow foolish over Cincinnati? Why, then, should America be so supersensitive on this point? Why should Paul Bourget still have to put it into his French text that we are so "touchy" — *au plus haut degré* "touchy"? [1]

Though the French and Germans note this trait, such natural history of our sensitiveness as can be traced has far more to do with our Mother Country than with that of any other or all others. In spite of vehement denial, we *cared* about English opinion. The historical relation with England, which covers the origin and close of two wars (1776 and 1812), did not wholly create this touchiness, but it helps

[1] "Outre-Mer," Vol. I, p. 68.

much to explain it. It is altogether impossible at this date to reproduce the enduring bitterness toward England which her attitude in these conflicts produced upon the American people. Almost more than the wars themselves was the prevailing tone of her official dealing with us, as well as the more general criticism seen in the last chapter. De Tocqueville, a quarter of a century after the War of 1812, says that it is incredible to what length this hatred of England went.

It is to the popular reading habit that we must first look. Dickens finds every American with his heels in the air and a newspaper in his hands. What sort of message did these readers find reprinted for them from the last batch of English papers? It was oftener than not coarse abuse of this country. Or it was a half-insolent ignoring of every national aspiration, and this was more galling still. It is a loyal Englishman who speaks of his own countrymen in these words:[1] —

"But it is just his calm, supercilious Philistinism, aggravated no doubt by his many years' experience as a ruler of submissive Orientals, that makes it no less a pleasure than a duty for a free and intelligent republican to resent and defy his criticism."

Until the forties, English opinion had been chiefly formed by books like those of Basil Hall, Hamilton, Dickens, and Mrs. Trollope. Books, still more

[1] "The Land of Contrasts."

recklessly hostile, like those of Parkinson and Smyth, were widely read by their countrymen. For years it was honestly believed in this country that vilifiers were hired by the British Ministers to discredit the United States. It was, of course, not true, but that it could have general belief indicates the state of feeling. It was also among our honest beliefs that many of these critics were here to gather discouraging evidence that might prevent English laborers from coming to this country.[1] This angered a certain class of employers who wanted cheap labor. That it was the adopted English policy to empty her poorhouses, orphan and insane asylums of their inmates and ship them to our shores, was also the commonest belief, and a belief that had plenty of apparently good evidence to sustain it. Indignant public meetings were held, with many investigations and lurid reports.

A fair sample of these reports was sent to the General Assembly in Baltimore (1831) by the mayor and city council. The report contained these words: "Of one thousand one hundred and sixty persons admitted to the almshouse in that city in 1831, four hundred and eighty-seven were foreigners; and of this number two hundred and eighty-one had been

[1] The son of Napoleon's general, Achille Murat, believed this, for he wrote in his "Moral and Political Sketch of the United States," in 1827, that the English Minister, wishing to stop emigration to the United States, descended so far as to induce mercenary writers to travel and promulgate through the press false statements against our people and Government.

in the country less than six months prior to their admission, and one hundred and twenty-one less than one week."

To recount these various sources of antipathy, jealousy, and misunderstanding explains much of our excessive self-consciousness under English criticism. I have heard the story of a sturdy-minded sea-captain on Cape Cod, whose boy brought word from school that an English grammar must be purchased. The old man, who lived through the period of 1812, shouted: "An English grammar! I wouldn't have the thing in the house. You will buy an American grammar!" January 17, 1808, in a despatch to Canning, the English Minister in this country mentioned that Congress contained one tailor, one weaver, six or seven tavern-keepers, four notorious swindlers, one butcher, one grazier, one curer of hams, and several schoolmasters and Baptist preachers. The tone of this was understood to be one of ill-concealed contempt. We have only to imagine amiabilities like this, copied in half the press of the United States, to understand what lively response would follow.

Into the American press came a steady stream of such quotations from English opinions. They were patronizing, contemptuous, or insulting, according to the humor of the writer. For more than a generation this was the food on which the American reader fed; De Tocqueville's word "incredible," as applied to these angers, is none too strong.

It is into this atmosphere that the English critic came. Nor is there much change until the nineteenth century is half spent. It was an atmosphere that heightened every one of our faults. It quite accounts for our early "suspicion." It throws a good deal of light on our bragging habits. The English traveller then seemed to us the embodied denial of every democratic ideal that we cherished. To assert ourselves against this chilling influence was too human to be avoided. In June, 1837, Jared Sparks wrote De Tocqueville that he was "vexed and mortified that an edition of your 'Démocratie' has not yet been published in America." Our newspapers had begun to copy extracts from English reviews which naturally emphasized De Tocqueville's more critical remarks. Mild as these were, they were enough to create an instant prejudice against the book in the United States.

That a good deal of this criticism was true, did not sweeten it to the taste. We had boldly and very conspicuously set up imposing ideals of political and social equality. Without the least restraint, we had raised these ideals before the world and made them the object of lofty and continuous declamation. It was therefore very rasping to have the ideals challenged. A yet sharper sting was in the frequent inquiry, "If you have a land of equality before the law, why do you continue slavery?" To the Northerner this passed endurance, and he usually makes a very poor figure in his attempts to show that slavery doesn't really conflict with these sacred phrases about liberty. One enraged Yankee replies that only a blockhead could see any inconsistency between slavery and liberty, and "besides, it's only down South, anyhow." An Englishman walking with his American host in New York, in 1825, sees the announcement of a dance on a placard bearing the words, "No colored people admitted." The guest says he remarked innocently, "It's pretty hard to practise equality, isn't it?" Whereupon his entertainer lost temper and said, "The Europeans are so spoiled by flunkeyism that they can't understand liberty when they see it."

Our treatment of the Indians also gave rise to many tart passages, as did our rancor and inhumanity against the Catholics which culminated in the burning of the nunnery in Charlestown.

There were indeed, at most periods when our visitors were present, some troublesome illustrations that seemed to give the lie to our fine speaking and writing. That Harriet Martineau, for instance, should come into Boston on the very day when Garrison was being dragged through the streets was awkward enough. She had given great attention before her coming to our political history and development. What interested her from the first was the Theory and Practice in our life and institutions. Here was her first rude shock. In this "land of the free" was liberty of speech so brutally denied? If men were thus assaulted, was

there no law? It was an eminent college president
who tried to soothe her in her disappointment.
He insisted that "it was all right, — *the mob having
been entirely composed of gentlemen.*" Lawyers tell
her that nothing can be done about it. "Ladies
were sure that the gentlemen of Boston would do
nothing improper." "Merchants thought the aboli-
tionists were served quite right." "What would
become of trade if such agitators were allowed to
anger the South?" "Clergymen excuse themselves
because the whole subject is so 'low.'" She writes
further, "And even Judge Story, when I asked him
whether there was not a public prosecutor who might
prosecute for the assault on Garrison, if the aboli-
tionists did not, replied that he had given his advice
(which had been formally asked) against any notice
whatever being taken of the outrage, — the feeling
being so strong against the discussion of slavery and
the rioters being so respectable in the city." [1]

Here was the rough awakening to this noble
woman. As one sees in Mrs. Chapman's Memoirs,
Miss Martineau was capable of commanding moral
courage.[2] She had every hospitality that Boston
and Cambridge could offer, but she did not flinch
from criticising these open affronts upon liberty,
law, and order. That the highest social and educational respectability should lead in these attacks
added gall to her pen. Her plain speaking stung

[1] "Autobiography," Vol. II, p. 24.
[2] "Autobiography," Vol. II, p. 30.

Boston to the quick.   It at once became the habit to
belittle her book and abuse her personally.   When
Captain Marryat came, he found her referred to as
"that deaf old woman with the trumpet."   He was
assured that "her volumes were full of blunders; that
her entertainers really had great fun in telling her big
stories which were solemnly written down."   One
eminent individual brings Miss Martineau's book
to Marryat, who says that he was "excessively delighted when he pointed out to me two pages of
fallacies, which he had told her with a grave face
and which she had duly recorded and printed." [1]

It was in this spirit that the injured self-love of the
community took its revenge.   It was very human,
but rather petty and ignoble.   There are errors in
Miss Martineau's book and too much dogmatism.
But at that time not two books had been written
on the United States so full of truth, so enriched
by careful observation and stated with more sobriety.[2]

I enlarge upon this special experience because it
faithfully represents that of many other visitors.

---

[1] "Diary in America," 1839, p. 9.

[2] That a college with religious traditions like those of Welles-
ley should honor itself, as it honors Miss Martineau, by giving her
statue so conspicuous a place in that institution, is the happiest sign
of enlarging intellectual life.   There are those living who remember her well and the obloquy that was heaped upon her.   She was
an object of "moral vituperation."   She was a "coarse infidel" and
even a "hardened atheist."   She was a "trifler with truth and all
sacred things" who "could not even write a single page without
several misstatements."

We had called so much attention to our political and social principles, had so emphasized their superiorities, and, at the same time, had taken such mocking liberties with the corresponding ideals among our effete neighbors in Europe that we laid ourselves bare to every shaft of the enemy. Were we actually realizing these ideals of liberty, justice, and equality with a success that justified our tone? Were our manners, morals, and social virtues, as set forth by the "cannon oratory" of July Fourth or by the politicians asking for votes, quite up to the representations? We had ourselves some searching doubts on this point. No one probably knew better than we that there was a great deal of buncombe in these pretensions. It was this uneasy consciousness of the gap between our proclaimed ideals and our observed social and political practices that created and maintained a great part of our "supersensitiveness" as a people. This condition was also a kind of hothouse in which our spirit of boasting reached its luxuriant growths. Both the sensitiveness and the bragging have diminished, partly at least, because we have been disciplined into a little humility. With many triumphs have come some sobering defeats. We have learned to look at our whole community life with fewer illusions. The Civil War, with its long aftermath of paralyzing difficulties, was the first awakening. That event, with the unavoidable blundering that followed far into the seventies, taught us the delicate complexity

of our political traditions; taught us slowly that
conflicting views on the most fundamental issues
could be honestly held, and that multitudes would
die as bravely as ever men died to maintain those
views. From the hard experience of that quarter
of a century, both North and South learned immeasurably through the *un*learning of prejudices.
The South had to learn the meaning of nationality.
It had to learn all that is meant by a reorganized
industrial life with its necessary readjustments to
the country as a whole. The North had surely no
less to learn and to unlearn. Tardily she came to
recognize that the struggle in the Southland was not
solely to save slave property. That quite apart from
this, there was an idealism which all fair men now
honor and history will respect. After the war, the
North had to learn within what narrow limits force
is a remedy, just as she had to learn that the South
must be governed by what is best in the South, and
as for all that is implied in the "negro question,"
the North had to learn its main lesson as a child has
to learn its alphabet. The intellectual and moral
adjustment to the whole legacy of war problems has
steadied and disciplined us as a nation.

Not wholly separated from the teaching of this
inheritance is the educational effect upon us of difficulties that seem inherent between the Federal
Government and the several States. It is not alone
the murdered Italians in New Orleans and the
confessed helplessness of the Government to enforce

CAPTAIN MARRYAT
English Novelist and Critic of American Institutions

justice or the reverberations from California over the Japanese in public schools; it is a whole nest of practical industrial and social problems that are seen to be grave because of our political structure. Sobering, too, are our immigration and Philippine problems with all that we are coming to associate with those heavy responsibilities.

These collective experiences have done much to show most thoughtful Americans that our deeper problems are not solved solely because of our form of government. Neither universal suffrage nor popular education has worked half the wonders that were expected of them. Better still, we are learning how futile a thing is the mere legislative act, unless the will of a dedicated citizenship lives in the enactment. In not one of these ideals has the light of our faith gone out, but a certain levity and briskness in our optimism has been subdued. It is no longer a fatality that works independent of our own acts.

We were reproved some years ago by a French guest for lacking "objectivity." In this academic dialect, he wished to inform us that we were sentimental about ourselves; too self-centred and without much capacity to see and criticise ourselves, as other people see us and criticise us. This, too, was doubtless true, but it is surely a little less true in the later years.

It is not a generation since Matthew Arnold wrote of the "American rhapsody of self-praise." In the

I

"elevated," the "beautiful," and the "interesting," he found our civilization in the United States lacking. He thought this lack unavoidable and natural, but saw it as an evil sign that we were sensitive and petulant when so obvious a truth about us was set down by the foreigner.

He said if we would only be frank about these shortcomings, and acknowledge that the rule of "the average man is a danger," no fair observer would find fault. "Even if a number of leading lights amongst them said," he continues, "Under the circumstances our civilization could not well have been expected to begin differently. What you see are *beginnings:* they are crude, they are too predominantly material, they omit much, leave much to be desired — but they could not have been otherwise. They have been inevitable, and we will rise above them; if the Americans frankly said this, one would not have a word to bring against them." [1]

The test which this passage submits, we may accept without the slightest misgiving. The rare distinctions of beauty, elevation, and the "interesting" were lacking in our civilization. They are still unachieved, but many more than "some leading spirits" now know this limitation and acknowledge it. The last quarter of a century has produced a literature of self-criticism and self-accusation that fully meets Arnold's test. Bryce's first visit was a few years after the war. He was here again in 1883.

[1] "Civilization in the United States," pp. 9, 182.

He says that between those dates the oversensitiveness "had sensibly diminished." In 1905 he could
say more strongly still that the early bounds to our
optimism have become "very different from self-
righteousness or vainglory."

CHAPTER VII

THE MOTHER COUNTRY AS CRITIC

If it is true that no quarrel may take on more virulence than that within one's own family, the fact accounts for the extreme rancor of feeling against England that continued a generation after the War of 1812. I do not see in the evidence a sign that England "hated the United States," as was so often said. Until after the Civil War we were not thought important enough to inspire that feeling. She had merely an unintelligent contempt for us. This led her to ignore or to trample on every sensitive nerve in the national body. Sir George Otto Trevelyan, who justifies our Revolution of '76 in three volumes with an extreme of gallantry that excites some astonishment, uses a truer word to characterize the English feeling — "antipathy." He says that the uniform picture of our character was "daubed in colors which resembled the original as little as they matched each other." The men of Massachusetts were said to be "sly and turbulent, puritans and scoundrels, pugnacious ruffians and arrant cowards." That was the constant theme of the newspapers and the favorite topic of those officers of the army of occupation whose letters had gone the round of London clubs and English country houses. "The archives of the Secretary of State were full of trite calumnies and foolish prophecies." [1] It was the worse because, he says, the governing classes had the least understanding of us. They represented the Americans as a "tumultuous rabble meddling with affairs of state which they were unable to understand." [2]

The touch of Matthew Arnold is perhaps just as true when he says: —

"The British rule which they threw off was not one of oppressors and tyrants which declaimers suppose, and the merit of the Americans was not that of oppressed men rising against tyrants, but rather of sensible young people getting rid of stupid and overweening guardians who misunderstood and mismanaged them." [3]

It was this "stupid and overweening" mismanagement and misunderstanding of national feeling in the United States that was England's real fault. On our side there was plenty of rancor and plain hatred. The evidence has to be supplemented by the "national sensitiveness," with which the last chapter dealt, before it is quite possible to appreciate the malignity which early English criticism stirred in this country. It would be ill-advised to call up these chattering ghosts, if both nations had not now grown sensible enough and strong enough to join

[1] "The American Revolution," Part I, p. 176.
[2] *Ibid.*, p. 178.
[3] "Civilization in the United States," p. 116.

in the laugh against those musty and heavy-witted animosities. If England exhibited an incredible lack of tact as to everything which concerned popular feeling in this country, we too were often overfussy and childish about our prerogatives. Under the subject of American supersensitiveness, we have seen how the newspaper habit among our people brought a steady down-pour of galling criticism from British sources. Nothing corresponding to this was happening in England, for ordinary folk.

A small part of the cultivated classes in England read the books written by their travellers.[1] In the great reviews, men of letters like Sydney Smith and Gifford were using this collected material to put us on the rack. The lengths to which these leaders of English opinion went will be believed by no one who does not look at the record. The *Edinburgh Quarterly*, *Blackwood*, and the *British Review* were all in it, as if there were a conspiracy to make the United States an object of common obloquy. It was believed in this country that the Poet Laureate Southey wrote one of the most contemptuous of these articles. The great Wordsworth penned lines like the following: —

> "All who revere the memory of Penn
> Grieve for the land on whose wild woods his name
> Was fondly grafted with a virtuous aim,

[1] Chevalier says, "Almost all English travellers in this country have seen a great deal that was bad and scarcely anything that is good." — p. 106.

> Renounced, abandoned, by degenerate men,
> For state-dishonor black as ever came
> To upper air from Mammon's loathsome den."

Again he puts into his gentle cadence such opinions about our society as this: —

> "Big passions strutting on a petty stage
> Which a detached spectator may regard
> Not unamused. But ridicule demands
> Quick change of objects; and to laugh alone
> In the very centre of the crowd
> To keep the secret of a poignant scorn," etc.

This venerable seer did not get his "poignant scorn" from local observation, but wholly from what English books and travellers had told him.

We had our own sins in this tradition of ill-will. We cannot omit minor irritants like the scandalous behavior of some of our states in the non-payment of their debts. It was this which gave venom to the slurs of Sydney Smith and the poet Wordsworth.[1] It was this which rankled in the minds of hundreds of English investors, and was so savagely reflected in at least ten years of this criticism. Nothing more nettled Americans than the English habit of scourging the entire country for the sins of exceptional states. To include Massachusetts, with her honorable record, in the same category with the shame of Mississippi seemed to inhabitants of the state which paid its debt an outrage on the country as a whole.

[1] See Sonnets VIII and IX, Vol. IV, "Poetical Works," Boston, 1864.

Neither can the natural wrath of the English over our long pirating of their books go unmentioned. The historian Sparks had a correspondence with De Tocqueville about the delays and difficulties in getting his book published in this country. He finds it unpleasant to explain why the author could expect no money from the publisher. An English author refuses to set foot in this country because of this "organized national thieving." Kipling reveals this feeling in the following: —

"Oliver Wendell Holmes says that the Yankee schoolmarm, the cider, and the salt codfish of the Eastern States are responsible for what he calls a nasal accent. I know better. They stole books from across the water without paying for 'em, and the snort of delight was fixed in their nostrils forever by a just Providence. That is why they talk a foreign tongue to-day." [1]

These incidental raspings do not, however, account for the main trouble.

As early as 1814 the *Quarterly Review* began this "crusade of vituperation." We were depicted as a people devoid of every common decency. We had neither religion, manners, nor morals. The replies of Timothy Dwight and J. K. Paulding published in New York, 1815, stimulated counter attacks in later English reviews.

We did not like being told that our ships could not fight; that the "*Frolic* surrendered without firing a shot"; that we were "the most vain, ego-

[1] "American Notes," p. 20, Boston, 1899.

tistical, insolent, rodomontade sort of people that
are anywhere to be found"; that "the supreme
felicity of a true-born American is inaction of body
and inactivity of mind." We were "techy," "way-
ward," and "abandoned to bad nurses," and, like
spoiled children, "educated to low habits." The
Quarterly Review printed pleasantries like these.
Franklin was idolized among us for gifts that are
thus characterized in that *Review* :—

"Franklin, in grinding his electrical machine and flying his
kite, did certainly elicit some useful discoveries in a branch of
science that had not much engaged the attention of the philosophers of Europe. But the foundation of Franklin's knowledge
was laid not in America, but in London. Besides, half of
what he wrote was stolen from others, and the greater part of
the rest was not worth preserving." [1]

We were "too proud to learn and too ignorant to
teach, and having established by act of Congress
that they are already the most enlightened people
in the world, they bid fair to retain their barbarism
from mere regard to consistency." This insolent
ribaldry is not from the pens of hungry journalists.
It is the expressed conviction of literary and socially
distinguished men. It continued pretty steadily for
a generation. Here are a few titbits from the
Foreign Quarterly as late as 1844. We have:
"Swagger and impudence"; "As yet the American
is horn-handed and pig-headed, hard, persevering,
unscrupulous, carnivorous; with a genius for lying."

[1] *Quarterly Review*, No. 20.

We are a "brigand confederation"; "Outrage and disorder and naked licentiousness" were rife, and everywhere was "that depravity that rots like a canker at the core of American society."

Thomas Brothers concludes thus, "I believe there to be in the United States more taxation, poverty, and general oppression than ever known in any other country."[1]

Three years later Dickens wrote, "That republic but yesterday let loose upon her noble course, and to-day so maimed and lame, so full of sores and ulcers, that her best friends turn from the loathsome creature in disgust."

There were nearly ten years of this inflamed scurrility before an attempt was made in *Blackwood's Magazine* to counteract the harm done by this English tone. A writer then warned the English that they would "turn into bitterness the last drops of good-will toward England that exist in the United States."[2]

One of the most careful of our critics who studied us for three years felt this danger. He cries out: —

"Why, in God's name, should we not give every assurance of respect and affection? Are they not our children, blood of our blood and bone of our bone? Are they not progressive,

[1] "The United States of North America as They Are," p. 228, Thomas Brothers, London, 1840.

[2] A little earlier this magazine said, —

"The tendencies of our Constitution toward democracy have been checked solely by the view of the tattered and insolent guise in which republicanism had appeared in America."

and fond of power, like ourselves? Are they not our best customers? Have they not the same old English, manly virtues? What is more befitting for us Englishmen than to watch with intense study and deepest sympathy the momentous strivings of this noble people? It is the same fight we ourselves are fighting — the true and absolute supremacy of Right. Surely nothing can more beseem two great and kindred nations than to aid and comfort one another in that career of self-ennoblement, which is the end of all national as well as individual existence." [1]

There is pathos, too, in the words of Washington Irving: —

"Is this golden bond of kindred sympathies, so rare between nations, to be broken forever? Perhaps it is for the best: it may dispel an illusion which might have kept us in mental vassalage; which might have interfered occasionally with our true interests, and prevented the growth of proper national pride. But it is hard to give up the kindred tie; and there are feelings dearer than interest, closer to the heart than pride, that will still make us cast back a look of regret, as we wander farther and farther from the paternal roof, and lament the waywardness of the parent that would repel the affections of the child."

It is clear to us at this distance that these English reviewers got a genuine pleasure out of the books which most roundly abused us (Fearon, Brothers, Welby, Ashe, Harris, Faux, and Bradbury). We had won our independence, and made it extremely uncomfortable for England in 1812. Her prestige and national vanity had suffered from these events. She suffered the more because of the trumpet tones

[1] James Sterling, "Letters from the Slave States."

in which we bragged over these victories. They
were organized into permanent memorials about
which the high tides of oratory, song, and editorials
flowed and ebbed as if by force of nature. An
Englishman, unhappy enough to arrive here a few
days before July 4, 1819, writes: —

"I know we came off rather lamely in the Revolutionary
War, but I never realized before that we began by being
cowards and bullies and ended by being annihilated in every
fight. I had always supposed we English whipped them at
Bunker Hill, but these Yankees have turned it into a victory
that ranks with Thermopylæ and Waterloo. Even our English warships were swept from the sea, and men that I never
heard of are greater than Nelson at Trafalgar."

As one follows these Englishmen about, it is
impossible to withhold sympathy for them. There
was not the slightest hesitation in rubbing in all
the old victories and in all ways belittling English
behavior in both wars.

Nor was our form of government less irritating,
especially when we insisted that the poor foreigner
should forthwith admire it. De Tocqueville inti-
mates that his approval would have had freer
expression, if he had not been so insistently *expected*
to approve. Our democracy was itself an affront
to all Tory sentiment. Whether it were to succeed
or fail, it was an embodied challenge to the mother
country. It was not merely the dropping of a king
and a hereditary House of Lords, but the separation
of Church and State, the doing away with primo-

geniture and property qualification for the vote, the wide extension of the suffrage, which seemed to strike at what were fundamental and venerated English traditions. There is a strong passage in Trevelyan which runs thus: —

"But in order to comprehend a policy which lay so far outside the known and ordinary limits of human infatuation, it must never be forgotten that there was a deeper and a more impassable gulf than the Atlantic between the colonists and their rulers. If Cabinet Ministers at home had known the Americans better, they would only have loved them less. The higher up in the peerage an Englishman stood, and the nearer to influence and power, the more unlikely it was that he would be in sympathy with his brethren across the seas, or that he would be capable of respecting their susceptibilities, and of apprehending their virtues, which were less to his taste even than their imperfections." [1]

The English statesman, John Morley, has this striking confirmation of these words in discussing Maine's "Popular Government": —

"The success of popular government across the Atlantic has been the strongest incentive to the extension of popular government here. We need go no farther back than the Reform Bill of 1867 to remind ourselves that the victory of the North over the South had more to do with the concession of the franchise to householders in boroughs than all the eloquence of Mr. Gladstone and all the diplomacies of Mr. Disraeli." [2]

We have learned, as in the case of murdered Italians in Louisiana and affronted Japanese in

[1] Part I, pp. 44 and 45.
[2] "Studies in Literature," pp. 125–126.

California, that our states are related to the Federal Government in ways that have been an honest perplexity to all foreigners, as they are becoming a very serious perplexity to ourselves.

During the period we are considering, there was practically no conception of this relation of state to the central government among the critics whose censure was most resented. We can therefore at last not only understand, but make some measure of allowance for the caviller. We can even forgive that shining wit, Sydney Smith, for saying that all our literature was imported; that Franklin's fame might possibly last for fifty years; and that "prairies, steamboats, grist-mills" were our proper heritage.

This long wordy tiff, with much spite and heartburning in it, continued until the middle of the century. The shrill note of it begins then to soften, partly, I think, because so many sensible men on both sides became tired and ashamed of it. Its humiliation was that cultivated men should lend themselves to such a cause. Among the average mass of men, anything like international amenity and real understanding is but just beginning on the earth. Think of two nations as advanced as England and France living century after century hard by each other, and until the most recent years having merely contempt for each other; the average Englishman thinking that a Frenchman was a kind of monkey with clothes on, and that chiefly because he had a different manner and speech from the

English.   Though from the same trunk and with a common speech, there was almost as much misapprehension between England and this country.   It was not caused by primitive race antagonism or too close national rivalry, as between England and France. The misunderstanding was, nevertheless, quite as natural and probably as inevitable.

In Chapter VIII we shall see it passing away for reasons that are humorous in their simplicity; chiefly because so many people in both countries have seen each other closely enough and often enough to gain a common respect one for the other.   A distinguished Englishman who has just been lecturing in this country put a world of good sense into these words, "I would not have believed that six weeks' good fellowship here in the States could have burned all out of me the amount of ignorance and prejudice that I brought to this country."   That has happened to many thousands in both countries since the Civil War.   This intelligent sympathy was never increasing so rapidly as at present, and it will continue with growing hopefulness in the future.   At least with peoples not too widely separated by cultural stages, this elementary understanding has infinite promise. The possibilities and business necessities of modern travel are rapidly doing this fundamental work of making people so far known to each other, as to train them into neighborly habits and into a toleration of superficial differences.

The chief change in this history of criticism is that

we have now reached a stage in which men of enlarged experience are writing books for the express purpose of creating an intelligent good-will among nations. Into this purposed brotherhood come men like Bryce, Trevelyan, Archer, Muirhead, Münsterberg, Abbé Klein, Von Polenz, De Rousier, with an interpreting message, every line of which is an added tie of friendly feeling and tolerance among peoples isolated by geographic lines but sundered even more by prejudice and ignorance. In the common darkness of this national and race misunderstanding, the devil's main work is now carried on in our present world. In this misunderstanding are the sustaining roots of the immense stupidity which still assumes that the permanent good of this or that nation is bought at the price of some other people's discomfiture or undoing. From the same source spring the low cruelties of modern warfare. Our continued bungling with defective children, delinquent youth, and large classes of criminals will end only when we learn to *understand*. Some brave steps have been taken toward this saving tolerance. Upon its extension at home and abroad depends all that is meant by the word civilization.

CHAPTER VIII

THE changes noted in this chapter are largely English, although French writers like Bourget, Madame Blanc, and Paul Adam; Germans like Münsterberg, Von Polenz, and Grillenberger, indicate a corresponding change of temper. The condescension is gone, or is rapidly disappearing. The visitor is studying a people that may disturb and irritate him, but our rough beginnings have taken on proportions that command a new kind of attention. It is not so much what we have definitely achieved, as it is the unmistakable promise of achievement, that arouses new homage. For a half century there has been no question of our material exploits. These have had compliments and marvelling enough. It is the whole cultural side of life in the United States that has been put in question. Could we create literature, develop science, paint pictures; could we reach first-rate educational standards or even learn to appreciate the best music? Values like these, with softened manners and a pleasant voice, were what seemed to older observers rather hopelessly beyond our attainment.

There are many still to deny our possession of

these gifts, but that we have proved our desire
for them and a very encouraging purpose to win
them, is heartily conceded by competent continental
judges.

The changes of judgment among the English
do not come through any of these refinements.
England began really to respect us because of the
national strength displayed in the Civil War. The
enduring valor, the sacrifice for an idea, both North
and South; the tenacity of the entire people and the
ready acceptance of the result, were, one and all,
arguments that are finalities to practical men of
Anglo-Saxon origin. Barring a few holiday skits,
the critical atmosphere changes after this date as by
some cleansing storm. Mr. Bryce says that philosophers from Plato to Sir Robert Lowe have attributed "weakness in emergencies" to democracies,
and further that Europeans had concluded (partly
from internal dissensions and our habit of too much
blustering) that we "lacked firmness and vigor."
The Civil War, he says, undeceived Europe. "The
North put forth its power with a suddenness and
resolution which surprised the world. The Southern people displayed no less vigor, even when the tide
had evidently begun to turn against them." This
Saxon trait of bowing to the hard fact of success
appeared again when the Spanish ships went to
pieces before American guns.[1]

[1] In 1856 Emerson said, "It is noticeable that England is beginning to interest us a little less."

The eye of the foreigner noted other events, like that of Northern and Southern armies quietly going to their ordinary tasks after Appomattox.   Especially England watched the popular frenzy that raged about the attempt to impeach Andrew Johnson.   One of the ablest of English publicists, Walter Bagehot, wrote, "Few nations, perhaps scarcely any nation, could have borne such a trial so easily and so perfectly."   The effect was no less telling when it appeared that a stupendous national debt was to be honestly met and rapidly paid off.   From Gladstone this resolute facing of debts won for us the following tribute : —

"In twelve years she [America] has reduced her debt by one hundred and fifty-eight million pounds, or at the rate of thirteen million pounds for each year.   In each twelve months she has done what we did in eight years; her self-command, self-denial, and wise forethought of the future have been, to say the least, eightfold ours.   These are facts which redounded greatly to her honor; and the historian will record with surprise that an enfranchised nation tolerated burdens which in this country a selected class, possessed of the representation, did not dare to face, and that the most unmitigated democracy known to the annals of the world resolutely reduced at its own cost prospective liabilities of the State which the aristocratic, and plutocratic, and monarchical Government of the United Kingdom had been contented ignobly to hand over to posterity."

Forty years after the war John Morley wrote : —

"Of this immense conflict Mr. Gladstone, like most of the leading statesmen of the time, and like the majority of his own countrymen, failed to take the true measure.   The error that

lay at the root of our English misconceptions of the American
struggle is now clear. We applied ordinary political maxims
to what was not merely a political contest, but a social
revolution." [1]

The change here indicated appears at once among
the writers who come after the war. They seem
for the first time really to *see* the United States. It
is as if most writers before this event had been
watching, not the United States, but some idea of
our country which they brought with them. From
now on there is a new deference; even a good show
of modesty in passing judgment on complicated
social phenomena. There is not only more regard
for American feeling, but a more conscientious
attempt to interpret the objects under observation.
The old platitudes are questioned; the conventional
repetition of supposed peculiarities no longer satis-
fies. This has to be shown through trivial illustrations and by repeating some of our alleged characteristics. Yet it is these very trivialities that occupy
half the space in these travel books. Whatever
space is still given to them, there is an altered attitude
as to their interpretation. "Why," says one, "should
a whole nation set itself so joyously to the rhythmic
use of the rocking-chair, unless this motion answers
some physiological need? I thought at first it was
devised for some special form of nervous diseases,
but I soon came to find how much solid comfort I
could have in it."

[1] "Life of Gladstone," Vol. II, p. 70.

SIR CHARLES LYELL
English Scientist and Traveller in America

A temper like that applied to every phase of a nation's life would give us a new critical standard. It reminds us of Huxley's definition of science, as "organized common sense." Its luminous advantage is that objects and experiences are so studied that one sees them in relation to the social and historic whole of which they are a part. There was in our Civil War an intensity of dramatic effect upon foreign observers that did much to create this new temper. There are many references to it in those who come after 1866. They seem to be saying: "Well, well, we had no idea that there was so much in you; that you had such reserves of strength; or that you cared so much for ideals. We shall have to make of you a new study." I heard a German writer say that the United States appeared to him absolutely destitute of all ideals until he followed the story of the war. "Then," he added, "I saw that no people had more stuff for heroism than the American." Our country had only been seen by bits. As a *whole* it had never been the object of study. I do not mean by this that one must live here twenty years or see every state, but that some conception of the infinite variation of life and problems here is fundamentally requisite. It is requisite for this reason, that without some sense of these differences in social structure and development no helpful comparison of things that properly go together is possible. I heard one of the most widely known of living Englishmen say, "There is no scenery in the

United States." Our coast-line, with one or two
slight exceptions (as on the coast of Maine), he
thought tame and uninteresting. The character
and grouping of our Rocky Mountains, he said,
were not "scenery" in any proper sense — and so
on.

Now this criticism, true or false, depends upon
comparison. The critic had in mind the varied
magnificence of Switzerland with its splendor of
color in snow, verdure, and water effects, or he was
bringing together in his imagination other parts of
the world side by side with his mental picture of this
country. If we could once agree upon a definition
of "scenery," these comparisons would assist us just
so far as our observations covered the ground. But
scenery is an affair of æsthetic taste, about which
the only certainty is that tastes will differ. It is not
alone a matter of coast-lines or mountain groupings.
Upon a score of our smaller rivers, with their soft
curves and stretching meadows; in a hundred dainty
nooks among the New England and Southern hills;
in the sweep and perspective of the great plains beyond the Mississippi, what is it that gives the thrill
if it is not scenery? This is a composite and inclusive term. Going south from Pueblo, Colorado,
the train seems to sink as into a vast shallow cup
with the Spanish Peaks on the far outer rim. I saw
it once in an evening light so gorgeous in its intensity, that it gave one a kind of pain to look upon it,
because there was no way to express the pressure of

emotion it excited.   If that was not scenery, what
name are we to give it?

Washington Irving had an eye for natural beauty.
He said, "Never need an American look beyond his
own country for the sublime and beautiful of natural
scenery."   Some varieties at their highest we may
lack, but other varieties surely are ours.

As we know our country better in quite other than
its natural aspects, we shall apply this same test to
all these critical decisions.   We shall ask in morals,
in education, in things social and material, that the
comparison recognize this almost measureless diversity in the totality of American life.   To see something of this completer relation requires long and
concentrated study or an imagination like that of
H. G. Wells.

This is a digression, but it should light up a little
this point; that the recent visitors (those with even
the least competence as critics) seem at last honestly
to feel and to confess some sense of the magnitude
and diversity of their task.

Let us appeal again to the trivialities.   Our
"national habit of drinking ice-water" was invariably spoken of earlier as an inexcusable freak.
Even Steevens in his "Land of the Dollar" continues
the tradition: —

"It is more indispensable than a napkin, and the waiter
who will keep you waiting ten minutes for bread, will rush
wildly for the bottle if your ice-water sinks half an inch below
the brim of the glass.   Ring a bell at any hour of the day or

night — a panting attendant dashes in with ice-water. Sip, sip, sip — men, women, and little children go pouring the noxious stuff into their insides. The effect of this ice-water habit on the national constitution can only be most disastrous." [1]

We have the new temper of which I speak in Mr. Muirhead's "Land of Contrasts," in which he begs to —

— "warn the British visitor to suspend his judgment until he has been some time in the country. I certainly was not prejudiced in favor of this chilly draught when I started for the United States, but I soon came to find it natural and even necessary, and as much so from the dry hot air of the stove-heated room in winter as from the natural ambition of the mercury in summer. On the whole, it may be philosophic to conclude that a universal habit in any country has some solid if cryptic reason for its existence, and to surmise that the drinking of ice-water is not so deadly in the States as it might be elsewhere."

Yes, it is "philosophic to conclude" that a "universal habit" among a people may have something to say for itself; that it is not to be accounted for by any snap-shot impressions. There is scarcely one of the commonplace parrot phrases that is not now being carefully revised.

"American houses and cars are like a lot of ovens." "You may travel a month without seeing a human being who seems to be at leisure." "Their politicians are invariably below the average in intelligence and morals." "They are gloomily silent." "The American voice has a grating quality that

[1] p. 177.

sets every nerve on edge." There is some truth in every one of these statements, and in two of them there is a great deal of truth. That our houses and cars are very generally overheated, we know well. It would be truer to say that we used our heat too jerkily; that it runs to extremes of heat and cold, as on our trains. But here at last comes an Englishman who "sees a great deal of home life in several cities during four months." He says: "I looked in vain for those stifling houses of which I had read all my life. Upon the whole, I was no more troubled by heat than I have been in London." We think he was pretty lucky, but he should go in as a witness to the change of opinions.

The third observation that no one of us seems to have any leisure must have far more qualifying. Some recent writers will give no countenance to the generalization whatever.[1] No one will watch the workers, even in such a whirlpool of activity as Pittsburg, without some amazement at the extremely leisurely air of whole sections of skilled workers, as well as among many heads of departments upon whom great responsibility falls. De Tocqueville has much to say of the feverish ardor with which the Americans pursue their welfare; of "the strange unrest of so many happy men, uneasy in the midst of abundance." Until the period

---

[1] This is also the strongly expressed opinion of the working-men members of the Mosley Commission to this country two years ago.

of discrimination came, this opinion is repeated by
nine out of every ten of our inspectors. Mr. Muirhead does not let the formula pass. He is much
more closely accurate in the following: —

"If an Englishman has a mile to go to an appointment, he
will take his leisurely twenty minutes to do the distance, and
then settle his business in two or three dozen sentences; an
American is much more likely to devour the ground in five
minutes, and then spend an hour or more in lively conversation not wholly pertinent to the matter in hand." [1]

That our politicians are invariably below the average morally and intellectually has a disheartening
truth, so far as attention is fixed on certain city and
state conditions. In our political life as a whole,
there is no sense in which our representatives can be
said to fall below the average. Both Bryce and
Münsterberg give strong statement to this effect.

What is meant again by the frequent assertion
that we are "the most silent people"? I have often
heard this said by foreigners, and it is many times
written. I asked one of the keenest of our observers
what he meant by our silence. He answered: "I
mean first, that in all public places, as you travel,
sit at table in hotels and restaurants, in your larger
stores, on the street and in crowds, you are strangely
silent.[2] I ask a policeman for a street, and all I

[1] "The Land of Contrasts," p. 90.

A New York paper comments thus: "Everything considered,
though, the real dementia Americana is hurryupitis."

[2] Bryce is more cautious in his statement. "They are not a
loquacious people." — Vol. II, p. 688.

get is, 'Second turn to your left.' I ask the conductor on the trolley-car to let me out at a certain
point, and, usually, he makes no reply whatever
but — *does let me off.*[1] I ask the girl behind the
counter for some article. Oftener than not she
serves me without a word, as if I didn't exist." He
hears that in our family life it is the exception to
have much conversation at meals; that we do not
get a pleasure out of common talk; that when the
meal is over, the evening paper or whist becomes a
substitute for conversation. Dickens says: "No one
speaks at meals. They all seem to have tremendous
secrets on their minds." One of the critics concludes that our joking habit spoils conversation.
"The funny man is a national calamity." Another
thinks that we are so busy that our nervous energy
is exhausted, and therefore we are too tired to talk.
A third carries this a step farther, saying that
"Americans have not yet had time to develop the
habits and forms of easy verbal intercourse." Still
another says, "The Americans are too afraid of
each other to talk much."[2]

[1] One wonders if this critic could have read De Amicis on the
land of William the Silent. In his chapter on The Hague, he describes at length this characteristic of silence or scanty response
to your inquiries. He tells of the great pains they will take to do
the things you ask, *but without words* — "sans proférer une pa-
role."

[2] It is of her own countrymen at table d'hôte that the English
writer, Miss Betham-Edwards, asks: "What deadly feud of blood,
caste, or religion could thus keep them apart? Whilst the little
knot of Gallic travellers at the farther end of the table straightway

I have quoted these views to several of our countrymen who have had large experience. If they reflect
with some care on the criticisms, they usually admit
their truth as applied to a great deal of our life.
On a coast steamer crowded with Americans, I
saw a French family sitting together at meals.
Their conversation among themselves was incessant,
and day after day so full of gaiety that everybody
showed a kind of fascination in watching the ani-
mated group. An American, observing it, asked:
"Why is it that we haven't sense enough at least to
cultivate a habit with so much charm and health
in it as that? It would cure us of our dyspepsia and
many other national vices."

But with whom are we compared? Do the English people, as a whole, talk more freely than we?
Do the Norwegians or the Germans? We know that
Latin people have a joy in conversation which
northern nations but poorly imitate. We know,
also, that to a large part of the Americans, "silence"
is as little a characteristic as sky-blue is of the com-
plexion. Professor Janet wishes to set history right
on this point by saying, "The Americans talk much
more freely than the English and the Dutch."

That "the Americans have the worst voices known
among civilized people " is a generalization much
nearer the fact than that we are silent. What can

fall into friendliest talk, the long rows of Britons of both sexes
and all ages speak only in subdued voices and to the members of
their own family."

have caused such a voice is many times an object of curious inquiry.[1] Climate, nervous tension, ill health, especially among the women, are the most frequent explanations. Another thinks overstraining of the vocal organs during our long life on the border, when the women had to strain their voices in calling the men-folks to meals, accounts for it. More astonishing is the theory that traces our irritating utterance to the absence of monarchy and a superior class. If we had been civilized enough to keep these hallowed possessions, we should have unconsciously preserved and cultivated a subdued and deferential vocalization. Another, perhaps with the same thought, says we have bad voices because we have a bad government. Believing in democracy and the equalities, we put gruffness, loudness, and bluster into the voice! As this is unnatural, it impairs the vocal organs. One other thing is full of inspiration: it is that which attributes this special inferiority to the lack of tipping waiters and dependants. The softening influence of a monarchy we have lost, but the tipping system may be made a substitute. Does it not cultivate graciousness in the giver, and mild and gentle ways in the receiver? We are told that this form of generosity, which acts automatically upwards and downwards, produces

[1] . . . I once said to a lady, "Why do you drawl out your words in that way?"

"Well," replied she, "I'd drawl all the way from Maine to Georgia rather than *clip* my words as you English people do." — MARRYAT, Vol. I, p. 222.

an atmosphere of good manners which includes a milder and more pliant voice. At the time of this happy exposition (1840) there was no tipping in sight, nor any hopeful sign of tipping to come. There is no doubt that the remedy is at last ours, or that it has a wide and contagious popularity. We may therefore free ourselves from this special source of worry.

I am not certain that Professor Freeman observed the effects of the tipping cure in its early stages, but he is one of the first to come to our defence in the way of intelligent and truthful observation. Instead of reckless generalization like "Americans speak with an intolerable quality of voice," he discriminates. He uses the comparative method, not alone as applied to one nation with another nation, but, of greater importance, he gets corresponding classes or sections in each country into some relation, section with section, so that a real comparison can be made. The earlier vice was to compare a selected and better class in England with the miscellaneous, rough and tumble life as seen in the American coach, train, or boarding-house. We come off less badly as to voice in what Professor Freeman says: —

"Some people have the twang very strongly; some have it not at all. Some, after speaking for a long time without it, will bring it in in a particular word or sentence; in others it is strongly marked when a few words are uttered suddenly, but dies off in the course of a longer conversation. And I distinctly marked that it was far more universal among women than among men."

Professor Mills (McGill University), speaking of indistinctness and muffling the voice, says, "It is found in English and German also. English speech is often hard and guttural, German unduly guttural, if not hard; and American slovenly and horribly nasal."[1] That method throws a little light on the general obscurity. It does not leave the whole sin at our doors.

At first the American press reporter is "as incredibly ignorant as he is incompetent and ill-mannered." The tone is now rather that of William Archer:[2] —

"All the pleasant expectations I brought with me to America have been realized, all the forebodings disappointed. Even the interviewer is far less terrible than I had been led to imagine. He always treated me with courtesy, sometimes with comprehension."

This is the spirit of Herbert Spencer and Dean Hole. Dean Hole says: —

"I was interviewed by more than two hundred journalists of both sexes, and so far from being bored by their tedious dulness or exasperated by their inquisitive curiosity, — as certain false prophets had foretold, — I was universally pleased by their courtesy and instructed by their information."[3]

Münsterberg, who has had much discipline at the hands of reporters, thus writes in his "Americans," "The American journalist is usually a gentleman and can be relied on to be discreet."

[1] "Voice Production," *Lippincott*, 1906, p. 146.
[2] "America To-day."
[3] "A Little Tour in America."

A final illustration will mark still better the change
of tone.   A sturdy volume could be filled with asser-
tions to the effect that beyond all nations we are
consumed by the greedy passion for money.   Several
books bear titles like "The Land of Dollars."
Many chapters either give exclusive attention to this
mad hunt for lucre, or dwell upon it at great length.
It may be admitted that other peoples have an incidental regard to their pecuniary interests, but we
Americans make it "a seven-day religion."   Harriet
Martineau, so far as my record shows, was the first
to challenge this criticism.

"I have studied with some care the minds and manners of
a variety of merchants, and other persons engaged in commerce, and have certainly found a regard to money a more
superficial and intermitting influence than various others." [1]

This is cautiously worded, as if she were not quite
sure of her ground.   Even De Tocqueville had laid
this sin of money-loving upon us with a heavy hand.
But this man of genius was comparing us to an upper
section of European society whose income was,
for the most part, earned by their tenants or other
people.   It has always been easy for such as these
to show the most graceful indifference to money.
Of the vast majority of hard-working Frenchmen
he is not thinking.   On this point the pages of
Balzac are like a mirror.[2]   We look into them and see
reflected there such a hungry regard for money and

[1] "Society in America," Vol. I, p. 142.
[2] These are words we owe to a French economist: "We buy

rentes as cannot be found in a page of American history. Chevalier was speaking of a wider class still in his country when he said, "Nowhere do you see specimens of that sordid avarice of which examples are so common among us."[1] This accurate truth-telling about the love of money in England is as pitiless in Thackeray's novels as it is in Balzac. America has no literature which shows the sin in grosser or more prevalent form than in these two masters as they lay bare this passion among their own people.

We can now appeal on this topic to other writers. Professor Münsterberg's estimate is as follows:—

"The American does not prize his possessions much unless he has worked for them himself; of this there are innumerable proofs, in spite of the opposite appearances on the surface. One of the most interesting of these is the absence of the bridal dower. In Germany or France the man looks on a wealthy marriage as one of the most reliable means of getting an income; there are whole professions which depend on a man's eking out his entirely inadequate salary from property which he inherits or gets by marriage; and the eager search for a handsome dowry— in fact, the general commercial character of marriage in reputable European society everywhere— always surprises Americans. Everywhere one sees the

a woman with our fortune, or we sell ourselves to her for her dower. The American chooses her, or rather offers himself to her, for her beauty, her intelligence, or her amiable qualities, and asks no other portion. Thus, whilst we make a traffic of what is most sacred, these shopkeepers exhibit a delicacy and loftiness of feeling, which have done honor to the most perfect models of chivalry."

[1] p. 303.

L

daughters of wealthy families stepping into the modest homes of their husbands, and these husbands would feel it to be a disgrace to depend on their prosperous fathers-in-law. An actual dowry received from the bride's parents during their lifetime is virtually unknown. Another instance of American contempt for unearned wealth, which especially contrasts with European customs, is the disapproval which the American always has for lotteries. If he were really bent on getting money, he would find the dowry and the lottery a ready means." [1]

"The American chases after money with all his might, exactly as on the tennis-court he tries to hit the ball, and it is the game he likes *and not the prize*. If he loses, he does not feel as if he had lost a part of himself, but only as if he had lost the last set in a tournament." [2]

Earlier still Mr. Bryce wrote: "A millionnaire has a better and easier social career open to him in England than in America. In America if his private character be bad, if he be mean, or openly immoral, or personally vulgar, or dishonest, the best society will keep its doors closed against him. In England great wealth, skilfully employed, will more readily force these doors to open. For in England great wealth can, by using the appropriate methods, practically buy rank from those who bestow it; or by obliging persons, whose position enables them to command fashionable society, can induce them to stand sponsors for the upstart, and force him into society, a thing which no person in America has the power to do." [3]

[1] "The Americans," p. 231.   [2] *Ibid.*, p. 234.
[3] "American Commonwealth," Vol. II, p. 604.

In general, what has increased this new tone in our favor is unquestionably the advent of the United States as a "World Power."   Whether this new rôle is to fit us or unfit us, is open to doubt, but the kind of impression it has made abroad, is not open to doubt.

At the opening of the twentieth century, one of the most brilliant of English journalists begins his Preface with the words,[1] "The advent of the United States of America as the greatest of world powers is the greatest political, social, and commercial phenomenon of our times."   He says, "That the United States of America have now arrived at such a pitch of power and prosperity as to have a right to claim the leading place among English-speaking nations, cannot be disputed."   Then with much vigor he pleads for a vitalized union of English and American interests.   He quotes Balfour's words, "The idea of a war with the United States of America carries with it something of the unnatural horror of civil war."   He adds passages from Gladstone and Cecil Rhodes which ring with the same world note. He even reports Lord Derby when in Gladstone's Cabinet as saying to Dr. Dillon, "The highest ideal I can look forward to in the future of my country is that the time may come when we may be admitted into the American Union as states in one great federation."[2]   This outsteps Professor Dicey's sug-

[1] W. T. Stead, "The Americanization of the World," London, 1902.

[2] Mr. Stead reproduces a famous English cartoon which

gestion of political representation of the United States in the English Parliament.[1]

Years before any of these words were spoken, Richard Cobden wrote, "Our only chance of national prosperity lies in the timely remodelling of our system so as to put it as nearly as possible upon an equality with the improved management of the Americans." The irresistible journalist, Mr. Stead, is not, however, to be outdone. He will have the English people to whom he belongs unite with us in *the celebration of July Fourth*. If we gasp at this suggestion he says, "The practice of hoisting flags on the birthday of the American Republic has been gaining ground in Great Britain, and here and there Britons have begun to set apart the sacred Fourth of July as a *fête*-day of the race." Not wishing to be oversanguine, he admits that the "ordinary British subject cannot be expected just yet to enter into this common rejoicing without some hesitation." But he adds, "As year after year passes he will come to celebrate the Fourth of July heartily and ungrudgingly." To remove the lingering prejudices, we on

dresses John Bull in Uncle Sam's attire, and puts upon the body of the American eagle a lion's head.

[1] This profound student of politics uses these words: "The plain truth is, that educated Englishmen are slowly learning that the American Republic accords the best example of a conservative democracy; and now that England is becoming democratic, respectable Englishmen are beginning to consider whether the Constitution of the United States may not afford means by which, under new democratic forms, may be preserved the political conservatism dear and habitual to the governing classes of England."

CHARLES DICKENS

our side must unite on Shakespeare's birthday and
on the day when Magna Charta was signed. And
one step farther in the general healing — we must
all unite on the third of September. "It was
Cromwell's great day, the day of Dunbar and
Worcester, the day on which he opened his Parliaments, the day on which he passed into the presence
of his Maker. Cromwell, the common hero of both
sections of the race, summoned his first Parliament
on the Fourth of July, and his inaugural address
was *the first Fourth of July oration that was ever
delivered*. It was instinct with the conviction of
the reality of the providential mission of the English-
speaking race. In his own words, "We have our
desire to see healing and looking forward (rather)
than to rake into sores and look backward." If the
interchange of courtesies and fête-day shouting is
to be made so easy as this, it is not for Americans to
hesitate.

In 1813 so responsible a person as the English
Ambassador Foster said of us publicly, "Generally
speaking, they are not a people we should be proud
to acknowleged as our relation." In 1829 the
author of "Tom Cringle's Log" [1] said in *Blackwood's Magazine:* "I don't like Americans. I never
did and never shall like them. I have seldom met
an American gentleman in the large and complete
sense of the term. I have no wish to eat with them,
drink with them, deal with them, or consort with
them in any way."

[1] Michael Scott.

Many and interesting things appear to have happened between this and Mr. Stead's invitation to international fête-days grouped about July the Fourth.

This "journalist who thinks in continents" does not after all take much higher flight than the Oxford scholar, Freeman, who could say: "It is indeed a thrilling thought for a man of the elder England to see what a home the newest home of his people is. The heart swells, the pride of kinship rises, as he sees that it is his own folk which has done more than any other folk to replenish the earth and to subdue it. He is no Englishman at heart, he has no true feeling of the abiding tie of kindred, who deems that the glory and greatness of the child is other than part of the glory and greatness of the parent."

CHAPTER IX

HIGHER CRITICISM

JOHN STUART MILL called De Tocqueville's "Democracy" "the first philosophical book ever written on democracy as it manifests itself in modern society." [1] Until 1888 no book at all comparable to it had been written. It was said that every thinking man in Europe had to read it, in order to avoid the constant confession that he had *not* read it. Alexis de Tocqueville, though the son of a peer of France, took his stand as a youth of twenty-five for the French Revolution of 1830. At the close of his school studies, he made a long tour in Italy and Sicily, where he worked at politics and institutions with "incredible pains," to use his own words. On his return, he was given, for a lad of twenty-one, an important position (*juge auditeur*). Political and social studies were from this time his pursuit. With no man can we less connect the word cranky or flighty. Only when he became convinced that Charles X either could not or would not understand constitutional freedom, did he yield to the Revolution

---

[1] He also says it is the first analytic inquiry into the influence of democracy.

of 1830. His moral and intellectual struggles at this period determined his career. He had become convinced that the permanent defeat of democracy was impossible. How, then, could he better equip himself for service to his country than go at once to America? He had already discovered the most competent man in this country, the historian Jared Sparks, to guide him in his first studies of the town-meeting. He reached New York in 1831, spending a year in travel and incessant study. He rose in France to be Minister of Foreign Affairs in 1849, receiving, for his moral courage, the honor of imprisonment at the hands of Louis Napoleon on the second of December, 1851.

It is better to put down first the critical word about these volumes. There is so much eloquence, so much elevation of tone, so much sympathy with every ideal aim of democracy, that one has to be a little on the defensive. For present usefulness, de Tocqueville does not equal some later authors who are far his inferiors. Even he came with a bias. He brought an ideal of political society with him. He had committed himself heart and hand to the constitutional hopes under Louis Philippe. He wanted evidence. He wished to show that the people could govern themselves. He had heard that this self-government resting in the town-meeting was triumphant in the United States.

With the vision of what he wanted, he came to prepare for his great book. There is a little line in

ALEXIS DE TOCQUEVILLE
Author of "Democracy in America"

his Introduction which tells all there is to tell about his bias, *"J'avoue que dans l'Amérique, j'ai vu plus que l'Amérique"* — "I grant that in America I saw more than was there." But more than this seeking of evidence that he was eager to find was his intellectual habit of dealing with large political abstractions. These never leave him quite free to follow the humbler indications of the facts before him. It was the method of his time. Even the hard-headed Chevalier cannot get his book under way, without imposing inferences drawn from all corners of the antique world. The two races supposed to flow from Japhet and Shem are essential to a true understanding of democracy in America, as are the Roman Empire, China, and Japan. We now know that two generations ago these august and sounding analogies, if applied to modern conditions, served chiefly to conceal the facts or to muddle and bewilder our relation to the facts. Even at the present time, it is only here and there that a scholar is wise enough to flourish those ancient societies before us without enveloping the audience in a general haze. I heard the president of an eastern college once say, "When we are discussing these modern political problems, if any one raises Greece and Rome, I always vote to adjourn." Mr. Dooley is of the same mind : "Whiniver I go to a pollytical meetin', an' th' laad with th' open-wurruk face mentions Rome or Athens, I grab for me hat. I know he's not goin' to say anything that ought to keep me out iv bed."

This was so the usage of de Tocqueville's time that, although very temperate, he cannot wholly avoid the temptation. Too frequently these classical analogies are a substitute for good argument. But this is only a part of de Tocqueville's real weakness. He has a delight in working out large formulas about liberty, equality, democracy, and public opinion. These become in his mind "principles," as they indeed are, but he gets them *too soon* and *too easily*. Above all, he gives them shape before the facts quite justify him. He is so tenacious of these principles, that he inclines to rule out facts, or not to see them, if they disturb his general position. His generalization often seems to drive him off his natural course, as when he conjures up his group of little political factions, or sees the steady decrease of the Federal Power.

He was led by his formula to fix upon us, as a democracy, certain matter-of-fact habits of mind which were precisely as true of England as of us. He wanted to endow the democratic mind with great capacity for *action*, but not for thought and reflection. We produced, forsooth, "no inventors." This cunning was not in the democratic mind. Very remarkable achievements were already at hand before a printed line of de Tocqueville had reached this country. Again, equality so reacts upon us that, as a democracy, we will not "recognize our faults." What government does? Are aristocracies eager to confess them? No one to-day could conceive of this disinclination to "recognize our faults" as in the least peculiar to democracies. Yet, as Newman said of some book, that "it was always open to criticism and always *above* criticism," so one must say of this master's study of democracy.

It would be unjust not to admit that his abstract method gives him in other ways and for other phases of his problem both strength and insight. A hand-to-mouth policy, cheap expediencies, and the dogmatism of common sense are such ever present weaknesses in democracy, that we should greet the more cordially a type of man to whom large principles have some sacredness.

De Tocqueville did not merely think in principles, but he acted upon them in his political career. He possessed those high and rare distinctions in a politician, *convictions*, and human sympathy without cant. It is because these were thought out and lived out, that his "Democracy in America" has for us such priceless value. As we follow his pages, we see our troubles as through mists, but the mists are radiant and the light of a great hope shoots through them. Critics have said that democracy, as a better form of government, was conceived of by de Tocqueville as a fatality; that it was bearing down upon us with forces so irresistible that argument and effort for or against it were alike futile. Few careful readers will draw this conclusion. Democracy is not to de Tocqueville necessarily a good. If it prove a good, it will be

so only because citizens do their part in directing
the forces that make for equality. Democracy
will bear fruit, sweet or sour, according to the soil
of character in which it grows. In this conception,
there is indeed "destiny," but it is the destiny of
character. Democracy rises or falls as men put
into it their best or their worst.

As a qualification for really enlightening national
criticism, I have laid great stress on a capacity for
common human sympathy. At least imaginatively,
de Tocqueville had this at a very early age, and it
deepens in him as a result of his social studies. He
conceived a kind of horror for the way in which
aristocratic classes had governed the masses. He
came to believe that the gradual softening of manners
was due largely to a growing social equality. He
says, "When the chroniclers of the Middle Ages,
who all belonged to the aristocracy by birth or
education, relate the tragical end of a Noble, their
grief flows apace; whereas they tell you at a breath,
and without wincing, of massacres and torture in-
flicted on the common sort of people.[1] To bring
this vividly before us, he quotes a letter as late in his
country's history as the time of Madame de Sévigné.
This brilliant and kindly woman is writing to her
daughter of what she had herself looked upon.
After a few affectionate pleasantries, she asks her
daughter,

[1] "Democracy in America," Vol. II, p. 301.

"Do you wish to hear the news from Rennes? A tax of a hundred thousand crowns has been imposed upon the citizens; and if this sum is not produced within four and twenty hours, it is to be doubled and collected by the soldiers. They have cleared the houses and sent away the occupants of one of the great streets, and forbidden anybody to receive them on pain of death; so that the poor wretches — old men, women near their confinement, and children included — may be seen wandering round and crying on their departure from this city, without knowing where to go, and without food or a place to lie in. Day before yesterday, a fiddler was broken on the wheel for getting up a dance and stealing some stamped paper. He was quartered after death, and his limbs exposed at the four corners of the city. Sixty citizens have been thrown into prison, and the business of punishing them is to begin to-morrow. This province sets a fine example to the others, teaching them above all things to respect their governors and not to throw any more stones into their garden." [1]

She then, as if passing to really important matters, tells of the visit of Madame de Tarente and the preparations for her coming; the lunch and festivities. Between the description of the gaieties in a later letter, she adds incidentally that they were at that moment "less jaded with capital punishments, only one a week, just to keep up appearances." "Hanging," she says, "seems to me quite a cooling entertainment."

De Tocqueville selects this famous lady because she was notably a kind person, neither "selfish nor cruel"; yet because of the caste system of which she was a part, she "had no clear notion of suffering in any one who was not a person of quality."

[1] "Democracy in America," Vol. II, p. 201.

As he comes to this country, one of his first impressions of the Americans is that "they are extremely open to compassion," [1] as shown, among other examples, in their administration of justice.

That the equalizing of social conditions under republican institutions is the one hope for the humanizing of the world, is the conviction of this converted aristocrat.

"When all the ranks of a community are nearly equal, as all men think and feel in nearly the same manner, each of them may judge in a moment of the sensations of all the others; — there is no wretchedness into which he cannot readily enter, and a secret instinct reveals to him its extent. . . . Something like a personal feeling is mingled with his pity and makes him suffer whilst the body of his fellow-creature is in pain."

What these qualities may at last do for the race in really civilizing them into a great brotherhood, is a dream that works powerfully upon the imagination of this great publicist. His book is not to be appreciated — neither its faults nor virtues — apart from this conception.

"The more I advanced in the study of American society, the more I perceived that the equality of conditions is the fundamental fact from which all others seem to be derived and the central point at which all my observations constantly terminated."

To think of de Tocqueville and to criticise him as if he were strictly the scientific investigator is to miss his highest quality. To think of him as in-

[1] Several foreigners note this kindness to animals as if it were new in their experience.

stinctively the *artist*, using his imagination to create
a model of democratic relationship among men,
is to see him as he is. His one sustained passion
is for freedom, which he calls the "*sainte et légitime
passion de l'homme.*" He writes to Mr. Reeve,
"*Je n'ai qu'une passion, l'amour de la liberté et de
la dignité humaine.*" It is this which keeps him
from being a good "party man." It was this which
made him fear that one of our own great dangers
was the possible tyranny of party majorities. It
was this which gave him a prophetic insight into the
essential dangers of slavery. And here we touch one
of those larger issues which is lighted up by seeing
it through a great principle. That a house divided
against itself could not stand was a principle with
Abraham Lincoln. If dark troubles are before us,
de Tocqueville says, "They will be brought about
by the presence of the black race on the soil of the
United States. That is, they (the troubles) will owe
their origin not to equality, but to the inequality
of conditions." [1] He sees that slavery must end,
but is under no illusions that race antagonism will
then cease. Those who think amalgamation is a
solution "delude themselves." "I am not led to
any such conclusion." When they are at last freed,
the social troubles will increase because the negro
will demand political rights. He reads the North
this lesson, "Whoever has inhabited the United
States must have perceived that in those parts of the

[1] "Democracy in America," Vol. II, p. 315.

Union in which negroes are no longer slaves, they
have in no wise drawn nearer to the whites.   On the
contrary, the prejudice of race appears to be stronger
in the States which have abolished slavery than in
those where it still exists; and nowhere is it so in-
tolerant as in those States where servitude has never
been known."

Here is no mere flaying of the South, as if the
North had no part in the slave evil, but a perfectly
true note from the point of view of the National
Whole.   To de Tocqueville democracy of *some
kind* was inevitable.   It was not to be argued with
any more than the passage of time.   It was not
perhaps the highest conceivable social relation.
It certainly held within itself the gravest perils, but
that it was becoming the *fact* to which peoples must
adjust themselves seemed to him like a fate.   This
is the clearer to us when we see what he meant by
democracy.   He is not thinking, like so many of
our critics, of democracy as a *form* of government.
He is thinking of social conditions in which the
utmost obtainable equality exists.   Renan in his
"Caliban" maintains that History is "a good
aristocrat."   To de Tocqueville, Destiny is a name
for the inevitable disappearance of aristocracy.   It
is fundamental to him that all sorts of people should
mingle and intervene more and more in government.
If they intervene wisely and with public spirit, it
will be a good government.   The equality of condi-

[1] "Democracy in America," Vol. II, p. 460.

tions which he found in this country was what most
attracted him. He told the French people that they
too would reach the same conditions even if they did
not "draw the same political consequences."

With this conception of democracy clearly in
mind, we better understand his opinions, his hopes,
and his fears. His gloom over the slavery question
was because he could not see how democracy could
develop here including the negro, even if the slaves
were freed. When they come to demand political
and other equalities, will the white race submit?
If not, how can a class rule, antagonistic to democracy, be avoided?

Equality of conditions and an increasing inter-
vention of *all* in government, is thus preliminary in
de Tocqueville's thought. Just as primary is it
that increase of liberty is good. Our safety in the
United States is this enlargement of freedom, and
nothing subtler or truer can be found in his volumes
than some of the practical inferences from this
principle of liberty, as applied to our political experience. He sees that changes in this country are to
come with extraordinary rapidity, but he does not
fear them. That we ourselves shall shrink before
the changes essential to our best growth, is to him
the real danger. That we shall accept the situation;
that we shall submit even with servility to existing
evils, is what threatens. To understand this peril,
if it be such, we are to see clearly what sort of people
we are. One passage shows this characteristic: —

M

"It is strange to see with what feverish ardor the Americans pursue their own welfare; and to watch the vague dread that constantly torments them lest they should not have chosen the shortest path which may lead to it. A native of the United States clings to this world's goods as if he were certain never to die, and is so hasty at grasping at all within his reach, that one would suppose he was constantly afraid of not living long enough to enjoy them. He clutches everything, he holds nothing fast, but soon loosens his grasp to pursue fresh gratification. . . .

"At first sight there is something surprising in this strange unrest of so many happy men, uneasy in the midst of abundance. The spectacle is, however, as old as the world; the novelty is to see *a whole people furnish an example of it.*"

Here we are in our entirety as a nation, no tempering class excepted, all devoted to business and commercial interests. But why should this fact lead to checks upon liberty, to submission, and even to servility?[1] The level from which de Tocqueville speaks is that of the National Whole and the Common Welfare. He has not in mind temporary interests; much less mere private interests. He is thinking of large public policies that include the general good and of long-range action that includes future social welfare.

We can to-day give a hundred illustrations of this peril where the author could have given a single one. Recently a flood devastated the City

[1] As it is so hopeless in a single chapter to touch one in a score of the Author's points, I select one of the most important in the hope of making his purpose and spirit clearer. I shall not depart from that spirit by translating it into the language of present political experience.

of Pittsburg. The enlightened chief of the Forestry Department, Gifford Pinchot, hastens to explain to the public what this means. Our losses as a nation have already run into millions beyond any calculating. From every part of the country, the men of science for two decades have been scattering among the people a wholly disinterested report of our "impending social dangers." It is true we have made a brave beginning in heeding warnings, but at the most important points, the public safety and future welfare are so fiercely opposed by pulp and timber interests as to defeat the most elementary work in safeguarding society. Pittsburg's jeopardy is but one among hundreds, but it strikes a great city and may be *seen*. That the people may get some hint of its meaning, Mr. Pinchot speaks through the press as follows: —

"The great flood which has wrought devastation and ruin to the Upper Ohio Valley is due fundamentally to the cutting away of the forests on the watersheds of the Allegheny and Monongahela rivers. These streams have their source in the heart of the Alleghany Mountains, which are high and steep and receive a heavy rainfall. The valleys through which these mountain streams flow are narrow and deep. Originally these steep mountain slopes contained as fine hardwood forests as existed in the country. Beneath the tree tops a heavy undergrowth and thick cover of leaves on the ground, and the intertwining roots of trees and shrubs so held back the water from rains and melting snow that dangerous floods seldom occurred.

"Cutting of the timber has gone on to such an extent that not enough oak and chestnut can be obtained now to supply

ties to the railroads which run through the region. Fire has
followed cutting and aided in the work of destruction by burning up the underbrush and leaf cover until many mountain
slopes are absolutely barren, and water rushes from them as
from a house roof. The ruin of the mountains is now accom-
plishing the ruin of the valley. All along the Allegheny and
Monongahela rivers and far down the Ohio Valley are wreck
and devastation. Disease will come when its fruitful germs
shall have multiplied over every foot of the inundated valley.

"The value of the property destroyed in this one flood is
probably sufficient to buy enough land at the head waters of
these streams to fully protect them. Great floods are becoming
common occurrences upon the eastern rivers which have their
sources in the high mountains. Such floods, with increasing
intensity, must be expected from year to year until the important watersheds are protected."

The fatuous outcry that a wise forestry policy is
"un-American"; that it is to be opposed because it
is "socialism," will, of course, continue, although the
most conservative governments in the world have
long practised it with such conspicuous success, from
the public point of view, that the very cranks of
conservatism no longer question it.

With careless prodigality, we have scattered these
most primary sources of wealth, precisely as we
scattered transportation and other franchises upon
which dangerous private monopolies were built.
With the franchises, we have in this generation come
to see clearly the kind of mistakes that have been
made. In the teeth of extreme difficulties, we are
trying to protect the public through legislative control of these corporations. We are learning the

same lesson in our forestry. We have the lesson still to learn as applied to the remaining mining, pasture, and oil lands. If it was a weakness, as we have seen, that de Tocqueville dealt too much with large abstract principles, it was also the source of strength, as in this instance. He knew that the "benevolent despot" could act for the nation as a whole. Could a large invertebrate democracy like ours escape from the clutch of short-range competing interests? Could such a democracy rise to this working conception of the *Commonwealth* as against the terrible political pressure of "the interests"?

It is this problem at the present moment that is testing our democracy as by fire. De Tocqueville saw the nature of it with the same seerlike vision with which he saw the real nature of the negro problem. It is not, he says, liberty that we have to fear, but the hesitations and conservatism of practical business interests. Whatever a wise monarch may do, no democracy realizes this kind of peril until population has so developed as to evoke a variety of interests, that finally come into conscious conflict. Lumber, grazing, mining, control of water powers, furnish such an illustration at the present moment. It is out of this narrower conflict that the larger public interest slowly emerges, so that it can be seen as something above and apart from any or all of these *immediate* pecuniary concerns. Nothing in the statesmanship of President Roosevelt will win him

surer laurels in the future than his pluck and consistency toward this policy which stands for the
whole people and for the future. For the first time
in our history, we have from the Chief Executive
the full purpose of this social policy outlined. "Min-
eral fields, like the forests and navigable streams,
should be treated as public utilities."

"It would surely be greatly to the advantage of this country
if some at least of the coal fields of the East, and especially of
the anthracite fields, had been left under the control of the
Government. Let us provide in the West against the recur-
rence of the conditions which we deplore in the East.

"The withdrawal of these coal lands would constitute a
policy analogous to that which has been followed in with-
drawing the forest lands from ordinary settlement. The
coal, like the forests, should be treated as the property of the
public and its disposal should be under conditions which
would go to the benefit of the public as a whole.

"This Government should not now repeat the mistakes of
the past. Let us not do what the next generation cannot
undo. We have a right to the proper use of both the forests
and the fuel during our lifetime, but we should not dispose
of the birthright of our children. If this Government sells its
remaining fuel lands, they pass out of its future control. If it
now leases them, we retain control, and a future Congress will
be at liberty to decide whether it will continue or change this
policy."

Will our legislators be strong enough and independent enough to act for all of us, rather than for
the few struggling for privilege? To know that our
dangers are in the servility of the politicians to local
and private business *at the points where these conflict*

with public weal, is to "see the enemy," as de Tocqueville conceives him in a democracy.

It was of de Tocqueville that Mill was thinking
when he used the term, "The American Many,"
as representing so exclusively the business class that
"impose upon all the rest of society its own type,
forcing all to submit to it or to imitate it." [1]   Yet
de Tocqueville does not abate one jot of his faith in
democracy.   He holds to liberty because it "corrects
the abuse of liberty."   "Extreme democracy ob-
viates the dangers of democracy." [2]   Yet the hand-
maid of freedom must be a vigilant and universal
discipline.   No one ever put more trust in popular
education as a remedy.   Nor does any incidental
evil discourage him.   There is extreme severity in
his judgment upon our Press : —

"The journalists of the United States are generally in a
very humble position, with a scanty education and a vulgar
turn of mind.[3]

"The characteristics of the American journalist consist in
an open and coarse appeal to the passions of his readers; he
abandons principles to assail the characters of individuals, to
track them into private life, and disclose all their weaknesses
and vices.

"Nothing can be more deplorable than this abuse of the
powers of thought."

"The personal opinions of the editors have no weight in the
eyes of the public: what they seek in a newspaper is a knowledge of facts, and it is only by altering or distorting those facts

[1] *Edinburgh Review*, October, 1840.
[2] "Democracy in America," p. 250.
[3] *Ibid.*, p. 237.

that a journalist can contribute to the support of his own views." [1]

Yet the principle of freedom means to him so much that no hand should be laid upon this press.

"The more I consider the independence of the press in its principal consequences, the more am I convinced that, in the modern world, it is the chief, and, so to speak, the constitutive element of liberty. A nation which is determined to remain free is therefore right in demanding, at any price, the exercise of this independence." [2]

De Tocqueville's faith in liberty is not academic; it is not merely a reasoned sentiment. It has in it something like a moral and religious trust. In spite of all that frightens him in the actual working of our institutions, his eye is steadily fixed upon the disciplinary value of an entire people exercising a free choice on all that determines their destinies. If the race is ever to be educated to self-government, it must be through the reaction of consequences of right and wrong acts. He speaks of "this perilous liberty," yet sees that already, as he compares us with Europe, the balance is on our side. It has great significance to him that while we have plenty of "factions," there was nowhere a sign of secret "conspiracies" such as have been the bane of many aristocracies. Everything comes to the surface — coarseness, clamor, bad taste, vituperation; but that all this *can* come out is our safety. More than any one thing, in his opinion, universal suffrage will

[1] "Democracy in America," p. 238.   [2] *Ibid.*, p. 245.

protect us from the real perils of a factional spirit, as it will guard us from other perils. It has, for example, become a platitude that, in spite of all our frailties, great and threatening emergencies bring out the real character and strength of the people. In proof of this, de Tocqueville had but a fraction of the evidence to which we may now appeal, yet he writes this eloquent passage: —

"But it is more common, both with nations and individuals, to find extraordinary virtues developed from the very imminence of the danger. Great characters are then brought into relief, as the edifices which are usually concealed by the gloom of night are illuminated by the glare of a conflagration. At those dangerous times, genius no longer hesitates to come forward; and the people, alarmed by the perils of their situation, bury their envious passions in a short oblivion. Great names may then be drawn from the urn of election." [1]

It adds to the impressiveness of de Tocqueville's faith in our destinies that with all his continuous study of the United States until the time of his death, his confidence increased rather than diminished. Had he lived to see the results of the Civil War, his most formidable fears would have disappeared. He could not help thinking of our States as little nations which would not hold together. They might still be democratic, but the territory was so vast and interests were so diverse, that all sorts of rivalries would break out to threaten the unity of the whole. "If the sovereignty of the Union," he says, "were to engage in a struggle with that of the States,

[1] *Ibid.*, p. 257.

at the present day, its defeat may be confidently predicted." [1] He, of course, could not see at that date, how steam transportation on land and water was to bind these "little nations" into a unity of recognized interests capable of resisting any probable strain.

Another misgiving was just as vain. Toward the close of the second volume, he reflects upon the chance of war. Would not the successful soldier seduce the imagination of democracy? He writes: —

"I foresee that all the military rulers who may rise up in great democratic nations will find it easier to conquer with their armies than to make their armies live at peace after conquest. There are two things which a democratic people will always find very difficult, — to begin a war *and to end it.*" [2]

These last words, "and to end it," have a strange sound as we remember what actually followed one of the most terrible conflicts in history: the rapid and peaceful return of armies North and South to their ordinary tasks.

Just as little did he foresee certain evils that were even then beginning to appear. He could not believe that we were to have great inequality of fortunes. He could see no paupers, nor any tendency to produce them. The party system with the rise of the boss and the spoils to the victor did not disturb his imagination. He had no intimation of the astounding growth of great cities and their reaction

[1] "Democracy in America," p. 497.
[2] *Ibid.*, p. 329.

on our national life. He was very confident that we were safe from dangerous bribery because "there are so many to be bought." If he could have "listened ahead" a single generation, he might have heard a railroad magnate say, "There are too many to buy in the legislature, I prefer to deal with the Boss." [1] It is also strange to us that the office of the President seemed to him so feeble a thing, and likely to remain so. People talked to him of their respective States, not of the Nation. They were proud of the State, thought about it, read about it, and showed little interest in affairs at the Capitol. As the average citizen takes up the morning paper to-day, what is it that claims his attention? Does he look first at the politics of his State? Is it the affairs of the State that first touch his imagination, or does he turn to the great events which centre in and radiate from the National Capitol? To answer this is to mark one of the profoundest changes in our recent history. We shall see it take even more dramatic form as measured from Mr. Bryce's comment less than twenty-five years ago.

If I were to summarize in a paragraph what seems to me of highest value in these volumes, it would be the revelation of the character and temper of the Author as he faces the thing called Democracy.

---

[1] *Ibid.*, p. 245.

"Perhaps in democracies, the number of men who might be bought is not smaller, but buyers are rarely to be found; and, besides, it would be necessary to buy so many persons at once, that the attempt would be useless." — *Ibid.*, p. 287.

He did not altogether like it. From some of its manifestations and some of its consequences he shrank. He did not, therefore, because of incidental evils, turn his back upon it or turn into that dreary nuisance, the chronic and petulant critic. There is a positive and constructive purpose in his sharpest thrusts. This high-born gentleman accepts without any fussy reserves the principle of self-government. The people and *all* the people are to learn the highest of all arts. They are to learn it through much suffering and through costly mistakes. Without one whining note, Alexis de Tocqueville took his part in the great discipline. So far as his example and precept count with men, Democracy is safe. Of the things threatening which he saw and prophesied, Bryce says: —

> "Of these clouds one rose till it covered the whole sky, broke in a thunderstorm and disappeared. Some have silently melted into the blue. Some still hang on the horizon, darkening large parts of the landscape."

What these remaining shadows are we shall see in the chapter on his peer and successor, James Bryce.

CHAPTER X

THE first French books that follow the Revolution are full of geniality and even flattery. It was long the custom to quote these genuine aristocrats "who knew what manners were," as an offset to the snubbing we received at the hands of the English writers.

A good example of this extreme amiability is in three volumes of travels by Brissot de Warville. As so many of the early English confess that their object in coming was to discredit us, this young aristocrat comes to study our social and political conditions for a purpose which glowingly appears in his preface as follows: —

"O Frenchmen, who wish for this valuable instruction, study the Americans of the present day. Open this book. You will see here to what degree of prosperity the blessings of freedom can elevate the industry of man; how they dignify his nature, and dispose him to universal fraternity. You will here learn by what means liberty is preserved; that the great secret of its duration is in good morals. It is a truth that the observation of the present state of America demonstrates at every step. Thus you will see in these travels, the prodigious effect of liberty on morals, on industry, and on the amelioration of men."

He lands in Boston: —

"With what joy, my good friend, did I leap to this shore
of liberty! . . . I flew from despotism, and came at last to
enjoy the spectacle of liberty among a people where nature,
education, and habit had engraved the equality of rights,
which everywhere else is treated as a chimera. With what
pleasure did I contemplate this town! . . . I thought myself
in that Salentum of which the lively pencil of Fénelon has left
us so charming an image. But the prosperity of this new
Salentum was not the work of one man, of King or Minister;
it is the fruit of liberty, that mother of industry."

The Bostonians unite simplicity of morals with
that French politeness and delicacy of manners
which renders virtue more amiable. They are
hospitable to strangers and obliging to friends.
They are tender husbands, fond and almost idolatrous
parents, and kind masters. Also "neatness without
luxury is a characteristic feature of this purity of
manners; and this neatness is seen everywhere at
Boston, in their dress, in their houses, and in their
churches."

Alas, this is not observation, it is rhapsody. It is
in so high a strain that this courtly gentleman moved
and spoke among us in those homespun days. There
are recorded compliments in the same key by
the Duke de la Rochefoucauld-Liancourt. He
says of the President's balls, that the "splendor
of the rooms and the variety and richness of
the dresses did not suffer in comparison with
Europe." De la Rochefoucauld was much in

Philadelphia society, of whose assemblies he writes,
"It is impossible to meet with what is called a plain
woman." No suspicion attaches to this gallantry;
but when Max O'Rell told us a few years ago that
he travelled six months in the United States without seeing one plain woman, we remember that
he was looking for lecture engagements.[1] There is
much of this benevolent myopia in the whole group
of French critics during the entire generation that
followed the Revolution. The French had helped
us largely because of their intense hatred and fear
of the English. The French became our literary
champions as naturally as they defended us with
their ships and arms. This impulse to vindicate
us against the English shows itself as late as de
Tocqueville. He finds American morals "very
superior to their progenitors, the English." [2]

Of the English abuse of our manners he says:[3] —

"The English make game of the manners of the Americans;
but it is singular that most of the writers who have drawn these
ludicrous delineations belonged themselves to the middle
classes in England, to whom the same delineations are ex-
ceedingly applicable; so that these pitiless censors furnish,
for the most part, an example of the very thing they blame in
the United States; they do not perceive that they are deriding
themselves to the great amusement of the aristocracy of their
own country."

[1] In " Jonathan and His Continent," p. 18.
[2] Vol. II, p. 249.
[3] *Ibid.*

So Sara Bernhardt, coming to fill her coffers, never lands in
New York without assuring the American people through the re-

It is thus, with regret, that we have to put aside these first Gallic flatteries. They have precisely the same value as the ultra fault-finding of the English. They are neither more nor less to be trusted as important critics. De Tocqueville is not to be classed among these overzealous friends. He sets the note of the discriminating but sympathetic student which continues through Chevalier until our own day, when it has become a fashion among the French to make flying trips to this country. Too many of them begin to write on the steamer coming out; take their first impressions as a finality, giving them literary form so rapidly that the book is on the Boulevards soon after their return. Even if the chapters totter with mistakes, they are likely to be more racily entertaining than English and German books of serious merit.

One wonders, nevertheless, why so many of them should be destitute of the slightest critical values.[1] I put this question to a professor of French in Harvard College. He replied that "they either had no real knowledge of English, or knew it just enough to deceive them into thinking they knew it — which was worse." Not a few of these latter-day writers are so slovenly and inaccurate that they serve admirably as books of humor. It is an ancient

porters that "no country touches the *heart* like America." At her last landing, she delights in the increase of gracious and delicate manners.

[1] The one exception in the most superficial of them is their comments on our theatre.

observation that the French care so little about
other countries, that they rarely learn to spell cor-
rectly the commonest names. There is such tenacity
in this habit that it finally surprises the reader if
now and then they get the word right. To avoid
extremes, here, for instance, is a new book by a
highly educated man who has been at least eight
years in this country. He was given every chance
to correct his proofs. A few of the spellings are
these: "Lettery; New Hawen, Coan, for New
Haven, Conn.; Boss Crotker; Tessenden for
Fessenden; Cark Schurtz." Arnold's first name
is now Mathew and then Matthew. Thus far the
case is extremely mild. "My Uncle Tom's Cabin,"
"Long-Fellow" (by one who had visited the poet),
"Athlantic Monthly"; the poor White House seriously turned into "Execution Mansion"; "Howard
College," for Harvard; the City of Churches trans-
formed into "Broakline"; the Nutmeg State into
"Conettocutt," and "New Jersia," fairly represent
the new spelling. "Teatotlar" is so often used that
it obviously conveys the idea to the writer that tea
was the adopted substitute for rum and thus gave
the name to the party. "Washington Irwing,"
"Rock-Chair," "Wahash," for Wabash, "Huddson
River," the "Poet Wittier," and proud Chicago tor-
tured into "Chicorgua"; the Mohawk, "Mohuwek,"
and the "*La cofoco* party" are others in the same
kind. These are a driblet in the main torrent of
misspellings. Even present-day philosophers write

N

"Williams" James. I had long believed that they were merely typographical errors, but there is authoritative proof that they represent, for the most part, indifference or sheer carelessness of observation. The quality which helps account for this is stated with great frankness by M. Blouet (Max O'Rell): [1] —

"Ask the first hundred Frenchmen you meet in the streets of Paris what is the name of the president of the United States; you will find ninety-nine of them unable to tell you. The Frenchman is exclusive to the point of stupidity, and that which is not French possesses no interest for him."

This is the stark provincialism for which Paris has long been noted.

No small part of this literature is by journalists who have in mind the group of French readers for whom they write. To entertain Parisians by pretty paradoxes and lively drolleries is as exclusively their aim as it was the aim of Tom Moore to amuse the English diners-out. They often follow so nearly the same route, see so nearly the same objects, and make merry with the same characteristics, that each newcomer seems to have read the same books and to have taken instructions from the previous voyager. They drive to the Waldorf-Astoria, of which a minute pen-picture never fails. The device in the room by which one may order thirty things, few of which any one ever wants, divides their attention with ice-water and the price of cabs. The next step is to hunt up a restaurant which reminds them enough

[1] "Jonathan and His Continent," p. 137.

of Paris to make life endurable. If the heaven of
the Smart Set at Newport or elsewhere is open to
them, the rest of the country grievously suffers.
One feels this even in so brilliant a writer as Paul
Bourget.[1] The next dash (by way of Niagara) is for
the West, where they struggle desperately with two
phenomena — Chicago and the Cowboy. They
are stunned by Chicago and the packing houses, but
the Cowboy electrifies them. The return trip is sure
to include the South for the sake of a chapter on the
Negro problem. This dark enigma is the only discomfiture. They do not even make it interesting.
There are at least twenty of these volumes from
which one could remove the various and picturesque
titles, replacing them by "A Whole Afternoon in the
United States." Of some of them one would have
to say that this half day was very ill spent.

One Paris exquisite, whose object was clearly to
create a sensation among his friends, lands in New
York, but is so instantly undone by our rude ways,
that he straightway returns to Paris. "*Je n'ai pas
pu supporter le coup*" — it was too insufferable.
This is far better than writing his book. He spared
himself that trouble, and yet gave the shock of surprise and delight to his friends.

Between this vivacious squad of journalists[2] and

[1] "Outre Mer," two volumes. It excites much curiosity, for instance, to know whether the lynching was really *seen* as described.

[2] Much better are two books, "Choses d'Amérique," by Max
Leclaire, with an interesting discussion of Catholicism in the United
States, and "La Femme aux États Unis," by M. C. de Varigny, in

serious inquirers like Le Play, Carlier,[1] Claudio
Janet, the Marquis de Rousier, and Madame Blanc[2]
the gap is like that between Brissot and de Tocqueville. Le Play's pioneer work in sociology has developed into an educational interest which has sent

which we are told why women have become the equals of our men.
"Flirt, amour, mariage," all get respectful attention.

[1] A work of extraordinary learning is "La République Américaine," by the French lawyer, Auguste Carlier. This savant came
in 1855, stayed two years, and formed intimate relations with men
like Sumner, Benton, Quincy, Ticknor, Everett, and Longfellow.
His larger work in four stiff volumes, if not in the class of Bryce
and de Tocqueville, is a profound study. He had before its publication written a volume on Marriage in the United States, 1860;
one on Slavery two years later; two volumes on general history,
especially in relation to the Indians, 1864; and still another, "The
Acclimatization of Races in the United States," 1868. Nearly a
quarter of a century was given to his crowning work, "The American Republic." Carlier is very critical of de Tocqueville because
of his taste for large and brilliant generalization, founded on what
is thought to be insufficient evidence. He does not even let Mr.
Bryce off without some strictures, chiefly because of the omissions
in the "American Commonwealth." No further use is here made
of Carlier because he is too exclusively for the student. The same
must also be said of Le Play.

[2] A brilliant exception to this troup of travelling dilettanti is
Madame Blanc, writing under the pseudonym of Th. Bentzon. She
was several times in this country preparing carefully such studies
as "Choses et Gens d'Amérique," "Récits Américains," "Questions Américaines," "Femmes d'Amérique," and "Nouvelle
France et Nouvelle Angleterre." She has an insistent purpose
"to make my own people really see the Americans as they are."
Writing for many years through the most distinguished literary
organ, the *Revue des Deux Mondes*, no one has done more than
Madame Blanc to get some elementary notions about the large
facts of American life into the French mind.

us some of the most conscientious students that have ever come. Through the service of the Musée Social they are making the life and institutions of this country known to France. Renan's horror of everything American has given way to honest desires at least to understand the United States.

From the dozen volumes that one would venture to recommend, I select a rather miscellaneous job-lot of observations that may do some critical service.

There is first the intelligent recognition that one does not get into real touch with us until one learns that to see the American at all, he must be seen in several places. This sounds commonplace, but how many travellers realize it, or act upon it in their judgments? A Dutch jurist spent some months in this country at tasks which compelled him to visit business men in their offices in the pressure of the day's work. He said, "Until I went into their homes and saw them off duty, I thought their manners outrageous. I was saved from stupid injustice by seeing them at their own tables and clubs." There is no class to which this does not apply. No perspective is true about morals, manners, or achievements that does not include several phases of the subject scrutinized. It is this same larger and more patient spirit in classifying impressions, upon which Le Play laid such emphasis, that enables de Rousier to read us a wholesome lesson.

For a growing number of American families, there is excellent educational material in some of the "shocks" which these gay Frenchmen suffer; as for instance, in that enduring superstition that the moral destiny of the family is really dependent upon rigid punctuality at a common and united breakfast table.

A French scholar is staying with a well-to-do family in which no exigency of business or school appointments, no lack of domestic service or tyrannous duties of the mistress could have been given as a reason, but because a daughter was ten minutes late for the seven o'clock breakfast, "the father showed great annoyance, which was all the more severe and disagreeable because he took on a high moral tone."

The visitor finds it an iron law in that household that all members shall be as punctual as at military dress-parade. He asks innocently why seven people should be expected to march in on stroke of the clock. The inquiry occasions great surprise. The parental explanations leave him less than ever convinced that the custom is good for this type of family. It had already gone into his docket as an American superstition, when the young lady found some opportunity to give her own exposition. "It *is* a superstition and a very immoral one. It always starts the day wrong at least for two of us. You may wake people up at the same time, but you can't wake up their *stomachs* at the same time. I am hungry and therefore happy if I can eat at eight or nine or when I like, and I am glad to get my own breakfast.

With this wicked punctuality, some of us are glum
or irritable, and almost the only family unpleasantness we ever have can be traced straight to this
seven o'clock breakfast." To this guest, the
daughter's outburst came as a gleam of hope. He
found us much too taciturn in our family life;
far too little given to affectionate gaieties of common conversation.

The one step to help this, he thinks, is "to individ-
ualize the breakfast; to allow sleep, the great healer,
to deal with each one after his needs." This hygienic
freedom will restore and give such nice balance to
the nerves that every one will be at his best. At the
meal (lunch or dinner), all things will go trip-
pingly because of this sagacious and humane
reform.

Many of the social troubles which we magnify are
troubles, according to him, because as individuals
we insist upon interpreting them solely by our tem-
poral personal convenience. The employer complains of high wages and shortened hours, yet these
are the very proofs of the industrial supremacy
which these critics grant us. The mistress groans
because the domestic is quick to leave; but that she
can leave, sure always of another place and, it may
be, a higher wage, is precisely what marks the
economic advantage of the country. That community leads which gives *opportunity* to the largest
number of its population. That opportunity is
here open to those classes which are elsewhere

narrowly held by custom, is the very sign of that progress which includes the nation as a whole.

It is, I think, de Rousier who expresses the humorous surprise that our democracy should have become the happy hunting-ground of the European nobility. As their rents fall and their castles decay; as the external symbols of class distinction become too costly to maintain, what happier resource have these titled pets than to save themselves at the expense of the well-dowered American girl? "Is your democracy," asked one visitor, "to be the chief protector and preserver of these man-made inequalities in Europe?"

It is full of interest to hear a Catholic scholar speculate with great open-mindedness upon the differences in the French and American ideals of the young woman's education. After many visits to the American schools he thus states his case: —

"The difference is revolutionary. We in France *assume* with our young women that they are to marry and live the family life. All our conceptions of the girl's training are consciously adjusted to this thought. The American ideal seems, on the other hand, to assume that the girl is to have a life of her own; that she is to be economically independent and make her way, marriage or no marriage."

If the family were to suffer from this, he sees in that fact the condemnation of this education in the United States. He is not convinced that this evil is to be feared, because of the indications that this very economic independence, with its enlarged freedom, may result in a sexual selection of a type that will secure better offspring and even a happier marriage. "The girl that is independent enough to refuse the man who can only offer economic support may later have her reward in the husband that nature means for her." This is like Jules Huret's discovery that the larger life opened to the American woman has made her so much nearer an intellectual mate of her husband that the offspring and society at large reap the advantage. The net energy and initiative of the country seem to him largely accounted for by this wider field of woman's activity.

Another reflection on our education, especially in the earlier grades, is that the imagination, the sense of mystery and of reverence, suffer much from our too positive methods. "Information and the fact" are thought to hold such sway in our schools that the more delicate qualities of mind and heart are hardened in the process. One of these writers [1] has a very penetrating passage upon this point. He says our education allows far too little for the unconscious resources in the young. He is sorry to find in the youth at school so little of the naïve, so little timidity, deference, and even awkwardness. He would see more capacity to blush, more "credulous simplicity" and less aggressive, conscious intensity. He gives this as one reason why many of our finest men of poetic and unworldly nature have such

[1] Paul Bourget, "Outre Mer," Vol. II, p. 135.

slight influence in the nation; — because "*cette vie est trop voluntaire, trop consciente, trop intensive.*"

It is this brilliant writer who turns many a neat phrase against us because of our lack of "*la mesure.*" Balance, perspective, proportion in our thinking and in that which thought expresses, he finds deplorably lacking in our inner and outer life. This evil is so inherent that nothing escapes it. Our architecture and theatre have as little harmony as our inner estimates of the spiritual values of life. We have a craze to count in vast numbers; cannot, he says, even show our new houses to strangers without insisting that they look into every room, toilet and linen closets included. The bulk of the Sunday papers is a fatal sign of this disease of "too much-ness." Reckless as to quality, the editor reckons well on his public by supplying a huge and promiscuous mass of print and pictures. Our houses are stuffed too full of ornament, too much is upon walls and tables. Roses, like the American Beauty, swaggering on stems four feet long, and the modest violet packed into bouquets that would fill the wash bowl; the length of the dinner, the amount of food and the waste connected with it; the height of the skyscraper; the "barbarous over-ornamenting of the Pullman car" and the last new hotel; the reckless speeding of specially advertised trains, are one and all unpleasant hints to this philosophic critic of our lack of "*la mesure.*" We are the most hospitable of people, yet cannot resist overdoing it for those whom we specially care to entertain, and thus over all is this trail of the serpent — exaggeration.

We cannot deny this altogether, but it is fair to reply that the standard which he sets us — harmony and proportion for the inner and the outer life — is the highest and most difficult that ever was or can be applied to a race. We have been told often enough that only the Greeks at their highest moment ever greatly approached its realization. Before this supreme test, no nation would go without whipping. The baby act, however, we will not play. The fault, beyond doubt, lies against us. Exaggeration and lack of *"measure"* are like a taint in the blood of our civilization.

Still, these fastidious connoisseurs leave us one crumb of comfort. As we saw a change and softening of tone in the English criticism, so in the French. Their most persuasive and confident strictures against us naturally concerned the realm of art. There is no relenting about our theatre. For our stage, their shafts still bear the poisoned tip. But architecture, painting, sculpture, literature, win most gracious praises from recent French guests.[1] Paul Adam,[2] in a recent volume of much charm, is unhesitating in his admiration for "the emerging

[1] M. Alfred D'Almbert, a half century ago, in his "Flanerie Parisienne," thinks it very clever to announce a chapter on the Beaux Arts en Amérique. As you turn the leaf you come upon a blank unprinted space.

[2] "Vues d'Amérique," Paris, 1906.

best" in these arts. Sargent has "incontestable mastery." We have "excellent art instruction." John La Farge is among the really great, and "*la grande simplicité*" of Saint Gaudens' figures is full of power and genius. In much of our sculpture there is "excellent technique." He says we have become the great art buyers of the world and that our rich men use their dollars far better than the rich men of France. He roundly says to the Latin people that they should be made to understand that the spirit of art "has definitely penetrated the soul of the Yankees." "Europe must look out if she would keep her supremacy in art." It is not less complimentary that he interprets much of our higher life through the philosophy of William James. Here, too, is a great artist whose thought fascinates him like the grand lines of the Lincoln statue.

In the genial book of the Catholic Professor, Abbé Klein,[1] we have an abandonment of appreciation for the spiritual tolerance which seems to that writer a sure solvent for many gritty obstacles, not alone on our shores, but for the future of a much

---

[1] "Au Pays de la Vie Intense." Though we say these things ourselves, it is more quickening to hear a large-minded French Catholic thinking aloud about the niggardly uses to which the great average of Protestant churches are put. That such a vast equipment throughout the land should have a leisurely Sunday morning opening with a possible prayer-meeting in the week, and then be locked tight as in fear of thieves! He finds multitudes of these costly structures used hardly more than half the hours of a single day during the entire week.

larger world in which the races must more and more live as in one common country.

There are few exceptions to the blank bewilderment of the abler French reporters, that the negro should excite the excess of feeling which they find in the North and South alike. This surprise is not in the least confined to those who have had no contact with the African and can therefore be said to know nothing about him. It is the same astonishment that the present Governor-General of Jamaica expresses. He has had long and intimate relations with negroes in various administrative capacities. That we should so *incessantly talk* about it; that we should so force the issue into the fierce light of controversy and debate; that reticence and self-control should be so rare, are what appear to him among the least excusable causes of the trouble. We act, he says, as if we were set upon creating two or three times as many difficulties as there are.

This is the tone of the most intelligent French observers. "If it is an uneasy ghost," asks one, "why can the Americans give it no rest? Why must they always assume that the hair by which the sword hangs is so soon to snap? Why do they shout so loudly that it must snap?" He is told by many best people in the South, that if the tongue of the politician should be struck by temporary paralysis whenever he appeals to this race feeling, the greatest obstacle to race improvement would be removed.

These sins appear to him, however, slight as compared to the "magnificent abandon" with which North and South alike are giving themselves to the education of the colored race. And thus we pass from the unchecked elation of Brissot at the closing of the eighteenth century to the more discriminating cordiality of these last writers who find it worth while to see us at our best rather than at our worst.

CHAPTER XI

THAT democracy is to deprive social relations of all delicacy and charm, is either taken for granted by many of the older critics, or they attempt to prove it by elaborate illustrations. "Democracy everywhere," says one, "has no soft words, no suppleness of forms; it has little address, little of management; it is apt to confound moderation with weakness, violence with heroism." As a democracy must be built up through trade and commerce in which the entire people takes part, no class remains to teach manners to the busy masses. This filled many of our observers with anxiety. If all must earn their own livelihood, how could they ever attain the ease and refinement of good behavior?

That those who produce the wealth upon which all must live could ever learn the gentilities in and through their work was not to be thought of. Enough of this has nevertheless come to pass that we see something of these rare values slowly emerging from the very jaws of the industrial monster. We have begun to see that manners are an excellent business asset. As business has lost its isolated and individual character; as it has come more and more to depend upon associated and corporate forms; in a word, as it becomes *socialized*, manners in the larger sense rise in value. To manage large bodies of men has come to require the kind of knowledge that includes manners of some sort. As for the general public and the greater corporations that depend upon its good-will, manners are coming to rank with ability. We have now to supplement the familiar formula "land, labor, and ability" by land, labor, ability and manners.

It was this larger use of the word that President Hadley had in mind when he said, "A large part of the railroad difficulties could be settled simply by good manners." That noble citizen, W. J. Baldwin, Jr., was also thinking of railroad problems when he said, "We shall be in hot water until we train up a set of men who know how to behave to each other and to the public." It has long been evident that a large part of our labor troubles spring from a lack of manners if the word is used in its larger sense. The best work brought about by arbitration has been through devices which enable the good manners of those most concerned to get effective expression. An American business man many years in Mexico gave this bit of his own history: —

"I was for months checked in my plans because I knew nothing of Mexican manners. My letters, my calls, my business propositions all seemed to freeze up the men with whom I wished to do business. A friendly Mexican to whom I appealed for help told me I was too abrupt. 'They don't understand you any better than you understand them. You must make a formal call and a leisurely one, before you say a word about your business proposition. You are beginning to use the telephone, but you offend people by not spending a minute first in careful inquiries as to health, etc.' Then he showed me all the flourishes that must adorn my letters, and slowly, and with great loss of time, I got on to a perfectly friendly footing with my Mexicans.'

This common ignorance of customs and traditions among another people accounts for a part at least of this sad tangle over the question of manners. A certain rare and occasional type of visitor brings the gift; — is it knowledge, imagination, sympathy, or a unifying of all these? — a gift at any rate which carries its happy possessor through every vexation of the journey, apparently without discerning that anybody has bad manners.

Almost exactly one hundred years ago John Bradbury, F.L.S., travelled one thousand miles in the United States. In his own words, he "never met with the least incivility or affront." We see the reason for this in a warning he gives to travellers from Europe. They must first *understand the character of the society to which they come,* especially if they have been in the habit of treating servants haughtily. "Let no one (in the United States) indulge himself in abusing the waiter or hostler at the inn," for these feel that they are citizens and are performing useful work.[1] De Tocqueville is, except now and then, just as philosophical. Even

[1] "Travels in 1809, 10, and 11," Liverpool, 1817, p. 355.

o

very ungracious differences in behavior interest him: —

> "There are many little attentions which an American does not care about; he thinks they are not due him, or he presumes that they are not known to be due; he therefore either does not perceive a rudeness, or he forgives it; his manners become less courteous, and his character more plain and masculine." [1]

With the large majority of these early travellers, our manners find no favor. Isaac Weld gives about the average acidity to his summary, "Civility cannot be purchased from them on any terms; they seem to think that it is incompatible with freedom." [2] Even the great ones discipline us, especially when we are caught out of our own country. In Lockhart's "Life of Scott," we find the great story-teller thus commenting on the Americans that sought him out, "They are as yet rude in their ideas of social intercourse, and totally ignorant, speaking generally, of all the art of good breeding, which consists chiefly in a postponement of one's own petty wishes or comforts to those of others. By rude questions and observations, an absolute disrespect to other people's feelings, and a ready indulgence of their own, they make one feverish in their company, though perhaps you may be ashamed to confess." This is mildly spoken compared to Tennyson's outburst against the steady stream of Americans that tried year after year to waylay him in and about

[1] "Democracy in America," Vol. II, p. 209.
[2] "Travels," p. 37.

HARRIET MARTINEAU
Author of " Society in America "

his home by the sea. Another benignant Englishman says the first thing an American does, when he
arrives at a London hotel, is to demonstrate his
inferiority to the waiters. He is so ignorant of the
fine art of tipping, that he gives a shilling where he
should give a penny, and to the man who should
get twopenny he donates two shillings. "The
consequence is that he is always in difficulties."
The growing insolence of English waiters he attributes wholly to the low-bred familiarity of the American tourists! This Londoner says it is a common
sight to see the entire business of a restaurant cease
while the man from Indiana loudly disputes the
extra price charged for bread, because "out in
Indiana they do not have such charges. Everybody
can have all the bread he wants. It's thrown in."

"Why," asks the English journalist, "is the American so well behaved at home, but such a consuming
terror in Europe?" He was given the well-worn
answer. "The noisy or conspicuously silly American
fixes attention upon himself. You English do not
notice the far greater number of quiet and decent
people for the very reason that they are well behaved." The American then asked, "Why can't
you understand that some millions of people in the
United States have the travelling habit; that thousands of them, from the humblest origin, go to Europe
as soon as they get money enough. In no country
in the world does this class sacrifice to see the world,
often with their families, as do Americans. That

among these, large numbers should make themselves officious and disagreeable is inevitable." This is true, but it is also inevitable that a very small minority of loud and objectionable folk, from any country, should set a common stamp on the entire people. Again and again, we see in our critics that they brought with them the idea of our manners from what they had already observed of American behavior in Europe.

We have good evidence that this offensive chip-on-the-shoulder attitude has disappeared from some classes of Americans. But for our continued shaming, a noisy and undisciplined contingent carries on the work of discrediting our country. On ship, in miscellaneous hotels and *pensions* in Europe, this plague still rages. A veteran conductor of Americans through Europe says, "I have my chief trouble with this infernal lugging of America along with them. I practically never get a party without some few who stir up bad blood by loud talk about 'the way we do things in the United States,' and the women are as bad as the men. The Italians and Swiss are good-natured about it; the English despise it, and if they can, avoid us altogether; the French shrug their shoulders and say, 'What can you expect? they are Americans.'" He adds, "I have often seen both French and English, when inquiring for rooms at *pensions* or small hotels, turn away upon learning that Americans were there."

An American who had to spend some years in

Italy admits that he changed his *pension* three times because he couldn't stand "so many kinds of bragging about his country. Four out of five of us can hold our own in decent behavior with other nationalities, but there is always that awful fifth to make mischief." In one *pension* from which he felt himself driven he says, a mother came with her three grown daughters. On their first entrance into the parlor in which several persons were reading or writing, one of the daughters said, as if no one were in the room, "Did you ever see such absurd ways of heating a house? It's almost as bad as those stuffy English grates. Why, in America—" "I didn't stop for the rest of the sentence, I hurried out to find some place where I should be free from this most intolerable way of making ourselves disagreeable on our travels."

Our task is, however, with that larger general public of which our critics are mostly writing. Especially in the first half of the century they rarely attempt any discrimination among different kinds of Americans. A French lecturer says, "He (the American) would be afraid of lowering himself by being polite. In his eyes politeness is a form of servility, and he imagines that, by being rude to well-bred people, he puts himself on a footing with them, and carries out the greatest principle of democracy, equality." [1] For more than half a century, we

[1] "Jonathan and His Continent," p. 278.
Hamerton speaks of certain classes among the Scots who

get almost unbroken chastisement, especially from the English. The French so far champion us as to say that, of all people, the English have the least qualification as instructors or censors of manners. But as this French view may arise from envy of the English, we will not take advantage of it.

It is, nevertheless, very vital to know as much as possible about the temper and idiosyncrasies of the critic. I have seen a good many Germans in that country (especially men classically trained) who had come to the United States, but for some reason failed to win their way. They returned embittered to the Fatherland. Henceforth it was a vocation to abuse American character and manners. But the root of this abuse was in their own remembered disappointment. If we add to causes like these, all sorts of personal bias, misadventure and injured vanities, we shall account for a good deal of the harsher comment on our manners.

There is no better illustration than Mrs. Trollope, who is selected because our manners were her special theme. It was these which gave the title to her book. Wherever she journeys, her eye seeks evidence of our ill breeding. She was standing by General Jackson when a good American thus accosted him: —

show "a sort of repugnance to polish of manner, as if it were an unmanly dandyism, a feeling that answers to a plain man's dislike of jewellery and fine clothes."

"'General Jackson, I guess?'

"The General bowed assent.

"'Why, they told me you was dead.'

"'No! Providence has hitherto preserved my life.'

"'And is your wife alive, too?'

"The General, apparently much hurt, signified the contrary, upon which the courtier concluded his harangue by saying, 'Ay, I thought it was one or the t'other of ye.'" [1]

She says, "The total and universal want of manners, both in males and females, is so remarkable that I was constantly endeavoring to account for it." [2] She is telling the truth for the most part, but she needs one correction. We are quite certain that her own peculiarities were so unyieldingly different from those among whom she lived, as to be a constant irritant. She was sturdily "sot" in her English ways; was very brusque and could not adapt herself to the life about her. She wishes to hire a domestic "by the year," as she did in England. She thinks it very absurd to hire by the month. The custom should be corrected; but she gets this response from the astonished maiden: —

"Oh Gimini!" exclaimed the damsel, with a loud laugh, "you be a downright Englisher, sure enough. I should like to see a young lady engage by the year in America! I hope I shall get a husband before many months, or I expect I shall be an outright old maid, for I be most seventeen already."

That the ways of men were rough and uncouth among the average folk with whom she had to do was as natural, at that time, as that pigs should run

---

[1] Page 201.   [2] Page 64.

in the streets, roads should be bad, houses built "like shells," and that there should be "a deplorable lack of sidewalks." We have to take her own conduct into account because manners are not alone an affair of the individual, they are a social relation. When Captain Marryat, who follows Mrs. Trollope, finds a group of Americans, jolly and companionable, it throws even more light on *him* than on the Americans. It is instant proof that the jovial author of "Peter Simple" was himself a lover of good fellowship; that he could "mix" with any company. This is a human approach that creates its own response.

Alexander Mackay, a few years later, says: —

"An American can be as reserved as anybody else, when he comes in contact with one he does not understand, or who will not understand him — and this is the reason why so many travellers in America, who forget to leave their European notions of exclusiveness at home, and traverse the republic wrapped in the cloak of European formalism, find the Americans so cold in their demeanor, and erroneously regard their particular conduct to themselves as the result of a general moodiness and reserve." [1]

This explains Mackay's temperamental equipment as a traveller. He will not insist upon hiring a domestic by the year, if that is not the custom. He will not insist upon the same [2] vocal intonation or openly rejoice, as one of his friends did, that our Hall of Representatives at Washington was perfect

---

[1] Page 126.

[2] "The Western World," 1846, p. 126. See also p. 283.

because you couldn't hear a word that was spoken in it. One Frenchman never sees a public official that was not coarse and brutal in his manners. Without defending all our officials, we yet know that about this same Frenchman there were peculiarities which, if we knew them, would qualify his sweeping judgment.

De Tocqueville, for example, shows us as in a mirror, in this little paragraph, what kind of a "mixer" he was: "A public officer in the United States is uniformly simple in his manners, accessible to all the world, attentive to all requests, and obliging in his replies." [1]

Sir James Caird was sent to this country by the English Government to report on the feeling of our people after the affair of the *Alabama*. He told me that on one of our trains he thought he had lost some luggage. He sent for the conductor, saying to him rather gruffly that his luggage must be looked up. "I assumed," said Sir James, "that your conductors were like the 'guards' on an English train. I at once found out my error. The tall Yankee took out his glasses and looked down at me with great deliberation, saying finally, 'Who in —— are you?' I lost my temper, saying to him that I was a 'member of Parliament, commissioned by my government,' etc., etc. To all of which the tall Yankee listened grimly till I had finished. He then said, as if examining a specimen, 'Well — I'll be ——, if you

[1] "Democracy in America," Vol. I, p. 263.

don't look just as I expected a member of Parliament to look. Good day.' He returned in a moment and said, 'If you go and ask the baggagemaster, perhaps he'll look after your trunk.'" Sir James added that he had never known before what degree of rage he was capable of. After some days he learned that the conductor was rather like the captain of a steamer and in no way like the guard of an English train. "I finally saw that I had made a fool of myself and after that never had the slightest trouble." This kindly English gentleman could, of course, have had that same circus every day of his stay in the United States, if he had not dropped that tone and air. His own misreckoning created the situation, just as thousands of Americans in Europe create all sorts of awkwardnesses and ill-feeling because in some moment of misunderstanding they have no key to the situation. They are in unwonted conditions where they have not learned the human approach.

As jovial a nature as Dickens certainly had not learned it on his first journey to this country. He had a great weakness for playing the dandy in his dress. He was much bejewelled and we have only to picture him, with his buttonhole bouquet, walking about in a town of the Mississippi valley in 1842. Every ultra effect of his person was bound to create among those rustics all manner of "impertinent curiosities." The gods could not have protected him. When, on his second trip, he said nothing would induce him to write another book, we see that he had learned something. Even so little a thing as the single eye-glass of Sir Charles Lyell explains some of the irreverent remarks that he did not like in that Western world.

Difficult as it is, there must be some understanding as to what is meant by manners. Renan says that no fact weighs so much in our human relations as manner. He is not asserting that manners are the highest or best in character, but that they practically count for more than other gifts among men. This has no more emphasis than in Emerson, who says that "the creation of the gentleman" is the most conspicuous fact in modern history. "Chivalry is that, and loyalty is that, and, in English literature, half the drama and all the novels from Sir Philip Sidney to Sir Walter Scott paint this figure." As we face the many charges that American manners are bad, what standard are we to have in mind? Has any nation as a whole good manners? We hear this said of some Eastern peoples, but in our Western world, are German or French or English manners good as totals of behavior? Or must we deal with a selected class or classes in each nation? We should find in every class in all of those countries gracious and most ungracious manners. In each community we should have to do with individuals. It is not unlikely that many more persons deserving the name of gentleman or lady, would be found in one nation than in another. But the question in

Europe as well as in the United States will be one of
ratios. The general statement that American manners are bad is like saying, "the American is fat or
temperate, or easily embarrassed." I heard an
Englishman in London, who did not like us, say that
he never failed to spot an American, because he had
"a wolf's face." I saw what he meant, but he was
depicting only a portion of his enemies. That
Europeans knocking about among our loosely settled
communities, as did Fearon, the two Halls, and
scores of others, should be concerned about our lack
of manners, is like their solicitude over our want
of cathedrals, castles, and good pictures. The slow
reaching out of our people toward the West with
all the burdens and hardships incident to pioneer
life, was no school for outward graces. Our popular
conception of liberty and equality unquestionably
added its touch of swagger to much of our
behavior. The hat-in-hand deference observable
among common folk in many parts of Europe could
not thrive in our atmosphere. That deference was
made in older countries by all sorts of forced subserviency. It is sweet to those who receive it, and
we often hear among us a toadying valuation set
upon the obsequious and bated homage of foreign
servants. This is called good manners. It is
said, they "know their places." But we cannot
continue to have those masks, and at the same time
have the best social manners.

As most of the early attacks on our ill-bred ways

ascribe them to democracy and equality, this charge especially has to be met. There is happily illustrious authority to which we may appeal. As great a man as Goethe declared that really good manners could only come with equality; not an inane literal equality, but an equality of native and achieved power; a social ranking according to social service, without any artificial aid of class flunkeyism. Many of the earliest critics insist that our theories of equality spoil manners. Our imperfections were very real, but they were not owing to any theory of equality, unless blatant exceptions here and there are to decide. We can appeal to the very highest authorities for this. In respect to our manner, James Bryce says, "Americans have gained more than they have lost by equality." [1] Then follows this admirable passage: —

"I do not think that the upper class loses in grace, I am sure that the humbler class gains in independence. The manners of the 'best people' are exactly those of England, with a thought more of consideration towards inferiors and of frankness towards equals. Among the masses there is, generally speaking, as much real courtesy and good nature as anywhere else in the world. There is less outward politeness than in some parts of Europe, Portugal, for instance, or Tuscany, or Sweden. There is a certain coolness or offhandness which at first annoys the European visitor, who still thinks himself 'a superior'; but when he perceives that it is not meant for insolence, and that native Americans do not notice it, he learns to acquiesce." [2]

[1] "American Commonwealth," p. 609.
[2] See de Tocqueville, "Democracy in America," Vol. II, p. 214. De Tocqueville puts this in more theoretic form: "The more equal

"The second charm of American life is one which some Europeans will smile at. It is social equality. To many Europeans — to Germans, let us say, or Englishmen — the word has an odious sound. It suggests a dirty fellow in a blouse elbowing his betters in a crowd, or an ill-conditioned villager shaking his fist at the parson or the squire; or, at any rate, it suggests obtrusiveness and bad manners. The exact contrary is the truth. Equality improves manners, for it strengthens the basis of all good manners, respect for other men and women simply as men and women, irrespective of their station in life."

Mr. Bryce admits that forty years ago the influence of equality may have impaired manners, but denies that this is any longer true. He says: —

"In those days there was an obtrusive self-assertiveness, among the less refined classes, especially towards those who, coming from the Old World, were assumed to come in a patronizing spirit. Now, however, social equality has grown so naturally out of the circumstances of the country, has been so long established, and is so ungrudgingly admitted, that all excuse for obtrusiveness has disappeared. People meet on a simple and natural footing, with more frankness and ease than is possible in countries where every one is either looking up or looking down." [1]

social conditions become, the more do men display this reciprocal disposition to oblige each other. In democracies, no great benefits are conferred, but good offices are constantly rendered; a man seldom displays self-devotion, but all men are ready to be of service to one another."

[1] Sir Charles Lyell on his later visit is struck by the advantage which the United States has over England in allowing men to take humbler business positions with no loss of social prestige. So many "younger sons" are driven from England by "aristocratic prejudice" as to what is genteel. — "North America," Vol. I, p. 20.

The spirit of all this accords with Hamerton's judgment that the French are "at once a very polite and a very rude people." He says the uses to which the upper class put their politeness is to defend themselves against the intimacies of people whom they do not want to know. He says his own countrymen, the English, do not care in the least about a reputation for politeness. They defend themselves against intimacies by "*roideur* and dignity." [1]

That democracy is to deform all life's graces is a kind of faith with the older writers. The most unrelated annoyance is sure to be traced to this source or to some supposed derivative, as for example, "woman's rights." That charming story-teller, Anthony Trollope, has his fling in this passage : —

"The woman, as she enters, drags after her a misshapen, dirty mass of battered wirework, which she calls her crinoline, and which adds as much to her grace and comfort as a log of wood does to a donkey, when tied to the animal's leg in a

---

[1] The French novelist, Marcel Prévost, writes an article in the *Figaro* on the English in which he says: "I should not belong to a Latin race if, in view of all this, I did not venture to compare ourselves with these conquerors. I find them less intelligent, less really cultivated than ourselves ; less cultivated and less laborious than the Germans. Nevertheless it is not the Germans, and it is certainly not ourselves, who, nowadays, give the world its rules of life. It is the English who do so. In a different order of things, but in an equal measure, they exercise upon the manners of the world the measure of authority which the French exercised in the eighteenth century.

"The English are now almost the sole people who have really national manners." He also finds the English, whom he calls "The Conquerors," more "adaptable" than the French.

paddock. Of this she takes much heed, not managing it so that it may be conveyed up to the carriage with some decency, but striking it about against men's legs, and heaving it with violence over people's knees. The touch of a real woman's dress is in itself delicate; but these blows from a harpy's fins are loathsome. If there be two of them, they talk loudly together, having a theory that modesty has been put out of court by women's rights."

De Tocqueville, in his chapter on the Relation of Democracy to Manners, says, "Equality of conditions and greater mildness in manners are, then, in my eyes not only contemporaneous occurrences, but correlative facts." [1] He opens the chapter with these words, "We perceive that for several centuries social conditions have tended to equality, and we discover that at the same time the manners of society have been softened."

Matthew Arnold deserves a place among these witnesses of the higher rank. In his "Impressions of America," this prince of critics pays merciless attention to some of our limitations and vulgarities. He does it in a tone of too much conscious ascendency over our poor humanity. This often rasps the soul. But no book ever written about us has, it seems to me, more truth that we need to know, packed into small space, like gold in the vein, than this little volume. Note the reason he gives why some of our women have better manners than English women of the same class.

[1] "Democracy in America," Vol. II, p. 198.

"I have often heard it observed that a perfectly natural manner is as rare among English women of the middle classes as it is general among American women of like condition with them. And so far as the observation is true, the reason of its truth no doubt is, that the English woman is living in presence of an upper class, as it is called — in presence, that is, of a class of women recognized as being the right thing in style and manner, and whom she imagines criticising *her* style and manner, finding this or that to be amiss with it, this or that to be vulgar. Hence, self-consciousness and constraint in her. The American woman lives in presence of no such class; there may be circles trying to pass themselves off as such a class, giving themselves airs as such, but they command no recognition, no authority."

I do not quote this because of the tribute in it, but to show his spirit toward manners as related to organized social snobbery. The manners that come from class subserviency we do not want. Even if long in the making, we desire the deportment that is not "humbled into shape" by artificial class distinctions.

To put this demeanor into a word or definition is at least as hard as to define religion. The paragon of manners would have that first indispensable requisite — delicate consideration of the feelings of other people. He would also have the graces of external carriage and behavior. If he were the paragon, he would show these gifts of sensitive regard to others, clothed in the outer charms of bearing, at all times and to all sorts of people. He would not show them in spots or upon occasion only. The Germans speak of "a street angel and a home

P

devil" — a man very popular in public, but a churl in his own family. In one of Cherbuliez's novels some swell of noble lineage is made mayor of his commune. A lot of miscellaneous citizens come to him with a request. He stands before them with the polished and smiling exterior moulded by his traditions. But while they are petitioning, the Mayor says to himself, "I wonder what this vulgar mob would think, if they could look into my mind and see, this minute, just how I am despising them?" This is the cad, yet he was some percentage of a gentleman. He had still the lacquered shell.

I was once on a very trying stage drive of several days in the West. More passengers than could be decently accommodated had to get through. A woman of the party had won every heart at the journey's end by a kindness and tact which prevented minor quarrels over the most desirable seats or rooms at the hotel. It was all done with entire unconsciousness. Yet she would openly chew gum by the hour, use the knife long and industriously upon her finger-nails, and, after each meal, elaborately remove the food from her teeth with her hatpin. One of the party, who would not speak to her on the first day, said at the end, "That is the most naturally *kind* person I ever saw. She carried us in her heart the whole way."

What are we to do between the French mayor with the human feeling all gone, and this woman with little besides human good-will? He is not a gentleman in spite of inherited gestures and grimaces and, what is more, there is no alchemy by which he can be made into a gentleman. And the woman who "carried us all in her heart," making rough ways smooth, neither is she quite a lady. But she has this greatly in her favor, that the most indispensable of all gifts was hers for the making of the lady. It is here that Harriet Martineau comes to our aid. She has heard of our imperfect ways and her decision is this, that as far as extreme good-will, consideration, and intelligence to help others are concerned, "they have the best manners I have ever seen." This at least is better than the most varnished shell.

Where the outer and inner perfection are united, we have the Paragon, but Emerson says this rare flower is seen "but once or twice in a lifetime." If an entire people is considered, this combination of outer and inner graces is extremely rare in all Western nations. Latin peoples censure the manners of all Northern races; but Eastern folk, India, China, Japan, are as critical of the brusque and discourteous ways of France. It is all so relative as to save something of our pride.

So far as improvement and right direction are concerned, the later critics give us gracious encouragement. It comes not alone from the new English ambassador. The historian Freeman, though he says, "No one teaches you your place so well as the

American hotel clerk," says of our outer life, "I
have never, on land at least, fallen in with the
pushing, questioning fellow-traveller, a dim tradition of whom we are likely to take out with us. As
for the American hotel, it is not an inn, but an
institution." And of our home manners, "In private life, the American strikes me as, on the whole,
more ceremonious than the Englishman on this
side of the ocean. I do not profess to know how
far this may be owing to the absence of acknowl-
edged artificial distinctions, but it seems not unlikely
that the two things may have something to do with
one another. It certainly did strike me on the whole
that, among those with whom I had to do in America,
there was not less, but more attention paid to minute
observances than there is in England." [1]

[1] "Impressions of the United States," 1883, pp. 235 and 203.
That other English historian, J. Anthony Froude, also wrote
these words, "Nowhere in America have I met with vulgarity in
its proper sense."

CHAPTER XII

OUR MONOPOLY OF WIT

ONE of our English visitors, after travelling several months in the United States, showed concern because of our lack of humor. When he reached the Mississippi, he expressed his delight because he met a new kind of American who "*sometimes understood a joke.*"

"In general, I thought they had less of the frigid, uninviting formality which characterizes the Americans further to the eastward. They were somewhat gruff, indeed, at times; but they seemed to trust themselves and us with more readiness, and *sometimes understood a joke*, which I hardly ever saw exemplified on this side of the Mississippi." [1]

I still recall the mental agitation roused by those four words, "sometimes understood a joke." That they fitly applied to other nations was something I had long taken for granted, but here they were fixed upon the funniest people in the world — the Americans. It proved very amusing to put this passage before friends whose patriotic pieties had never been disturbed. I had lived half a life without once asking why the Americans should have engrossed a possession so precious as the world's wit

[1] "Travels in North America," Vol. III, p. 355.

and humor. Had it come to this, that, of all the
world, an English tourist was to lay rough hands on
a belief so sanctified? I read the passage to one of
the most amusing of our countrymen. He listened
to it as if dazed. When it was repeated to him, he
said, "Is that his way of being funny?" When
it was shown that Captain Hall was not trifling, the
American replied, "Well, what would you expect
of an Englishman?" This is the American attitude.
By some alchemy, nature has endowed us with
capacities for humor that makes us lonely among
the nations. We have all been brought up on
sallies against the English for the leisurely way in
which they respond to Yankee wit. Few of us have
not heard at least a thousand of those merry tales
to illustrate the sluggish ways of the British in
"seeing" our jokes. It is, therefore, with unusual
emotion that we read of Hall's discovery, — an
American who "sometimes understood a joke."

A German meant to compliment us when he wrote
that he noticed an improvement in the appreciation
of humor in the United States, as if there were, after
all, hope for us in this respect. Edmond de Nevers
is struck by "the absence of the sense of the ridiculous." He thinks we owe such prestige as we have
to the Irish. Even our pleasantries against the
Paddy "are mostly by the descendants of the
Irish," though he makes no reference to Mr. Dooley.
Dickens wrote of us, "They certainly are not a
humorous people," though he admitted that we had

"a certain cast-iron quaintness" in which the New England Yankee "takes the lead." [1]

An American much in Oxford confesses to have told one of his most irresistible stories at a college dinner given by one of the Dons. "When I finished," he said, "there wasn't a laugh around the table. I attributed it to the habitual stolidity of the English in the presence of a good joke. I hinted as much to the man next me, who said, 'Oh, but we have been telling that ever since the Master of Trinity got it off.'" The American added, "That was my first shock. I honestly thought we had a monopoly of humor that nobody even questioned." That is probably still the opinion of most good Americans. [2]

Even if true, it is stiffly gainsaid by many of these foreign critics. One of the French writers makes a special study of our funny papers. After spending a good deal of time on the files of *Puck* and *Judge*, he says, "If these are supposed by their readers to be examples of humor, those who read them have that sense only in its most elemental stage of develop-

---

[1] "American Notes," p. 206.

[2] This is like the angered surprise of an Englishman as he read the advice in an American paper, that a party just off for England should keep with their own countrymen and "so avoid the horrid English intonation." To suggest that the English people had either accent or intonation seemed to him an indignity.

An American in Austria has a kindred emotion in reading in a restaurant a placard on which was written, "English spoken and American understood."

ment. How can a really intelligent people think such horseplay — *des grosses plaisanteries* — witty?" Harriet Martineau says we have a kind of drollery that is neither English humor nor French wit, and Captain Marryat, who certainly did not lack humor, says, "There is no country, perhaps, in which the habit of deceiving for amusement, or what is termed hoaxing, is so common.   Indeed, this and the hyperbole constitute the major part of the American humor." [1]

When Miss Martineau speaks of a kind of jesting "in conformity with our institutions," she throws light on this whole dark problem.   I once heard a Greek scholar read from a collection of Greek jokes. To the hearers, nine out of ten of these ancient humors were of such exceeding solemnity that all were puzzled to know why they should be classed among things called funny.   But in the audience not six of us knew enough of Greek institutions and life to get the local color and contrasts that created the humorous element.   An American, caring enough for the English *Punch* to subscribe for it, told me, "We have no wittier sheet, but the regular succession of horse and racing jokes bores me."   He added, "I neither know anything nor care anything about horses," which gives us all the explanation we need. This is offset by a German who thought our *Life* the very limit of dulness, until he had lived a year in this country: "When I understood something of

[1] "A Diary in America," Vol. I, p. 8.

the inner life of the nation, its politics, industry, and leading social events, I discovered why I could not at first appreciate the wit."

That hurrying travellers in foreign countries should not keep in mind a fact so elementary as this, has a grim humor of its own. A college instructor in the East, returning from his first summer tour on the continent, gravely said that among other impressions he was struck by the absence of humor abroad. This penetrating voyager had a slight Ollendorff capacity to make sentences in two or three languages. With the subtle and pliant idiom of these tongues, he had not even a nodding acquaintance. Of the current political and social happenings among these peoples, he also knew little. Yet it was his apparent expectation to be admitted forthwith among those intimacies of light and shade in national experience, that alone can give the key to wit and humor. The "Souvenirs à la Main" in the Paris *Figaro* are not explosively entertaining to one who knows nothing of what happens from day to day in the French metropolis.

An American who had lived so far into the Parisian life as to catch the zest of French wit, subscribed, when he returned home, for the *Figaro*. . . . Within a few weeks the sheet had lost all interest for him so far as the witticisms were concerned. To read them in his New England home was to lose the whole atmosphere from which they took their flavor.

We need not, therefore, be utterly cast down by
the chilling tone of these foreigners about our own
limitations.   They do embarrass us about one proud
and confident claim, namely, that we possess in
some supreme and exclusive degree the gift of being
funny.   That we have varieties of wit and humor
peculiar to our traditions, is very generally admitted.   Here, for example, is an attempt at a
definition of English as against Yankee humor: —

"And we must avow that in our opinion the Yankee humor
has not the ruddy health, the abounding animal spirits, the
glow and glory of healthful and hearty life of our greatest
English.   As the Yankee has a leaner look, a thinner humanity,
than the typical Englishman who gives such a fleshy and burly
embodiment to his love of beef and beer, so the humor is less
plump and rubicund.   It does not revel in the same richness
nor enjoy its wealth in the same happy unconscious way, nor
attain to the like fulness and play of power.   We cannot
imagine Yankee humor, with its dry drollery, its shrewd
keeking, shut-eyed way of looking at things, ever embodying
such a mountain of mirth as we have in Falstaff."

A visitor professes to have cut the next example
from an Ohio paper.   He says our bragging habits
have produced a humor of "rare and special flavor."
He assumes that the writer is making merry at the
expense of some boasting rival editor: —

"This is a glorious country!   It has longer rivers and more
of them, and they are muddier and deeper, and run faster and
rise higher, and make more noise, and fall lower, and do more
damage than anybody else's rivers.   It has more lakes, and
they are bigger and deeper, and clearer and wetter than those
of any other country.   Our rail-cars are bigger, and run faster,

and pitch off the track oftener, and kill more people than all other rail-cars in this and every other country. Our steamboats carry bigger loads, are longer and broader, burst their boilers oftener, and send up their passengers higher, and the captains swear harder than steamboat captains in any other country. Our men are bigger and longer and thicker; can fight harder and faster, drink more mean whiskey, chew more bad tobacco, and spit more, and spit further than in any other country. Our ladies are richer, prettier, dress finer, spend more money, break more hearts, wear bigger hoops, shorter dresses, and kick up the devil generally to a greater extent than all other ladies in all other countries. Our children squall louder, grow faster, get too expansive for their pantaloons, and become twenty years old sooner by some months than any other children of any other country on the earth."

Earlier in the century the Yankee trader is thought to have developed a form of humor of which this is given as an example: —

"Reckon I couldn't drive a trade with you to-day, Square," said a genuine specimen of the Yankee pedler as he stood at the door of a merchant in St. Louis.

"I reckon you calculate about right, for you *can't* noways."

"Wall, guess you needn't git huffy, 'beout it. Now, here's a dozen ginooine razor-strops — wuth two dollars and a half — you may hev 'em for two dollars."

"I tell you I don't want any of your traps, so you may as well be going along."

"Wall, now, look here, Square. I'll bet you five dollars that if you make me an offer for them 'ere strops, we'll have a trade yet."

"Done," said the merchant, and he staked the money. "Now," says he chaffingly, "I'll give you *sixpence* for the strops."

"They're your'n!" said the Yankee, as he quietly pocketed

the stakes! "but," continued he, after a little reflection, and with a burst of frankness, "I calculate a joke's a joke; and if you don't *want* them strops, I'll trade back." The merchant looked brighter. "You're not so bad a chap after all," said he. "Here are your strops— give me the money." "There it is," said the Yankee, as he took the strops and handed back *the sixpence.* "A trade is a trade, and a bet a bet. Next time you trade with that 'ere sixpence, don't you buy razor-strops."

It is, however, often granted that this endowment is more widely diffused among our people than in England. Further than this, most of the critics do not go. That we have any monopoly of what is essential to the soul of wit and humor is rather cavalierly denied. An American essayist, the charm and delicacy of whose humor has such growing recognition, has recently returned from six months in England, where he was in much popular demand as a lecturer.[1] He tells me that the response of an English audience to humor seems to him on the whole quicker than that of an American audience. This is probably also a tribute to the quality of the lecturer's humor.

Our prolific pleasantries to prove the poverty of the English capacity to "catch on" are really very amazing. Not to mention Shakespeare and the wits of his age, what is to be said of Sydney Smith, Charles Lamb, Jerrold, Monckton Milnes, Thackeray, Dickens, Tom Taylor, and many others?

[1] Dr. Samuel M. Crothers, author of "The Gentle Reader," "The Pardoner's Wallet," etc.

We have not alone to think of these individuals, but to think also that England furnished the audience to appreciate them, which is even more to the purpose. Let the American set down his most patriotic list and balance them against the English wits. Can we outmatch Sydney Smith, Charles Lamb, or Dickens by any three of our most glittering names? Any summing up of the subtleties of French wit would embarrass us at least as much. I select England especially, because it has long amused us to banter her for her general density in these matters.

There is much agreement among our critics that the quality of American humor suffers chiefly from exaggeration; that the elements of contrast and surprise are put to great strain; that too little appeal is made to the imagination. William Archer gives us an illustration: A Chicago man travelling in Louisiana wrote to his sweetheart: "Dear Mamie, — I have shot an alligator. When I have shot another, I will send you a pair of slippers." [1]

Again. A tired traveller arrives at a country hotel and calls for a bootjack to remove his boots. The proprietor noticing the size of his guest's feet says, "You come by the Croyden road, didn't ye?" "Yes." "Wall, you noticed that one road forked off toward Westbridge. I'm tellin' you this, because no bootjack made by the hand of man will git them boots off. You've got to go back to the fork in them roads."

[1] "America To-day," p. 99.

The French find most fault with this extravagance, especially as seen upon the stage. If they
find it on the ranch or in a Western paper, the
setting appears to them perfect. One boasts that
he has discovered the essence of American fun in
this exaggeration coupled with our inveterate good
nature. "They show a droll solicitude not to injure
any one's feelings, even though he be an arrant
scamp." This Frenchman, staying in a small
California hotel, is tricked out of a sum of money by
a sharper who lived on friendly terms with everybody
in the town. The victim rushes to the landlord.
"But this fellow is what you call a crook. Is it
not so? Is he not a thief, a thief?" The landlord,
quite undisturbed, replies, "Wall, that's a purty
strong word you're usin'. I shouldn't like to call
him a thief, though after I shake hands with him,
I do generally count my fingers." [1]

Another variation attributed to us is a tendency to
make one's self out very vicious in order to heighten

[1] This guest reports an instance in still milder form. "But
did you ever see a stingier old skinflint?" To which is replied, "I
don't know's he's stingy exactly, but he does keep his benevolent
impulses pretty well under control."

A very recent traveller, whose chief interest was the study of
Christian Science, hears of some one who has abandoned his connection with this faith. The investigator eagerly seeks to know
the reasons for the man's apostasy. "But why," he asks, "having
enjoyed such an experience, did you give up?" "Well, to tell you
the truth," was the reply, "I just got tired out being so d—d happy
all the time." This was at once classed as American humor, and
would be very pointless in any community which knew nothing of
what is at least popularly attributed to this faith.

the effect. A newly arrived English prelate, with much clerical excess in his appearance, boards a trolley car in New York. He is on the alert for information. Seeing what he supposes to be a vigorous working-class specimen, he sits down by him with the question, "I hear you have been having very interesting political events here in New York during the last week or two." The gentleman from the Bowery turned to take a leisurely but rather consuming look at his questioner, "I don't know," was the answer, "I've been drunk the last fortnight," and the conversation closed.

Another variety is left without definition, but this French inquisitor thinks, I know not why, that it could have happened nowhere out of America. A Western paper notices the death of "our old friend and neighbor Lyman Rogers." Sympathy is expressed for the bereaved wife, followed by a tribute to the dead, and closing with the words, "He has gone to a better home." Whereupon the newly made widow brings instant action for libel against the editor.

One reviewer writes that the most peculiar form of American humor is the "high falutin." The following, which he thinks is by Webster, "is the best of its kind": —

"Men of Rochester, I am glad to see you; and I am glad to see your noble city. Gentlemen, I saw your falls, which I am told are one hundred and fifty feet high. This is a very interesting fact. Gentlemen, Rome had her Cæsar, her Scipio, her Brutus, but Rome in her proudest days had *never* a water-fall a hundred and fifty feet high! Gentlemen, Greece had her Pericles, her Demosthenes, and her Socrates, but Greece in her palmiest days NEVER had a waterfall a hundred and fifty feet high! Men of Rochester, *go on.* No people ever lost their liberties who had a waterfall one hundred and fifty feet high!"

From frontier life an Englishman quotes this as "impossible in any other country." An elderly lady from the East, with a passion for botanical studies, goes into the cowboy's country, builds a small house, and begins her work of collecting speci-mens. Absorbed one day at her work far out on the prairie, she sees a cowboy riding toward her as for life. When within call, he cries out, "Your house is on fire!" What the botanic lady expected in way of news is unreported, but she said to the cowboy, "Oh, is that all?" Whereupon the amazed ranchman exclaimed, "Well, God bless my soul, Madam, that's all I think of at the present moment, but I'll look round the country and see if I can find something to interest you," and rides away.

Another visitor is told by a Southern teacher, the late Dr. McIver, that our travelling salesmen — drummers — are the reservoirs of what is most peculiar in American wit. Dr. McIver added that the drummers, immediately after the Civil War, were the first real peacemakers. They went in large numbers through the Southland seeking trade. There was the never failing resource of a batch of good stories. "During these first bitter years," said the Doctor, "when the clergy, editors, and politicians were fighting each other across the line, the drummer was the real brother and neighbor, and it convinces me that the Good Samaritan was himself a drummer. You remember that the church folk came upon the poor fellow and the first said, 'This is too bad, but I have an appointment in Jericho, so I will ask some one from the Christian Association to look out for him.' The next man — probably a deacon — has to meet his wife in Jericho at five o'clock, and thinks he will telephone to the Associated Charities to take up the case. Finally comes the drummer, who is touched by compassion. He takes the poor fellow in hand, according to scripture. The internal evidence that he was a drummer is complete. He knew where the best hotel was; he was coming that way again, and he had liquor by him."

From the press an Englishman cuts out the two following as "very characteristic": "Wanted, a servant girl that isn't above living on an equality with the family." Seeing a large number of hacks in a funeral, the traveller asks a man on the street, if some important citizen has died. "No, not very; and you know, Stranger, you can't always tell just what estimate the Almighty puts on a departed soul, by the number of hacks."

Another selects as "peculiarly American" the following from Josh Billings: —

"The mule is half horse and half jackass, and then comes

Q

to a full stop, Nature discovering her mistake.   The only way
to keep a mule in a pasture is to turn it into a meadow adjoin-
ing, and let it jump out.   They are like some men, very corrupt at heart.   I've known them to be good mules for six
months, just to get a good chance to kick somebody."

"Some people are fond of bragging about their ancestors,
and their great descent, when in fact their great descent is just
what is the matter with them."

"God save the fools, and don't let them run out! for if it
wasn't for them, wise men couldn't get a living."

"It is true that wealth won't make a man virtuous, but I
notice there ain't anybody who wants to be poor just for the
purpose of being good."

It is drolleries like these that attract attention,
especially from the English. A Frenchman confesses that he "spent days trying, without success,
to see why Mr. Dooley should be given such high
rank." All readers of "Tartarin" know that Al-
phonse Daudet did not lack humor, yet he is said
to have done his best to laugh over the pages of
Mark Twain, but always in vain.

One critic cuts from a Pittsburg paper an account
of a suicide who left ample justification for taking his
life in the following culmination of misfortunes : —

"I married a widow who had a grown-up daughter.   My
father visited our house very often, fell in love with my step-
daughter and married her.   So my father became my son-in-
law, and my step-daughter my mother, because she was my
father's wife.   Some time afterwards my wife had a son —
he was my father's brother-in-law and my uncle, for he was
the brother of my step-mother.   My father's wife, *i.e.* my
step-daughter, had also a son; he was, of course, my brother,

and in the meantime my grandchild, for he was the son of my daughter. My wife was my grandmother, because she was my mother's mother. I was my wife's husband and grandchild at the same time. And as the husband of a person's grandmother is his grandfather, I was my own grandfather."

If there are shades of difference in American humor, Miss Martineau's suggestion is right, that the differences are largely traceable to whatever is peculiar in our institutions and national experience. This is the commonplace with which we began, but which very few travellers among foreign peoples appear to realize in their attempts to standardize wit.[1] I have heard several Americans, still cutting their teeth upon the language, insist that the German funny paper, *Fliegende Blaetter*, was very heavy and not in the least to be compared with some humorous American sheet. But how could a callow provincialism like this justify itself? If there is anywhere in the world a detached and cosmopolitan genius competent to act as umpire, it is conceivable that he would declare *Life* funnier than *Fliegende Blaetter* or *vice versa* — but it is not conceivable that outsiders, such as these American students still were, should have any opinion of the slightest value on that subject. To know whether the German sheet is

---

[1] I have heard very sniffy comments by an outsider on the merry works of Wilhelm Busch, author of Max and Moritz, etc. It could not be compared to the "high quality" of the Frenchman Caran d'Ache, for example. But to "democratize laughter," to add to the jollity of an entire nation decade after decade is a fact behind which we cannot go.

witty or otherwise requires an intimacy of touch with
delicate phases of life and thought that only years
can give. I listened to a play in Paris, which at
two points brought out from the audience a tumult
of merriment., I had carefully read the play and
perfectly understood the laughter-provoking sentences, but it was several days before I could fall in
with the gaiety. I found the explanation at last
in the grotesque awkwardness in which a pompous
local mayor had entangled himself. I stood quite
as much in need of a surgical operation to admit the
joke as Sydney Smith's Scotchman. But that need
is common to all the world until it is admitted into
this inner and familiar life of a people. Not only
have the general currents of national experience
to be known, but also the more hidden currents of
tradition, custom, and prejudice as these express
themselves in the emotions of the hour. It was only
after several years of continuous life in France that
Hamerton could get the full humor of a provincial
theatre.

If we are content with modest tributes, they do not
fail. I asked an English author of one of the really
good books upon the United States [1] how he would
state the difference between the English and American appreciation of humor. This gentleman has
lived long in this country and his book shows an
admirable competence to judge. He said, "I think
the difference is a real one, that the people of this

[1] "The Land of Contrasts."

country have a more generally diffused sense of humor than in England." Professor Münsterberg gives his judgment as follows. He has also been here long enough to give weight to his words. He characterizes the quality as "whimsical," but adds that it is a great social equalizer.

"There is only one more sovereign power than the spirit of sport in breaking down all social distinctions; it is American humor. We could not speak of political or intellectual life without emphasizing this irrepressible humor; but we must not forget it for a moment in speaking of social life, for its influence pervades every social situation. The only question is whether it is the humor which overcomes every disturbance of social equilibrium and so restores the consciousness of free and equal self-assertion, or whether it is this consciousness which fosters humor and seeks expression in a good-natured lack of respect. No immoderation, no improper presumption, and no pomposity can survive the first humorous comment, and the American does not wait long for this. The soap-bubble is pricked amid genial laughter, and equality is restored. Whether it is in a small matter or whether in a question of national importance, a latent humor pervades all social life.

"A happy humorous turn will remind them all that they are equal fellow-citizens, and that they are not to take their different functions in life too solemnly, nor to suppose that their varied outward circumstances introduce any real inequality. As soon as Americans hear a good story, they come at once to an understanding, and it is well known that many political personalities have succeeded because of their wit, even if its quantity was more than its quality." [1]

Mr. Bryce's experience has so much in common

[1] "The Americans," pp. 543-544.

with our own, that we listen to him on this delicate point without pique.

"There is a difference, slight yet perceptible, in the part which both sentiment and humor play in American books, when we compare them with English books of equivalent strength. The humor has a vein of oddity, and the contrast between the soft copiousness of the sentiment and the rigid lines of lingering Puritanism which it suffuses, is rarely met with in England. Perhaps there is less repose in the American style; there is certainly a curious unrestfulness in the effort, less common in English writers, to bend metaphors to unwonted uses." [1]

"Humor is a sweetener of temper, a copious spring of charity, for it makes the good side of bad things even more visible than the weak side of good things; but humor in Americans may be as much a result of an easy and kindly turn as their kindliness is of their humor." [2]

This partial analysis which our critics help us to make does not deprive us of a single jocose talent. It is not that we are lacking, but rather that others are more richly endowed than we were aware. It looks as if we had preened ourselves upon a far too exclusive possession of the "rare sweetener of life's severities." To know that our foreign neighbors have this solace, even as we have it, ought to be good news to us. To be cocksure that we are the funniest among nations would too surely bring upon us from impartial outsiders that most damning criticism, "lack of humor" on our own part.

[1] "The American Commonwealth," Vol. II, p. 618.
[2] *Ibid.*, p. 666.

CHAPTER XIII

OUR GREATEST CRITIC

In the Introduction to "The American Commonwealth" Mr. Bryce says, "When I first visited America eighteen years ago, I brought home a swarm of bold generalizations. Half of them were thrown overboard after a second visit in 1881. Of the half that remained, some were dropped into the Atlantic when I returned across it after a third visit in 1883–1884; and although the two later journeys gave birth to some new views, these views are fewer and more discreetly cautious than their departed sisters of 1870."[1]

If this openness and flexibility of mind are indispensable to the critic's judgment, another qualification already noted is not less so. It is an unforced human sympathy with one's fellowmen. I heard a snobbish American ask Phillips Brooks in Europe how he managed to avoid the crowd of his fellow-countrymen. The great preacher's answer had in it an edge of rebuke and severity which the printed reply does not convey. "I do not try to avoid them, because I like them." "Because I like them!" There are not many critics who can

[1] Vol. I, p. 4.

say that without telling lies. Some subtle and clever books in my list are rich in entertainment, but one closes them with the feeling that the writers do not like their kind; that they rather fear and dislike too close contact with them.

This feeling of good-will toward one's kind may be instantly detected in every first-rate foreign observer. It is in Sir Charles Lyell, it is in Chevalier, it is in de Tocqueville, it is in James Bryce. There is a largeness about these men which enables them to deal with human nature in another country, at least as generously as they would deal with it in their own. If they note differences in habits, customs, and behavior, they are not merely pestered by them, but rather interested to account for and explain them. Lyell finds himself in a small town of the Middle West at a time when it was literally frontier. He is annoyed by curious and persistent questions, — but he does not pillory the whole town, like Mrs. Trollope, as intolerable nuisances. He does not, like the author of "Cyril Thornton," look upon the annoyance merely as impertinence. As a man of science, even a prying inquisitiveness interests him. It is a pity that its exercise must be quite so personally directed to his clothes and glass, but the narrowness and monotony of their lives explain this. Curiosity is excellent intellectual material. When the community has more varied interests, this eagerness to know things will have its higher and more impersonal expression. To philoso-

JAMES BRYCE
Author of "The American Commonwealth"

phize about one's kind in so kindly a temper as this, in the very midst of discomforts and awkward intrusions, is given to no man who does not like his fellows. One could quote many passages from "The American Commonwealth" to show this spirit of cosmopolitan good-fellowship with which the author enters into broad human relations with Americans. In his chapter on "The Pleasantness of American Life," he says: —

"This naturalness of intercourse is a distinct addition to the pleasure of social life.   It enlarges the circle of possible friendship by removing the *gêne* which in most parts of Europe persons of different ranks feel in exchanging their thoughts on any matters save those of business.   It raises the humbler classes without lowering the upper; indeed, it improves the upper no less than the lower by expunging that latent insolence which deforms the manners of so many of the European rich or great.   It relieves women in particular, who in Europe are especially apt to think of class distinctions, from that sense of constraint and uneasiness which is produced by the knowledge that other women with whom they come in contact are either looking down on them, or at any rate trying to gauge and determine their social position.   It expands the range of a man's sympathies, and makes it easier for him to enter into the sentiments of other classes than his own." [1]

Here is none of the arch snobbery that prides itself on the exclusiveness of one's friendships. That is good which enlarges the circle.   "Equality improves manners, for it strengthens the basis of all good manners, respect for other men and women *simply as men and women irrespective of their station*

[1] Vol. II, p. 663.

in life." This is the inclusive kindliness which
makes democracy possible.   There is neither vaporing nor cant when he approves the social condition
in which the shoemaker and the factory hand
address you as an equal.

In the first few days Mr. Bryce confesses to the
unpleasantness he felt at the brusque and careless
disregard with which some officials treated his
inquiries.   He soon saw that this was without in-
tended offence and it ceased to vex or even disquiet
him.

The smaller critic does not forgive a wounded
personal vanity.   The defence of his own little
dignity becomes at once his main concern.   One of
these in a western town asks a man, "who looked
as if he needed a shilling," to take his valise to the
hotel.   The needy individual turned upon him with
the question, "Stranger, does that pack require
two folks to carry it?"   "No, one person can carry
it."   "Well, then, I guess you'll take it yourself;
you are as big as I be and look as if you'd been
livin' at a better boardin'-house than mine."
The victim of this retort was incensed beyond measure.   "I even put myself out a little," he says, "to
do him a good turn, only to meet this brutal rebuff."
Mr. Bryce would have paid money to get such a
reply.   He would even have stayed over a train to
make the man's acquaintance.   It is, however,
certain that Mr. Bryce's tone and manner would
never have called forth the rebuff.

I have known an American scholar to travel some weeks in Germany in a chronic state of disgust at the brusqueness of the lesser German officials. He returned for a longer stay in that country to learn, in his own words, that "I had lost half the pleasure of that first trip by being a plain — fool. I finally learned why those officials take themselves and their work a good deal more seriously than we do in our country, and I also learned that behind the manner, there is an admirable conscientiousness and willingness to take great trouble to help you out of difficulties."

It is the distinction of the first-rate critic to *assume* this good-will at the start. He assumes it and acts upon it without waiting for the proofs.

In the middle of the last century a German by the name of Platenius thus comments on the American habit of sitting with the feet elevated on railings and tables. "I have not yet found the cause of this very common practice, but I am confident it is explained and justified by some physiological reason like that of imperfect digestion or circulation." This diagnosis may be at fault, but the temper is that of the perfect traveller. Mr. Bryce has this temper; he has the human good-will; he has done his work of investigation with unmatched thoroughness. From lifelong study and travel his grasp of "world politics" long since put him easily in the first rank of publicists. He has travelled widely enough and intelligently enough to apply the comparative method in making up a human document. If he is discussing American manners or morals, his judgment means something because he has watched manners and morals in many countries. If he deals with our asserted passion for dollars, he has had experience enough among many people to apply some intelligent test to the criticism. It is this large mastery of contemporary political and social experience which makes Mr. Bryce, not only superior to de Tocqueville, but clearly our greatest critic.

It is not only that the author of "The American Commonwealth" paid many visits to this country, it is also because here and in England he kept in the closest intellectual touch with those Americans who were competent and glad to assist him. His inquiries were so definite and so penetrating; they so touched the "live-wire" issues of the time, that it was an honor and intellectual pleasure to get information for him. One of his American friends and helpers said, "We never get such good talk about our own home problems as when Mr. Bryce is present to ask questions." This gentlemanly temper, this sympathy and searching observation, are not absent in a single critic who ranks with Lyell, de Tocqueville, Chevalier, and Bryce.

This is not a ranking of critics according to their good opinion of this country. The weakest and untruest things about us are often the hasty and indiscriminate praises. Lyell, Chevalier, de Tocqueville, have admonitions enough, but they so stand out

on a background of proper information and human
good-will that only the pettiest provincialism will
take offence.   No man has given more final tests of
sincerity in his democratic sympathies than Mr.
Bryce.   His attitude toward Irish Home Rule and
even more the moral bravery he showed during the
Boer War (whatever the merits of that struggle
may have been) are even better proofs than passages
like this: "When the humbler classes have differed
in opinion from the higher, they have often proved
by the event to have been right and their so-called
betters wrong."   But to this inborn spirit of democratic good-fellowship and breeding, must be added
a training for his task that few men living or dead
have received.   We have to think of "The American
Commonwealth" not as a study finished in 1887,
but, through its revisions and later letters, as the
sustained and coherent judgment of more than thirty
years.   He is not in the least a mere bookworm.
His academic distinction was eminent, but as a globe
trotter he was as intelligently the student as in writing
the Holy Roman Empire.   It was these large studies,
together with his knowledge of comparative politics
and his arduous labor as a practical politician, that
have given him a supreme fitness to report upon the
political structure and social spirit of this country.

Not the least among the services of this monu-
mental work is, that hundreds of Europeans read it
as a preparation for their coming to this country.
I once heard from a foreign scholar this admirable

word: "To read Bryce before you leave home, and then, with your own notes and memories, to read it again when you return, is the surest way to know America and to know it at its best." I have also heard one of our own scholars say that "he knew no single study that so effectively helped an American to know his own country as he ought to know it, as 'The American Commonwealth.'" [1]

As one looks back upon the universal touchiness under foreign comment, it is the more surprising that scarcely a protest has been raised against Bryce's strictures. In spite of the uniform cordiality and appreciation, there is a good deal of plain speaking that would have aroused resentment even a generation before the work appeared. One angry verbal protest I do remember: that "Bryce must have been blind in *at least* one eye to say that 'neither the Rocky Mountains, with their dependent ranges, nor the Sierra Nevada, can be compared for variety of grandeur and beauty with the Alps.'" Goldwin Smith says this more strongly still and it is probably true. But Bryce refers also to our cities: "Their monotony haunts one like a nightmare." He makes a few exceptions, but says: [2] —

"In all, the same shops, arranged on the same plan, the same Chinese laundries, with Li Kow visible through the window, the same ice-cream stores, the same large hotels with seedy

[1] It is perhaps a trivial warning, but I have found that the average person is more likely to read both volumes if he begins with Part IV of the second volume.

[2] "The American Commonwealth," Vol. II, p. 670.

men hovering about in the dreary entrance-hall, the same street-cars passing to and fro, with passengers clinging to the door-step."

"Travel where you will, you feel that what you have found in one place, that you will find in another. The thing which hath been, will be: you can no more escape from it than you can quit the land to live in the sea." [1]

Nor is this "monotony" an affair alone of externals. It appears in our mental habits, where it may be merely tiresome, or dangerous if it express itself in our political thinking. Like de Tocqueville, Bryce fears our lack of independence in politics; that there are "so few independent schools of opinion." "The structure of the party discipline leaves little freedom of individual thought or action to the member of the legislature." It is our "weak point" that free and unbiassed political opinion finds such difficulty in "bringing itself to bear upon those who govern either as legislators or executive officers."[2] Outside the line of party interests, there may be the bravest shoutings and display of intellectual courage, as if to call off the attention from vital issues. So vigorous a party Republican as Congressman Littlefield is reported recently as saying, "If there is anything more cowardly than one Congressman, it is two Congressmen:" —

"It is a humiliating fact that the House of Representatives is the most cowardly political body in the United States. It is not even equal to the ordinary State Legislature. The ordi-

---

[1] "The American Commonwealth," Vol. II, p. 674.
[2] *Ibid.*, p. 288.

nary congressman, when he is elected, gets the notion that there is a career before him.　It is almost impossible to get any member of Congress to vote against any proposition that seems to imperil his chances of return." [1]

This is what Mr. Bryce points out.　We have seen the same criticism in de Tocqueville.　We shall see it later in other form in Münsterberg and more powerfully still in Ostrogorski.

Mr. Bryce also speaks of the "commonness of mind and tone, a want of dignity and elevation in and about the conduct of public affairs, an insensibility to the nobler aspects and finer responsibilities of national life."　This is also true; but that so great a multitude of American readers should accept these and other strictures while showering praises on the author's head, is a new and extremely hopeful fact.

In the half century which separates de Tocqueville from Bryce, no one had attempted to cope with the whole theory and practice of our political life, as well as to enter minutely into questions of manners, habits, and ideas.　Mr. Bryce does this in his first edition of 1888, more completely in the third edition and in the letters published in 1905, in which he reviews the changes observable in the United States between his first visit in 1870 and that of 1905.[2]　No one of our critics has given any such extensive and

[1] Reported from address before the Providence, R.I., Commercial Club, April 23, 1907.

[2] *Outlook*, March and April, 1905.

intensive study of political structure in this country.
No one has entered more intimately into the whole
spiritual life of the nation. That the net judgment
of this profound study should be (I cannot help using
the word) so *doggedly* hopeful; that it should be
informed by a certain gaiety of good cheer and confidence that all is to turn out well with us in the
United States, has of course much to do with the
supreme rank accorded to Mr. Bryce's books. The
serenity of the author's optimism falls in with that
most persistent trait of the American character,
hopefulness. Scarcely a critic fails to note this
insistent American characteristic. Mr. Bryce not
only gives voice to this, but he adduces an ordered
host of reasons which he believes justifies our optimism. In the Introduction he writes of the doubters who fail "to realize the existence in the American
people of a reserve of force and patriotism more than
sufficient to sweep away all the evils which are now
tolerated, and to make the politics of the country
worthy of its material grandeur and of the private
virtues of its inhabitants. America excites an
admiration which must be felt on the spot to be
understood. The hopefulness of her people com-
municates itself to one who moves among them, and
makes him perceive that the graver faults of politics
may be far less dangerous there than they would be
in Europe. A hundred times in writing this book
have I been disheartened by the facts I was stating;
a hundred times has the recollection of the abounding

R

strength and vitality of the nation chased away these
tremors." [1]

I was once asked by an English friend, much in this
country, if there were any way in which this obstinate
residuum of American optimism could be explained.

"You have men who make a bluff at pessimism. They
talk fiercely against all sorts of things in their own country,
but they always surprise you finally by adding 'Still it's all
coming out right in the end.' Nothing impresses me in the
United States more than this characteristic. But I do not
understand it, nor does Mr. Bryce satisfy me. If your politics
are as bad as he implies and as most of you say they are; if
so much of your business is polluted, as your best witnesses
insist, why does every discussion among you have the same
refrain, 'Yes, it's bad, but it's sure to turn out all right in the
end'?"

This seems to me to touch the one critical weakness in Mr. Bryce's volumes. Again and again he
brings the reader to a yawning gulf of perplexities.
We are allowed to take one frightened glimpse
into the depths, only to be hurried instantly back on
to high safe ground. Nothing is more momentous
in the national life than the character and influence
of large cities. Yet our political method appears
to have failed in managing these moulding centres
in our common life. The main ground of Mr.
Bryce's optimism about us is our inveterate, under-
lying hopefulness.

From a good many wise people, I have tried to get

---

[1] "The American Commonwealth," Vol. I, p. 10.

some answer to this question, Does the *evidence* in Mr. Bryce's books justify his optimism?[1]

One is quick to note that the answers take the form of religious faith rather than of a reasoned conviction that appeals to definite proofs. One of our first-rate scholars of American politics tells me, "It is very discouraging that Pennsylvania, after the moral rousing of last year, should apparently sink back helpless under the same contemptible party tyranny. But," he hastens to add, "I am sure it will all come out right." Yes, most of us *believe* that, but do the volumes of Mr. Bryce contain the evidences of these things not seen?

Thirty-five years after his first coming, Mr. Bryce reviewed the most important changes observable in the United States since 1870. His summary is the more remarkable because he had seen much of the "Shame of Cities" as it had been reported by men like Lincoln Steffens. Most of this relentless inquisition into our political and business life was as truthfully as it was ably done. In spite of the direct personal character of the evidence, no important part of it has been in the least shaken by those under fire. Everywhere one heard angry and scornful denial in private. I heard a United States Senator say, "It's sewer-water, — mere sewer-water, not fit for a human being to touch." But if it is false,

---

[1] In the final chapters on Progress, an attempt is made to add evidence on this point from authentic changes which our critics enable us to see and measure through the century.

why not answer it, that the people may have some authentic statement? "Well," was the reply, "there is, of course, a lot of unpleasant facts so mixed up with these charges as to make it very difficult to reply." Yes, "such a lot of unpleasant facts" which no one dared to face in open public discussion. They were facts which did this service: they laid bare the whole organized intimacy between privileged business and politics. We had all been taught that our political corruption was in some dark way peculiar to large cities. Investigation during the last seven or eight years has destroyed that illusion. The large city merely gave concentrated and dramatic expression to evils that inhere in large business activities that depend on legislative and other favors.

Public service corporations with affiliated businesses like mines and other primary natural resources have set the pace in this subjection of the politician to private rather than public interests. That these powers should have become in recent years so centred in speculative markets; that business distinction should be now largely tested by capacity to manipulate securities; that the most precious wealth-resources should be like the stake in a gambler's game, are dangers that only selfish interest or mental dulness now fails to recognize. "Bad politics" follows and reflects the deeper evils of a grossly unfair competitive business; unfair in the sense that our excessive inequalities of wealth are known to be due largely to special favors or outright theft of public domain in mining, grazing, and lumbering. An excessive tariff is behind specific large fortunes "in iron." The tariff, together with rebates, has made several Steel Kings. Great mastery in the securing of rebates has made other vast fortunes. With a few distinct exceptions, this whole natural history of multimillionnairedom is a story, no line of which can be told apart from a political corruption which these businesses *started*. This corruption did not *begin* with the blackmailer or the people. These are developed as later and consequent evils.

Better than with oil, mines, lumber, cattle, or steel, railway transportation is that through which we may best see this evil. Dr. Albert Shaw is not an alarmist, neither is he a general scold. He knows about our railroads. Without wishing to do them injury, here are his deliberate opinions expressed in his *Review of Reviews:* —

"The mismanagement of insurance companies has been a mere passing trifle when compared with the mismanagement of American railroad interests.

"We have a small and select population of plutocrats who control our railroads and have somehow managed to put into their private pockets some hundreds of thousands of millions of dollars through their ability to skim the cream off the country's prosperity.

"Many of those in control 'have juggled with securities, have played the stock-market up and down, have played tricks with their dividend policies, have so falsified their bookkeeping as to conceal surpluses, and have virtually confiscated the property of the confiding stockholders by the use they have made of the proxies which they themselves have solicited through the mails at the stockholders' expense.' They 'have got control of the American railroad system, have bled it unmercifully for their own benefit, and the result is that it no longer serves the practical purposes for which railroads exist.'"

Though himself seeing great objection to government management of railroads, he concludes: —

"Whatever may be the objections to government ownership — and those objections are very great — it would be better than the indefinite continuance of an irresponsible and uncontrolled private management in the interest of a ring of plutocrats."

That judgment is caustic, but it is not exaggerated. If we add to it, that the partnership between the railroad and iron, oil, lumber, cattle, mines, etc., has been through local and federal legislation in such dark and covered ways as to infect the very sources of our political life, we have merely a further and complete statement of the fact. This digression is only to make the question a little more intelligent: Does Mr. Bryce take this evil thing fully and fairly into account? Seeing it all, has the bravery of his optimism good warrant?

One cannot answer it with satisfaction, because it is uncertain how far he is looking to the future rather than to the present. He seems to be saying, as he faces the evil, "Ugly as it is, you will throw it off. Your buoyancy, health, and confidence will cut out that rottenness as we in England cut out our 'rotten boroughs' and recognized debaucheries that were blacker than America ever knew."

For this faith he gives two forceful reasons. First, the strategic advantage which public opinion has in this country. As compared to other countries, he finds its peculiarity in this, that our public opinion "stands above the parties, being cooler and larger minded than they are; it awes party leaders and holds in check party organizations. No one openly ventures to resist it. It determines the direction and the character of national policy. It is the product of a greater number of minds than in any other country, and it is more indisputably sovereign. It is the central point of the whole American policy. To describe it, that is, to sketch the leading political ideas, habits, and tendencies of the American people, and show how they express themselves in action, is the most difficult and also the most vital part of my task."

This is a preliminary word in his Introduction in explanation of the detailed study of public opinion in several later chapters.[1]

In noting the powers of the President, he says, "Nowhere is the rule of public opinion so complete as in America, nor so direct, that is to say, so independent of the ordinary machinery of government." [2]

The really great changes since Bryce's first edition strengthen every opinion he has expressed on this point. De Tocqueville finds the President almost a

[1] Vol. II, Part IV.
[2] "The American Commonwealth," Vol. I, p. 63.

weakling in using public opinion. Ten years after
de Tocqueville, the French Ambassador de Bacourt
wrote his sister, "The State minds its own business
so much that I have nothing to do." Mr. Bryce
first writes: —

"An American may, through a long life, never be reminded
of the Federal Government except when he votes at Presidential and Congressional elections, lodges a complaint against
the Post-Office, and opens his trunk for a Custom-House officer on the pier at New York when he returns from a tour of
Europe."

As he comes now to a wide-armed welcome as
ambassador, he finds

"The Federal power in some of the most ordinary minutiæ
of daily life — when he buys a pound of meat, goes to the drug-
gist for medicine, buys coffee at the corner grocery, or secures
a railroad ticket."

He finds the immense hopefulness of public opinion
here to be in the fact that its directive power is more
and more *consciously active* in the entire body of
the people.

President Woodrow Wilson at Columbia University
says of this extraordinary growth that —

"In nothing has it grown more than in the development of
the presidency. His cabinet becomes more and more dependent upon him; upon his single office, more and more the
centre of the vital forces of opinion and political initiative.

"The President alone is elected by the people as a whole,
has no local constituency, speaks for no special interest. If
he truly interpret the national thought and boldly enough
insist upon it, he is irresistible."

Professor Münsterberg goes so far in agreement with Mr. Bryce as to say that "the parties with all their paraphernalia are merely the lower house of the nation, while Public Opinion is the upper house." He says again, "Most of all, it must be insisted that public opinion is all the time following up these excrescences on party life, and that public opinion presses forward year by year at an absolutely sure pace."

In no way has Mr. Bryce more helped us than in showing the folly of that long list of critics who glee-fully traced our frailties to the *kind* of government we had chosen. I tried to keep a list of the specific degeneracies that writers connected with our *form* of government. We had set up as a Republic and *therefore* were becoming "godless," "irreverent," "mannerless," "silent," "monotonous," "super-sensitive." We were "flighty" and "headstrong," "miserly in some directions and wasteful in others," all because we had cut loose from aristocracies. That five of our States repudiated their debts, or long threatened to do so, was an "inevitable result of democracy." Poletika gives his reasons why our inordinate boasting follows from our type of govern-ment.[1] As he says, the effect of democracy is "to make men turbulent citizens, abandoned Chris-tians, inconstant husbands, and treacherous friends." Captain Marryat says, "Slander and detraction are the inseparable evils of a democracy." [2]

---

[1] "Aperçu," p. 155.   [2] "Diary," Vol. I, p. 17.

We are shown how inevitable it is that we should consume such enormous quantities of cheap liquor, "because we are a democracy." Without the influence of aristocracy, we cannot produce art or literature.

Of all this shallowness Mr. Bryce makes short work. "One of the most polished and aristocratic societies in Europe has for two centuries been that of Vienna; yet what society could have been intellectually duller or less productive?" He says these theorizers about democracy are like Daniel giving us a dream and his own interpretation of it.[1]

"Few mistakes are more common than that of exaggerating the influence of forms of government. As there are historians and politicians who, when they come across a trait of national character for which no obvious explanation presents itself, set it down to 'race,' so there are writers and speakers who, too indolent to examine the whole facts of the case, or too ill-trained to feel the need of such examination, pounce upon the political institutions of a country as the easiest way to account for its social and intellectual, perhaps even for its moral and religious peculiarities." [2]

"Let any one study the portrait of the democratic man and democratic city which the first and greatest of all hostile critics of democracy has left us, and compare it with the very different descriptions of life and culture under a popular government in which European speculation has deported itself since de

[1] Professor Freeman writes: "It is absurd to infer that a democratic federal form of government has a necessary and special tendency to corruption, when it is certain that corruption has been and is just as rife under governments of other kinds." — "Impressions of the United States," p. 123.

[2] "The American Commonwealth," Vol. II, p. 612.

Tocqueville's time. He will find each theory plausible in the abstract, and each equally unlike the facts which contemporary America sets before us."

Mr. Bryce's second source of confidence is in the character of our education which works through this public opinion. More than twenty years ago he wrote of the new forms of education in the United States, "as powerfully affecting politics, the development not only of literary, scientific, and historical studies, but in particular of a new school of publicists, who discuss constitutional and economic questions in a philosophic spirit; closer intellectual relationship with Europe, and particularly with England and Germany; increased interest of the best class of citizens in politics; improved literary quality of the newspapers and the periodicals." In 1905 he turns with still greater reliance to these educational hopes. His running comparison between our best and the best in Europe adds interest to his estimate.

"There has been within these last thirty-five years a development of the higher education in the United States perhaps without a parallel in the world.

"The interest taken in the constitutional topics and economic questions, indeed in everything that belongs to the sphere of political science, is as great as it is in Germany or France, and greater than in Britain.

"America has now not less than fifteen or perhaps even twenty seats of learning fit to be ranked beside the universities of Germany, France, and England as respects the completeness of the instruction which they provide and the thoroughness at which they aim.

"Even more noticeable is the amplitude of the provision now made for the study of natural sciences, and of those arts in which science is applied to practical ends. In this respect the United States has gone ahead of Great Britain." [1]

That the remaining shadows neither discourage nor seriously alarm him is the message for which we have most to thank this writer. That his hopes for us are based upon the strengthening and enriching of our education as it acts upon public opinion brings this cheer; a steadying and informing education is a remedy and a responsibility over which we have control. It is the distinction of Mr. Bryce to have shown better than any of our critics how direct a bearing this educated opinion has upon every destiny that is to constitute the enduring greatness of our common country.

[1] "America Revisited," *Outlook*, March, 1905.

These words too are reassuring: "The notion which has obtained currency in Europe that the people of the United States, conscious that they have become a great World Power, are planning, and preparing to build up, a vast dominion over subject States or tribes seems ludicrous to any one who keeps his ears and eyes open in the country."

CHAPTER XIV

A PHILOSOPHER AS MEDIATOR

To Professor Hugo Münsterberg we are indebted for two books, one written for our instruction, one for the instruction of Germany. Each country is overburdened with prejudices against the other. To clear the common air of these absurdities, to help each to understand the other, to encourage and enlighten friendly relations between Germany and the United States, is the generous purpose of these complementary studies.

This scholar has been so many years in our country, he has travelled so widely, his activities are so variously related, as to give him skill as mediator and interpreter.

After seven years' teaching in Harvard University, he published "American Traits," in which the direct appeal is to us in America. Hundreds of students returning year by year from German universities learn something of the deeper life of that country, but the "average American ignorance" is not only dense but often increased by hurried trips through German territory. That they are frowsy, unpractical, and given to cloudy philosophies, that

their food swims in grease, that their pompous officials are perpetually interfering in your private
affairs, is a mental picture very common in this
country. The Americans' complaint of this petty
interference I have heard oftener than any other
criticism. We turn to Professor Münsterberg to
find him critical of this same evil in the United States.
He complains of our "restrictions and prohibitions
and a continuous meddling with private affairs."
Our policemen do not come in to insist that the
heating arrangements should be thus or so; they
do not get serious and bureaucratic over the baby
carriage, or over the way you carry a cane in the
street; but we have our petty legal interferences
quite as intolerable to Germans. We are used to
these and do not notice them.

To illustrate these international densities, the
author writes: —

"An American who has never been abroad invited me, the
other day, to a German luncheon. I had to work my way
through a series of so-called German dishes, which I had
never tasted or smelled before; and when finally imported
sauer-kraut appeared, and I had to confess that I had never
tried it in my life and had never seen any one else eating it,
my host assured me that I did not know anything about
Germany: it was the favorite dish of every Prussian. The
habits of the Prussian sauer-kraut eater are well known. He
goes shabbily dressed, never takes a bath, drinks beer at his
breakfast, plays skat, smokes a long pipe, wears spectacles,
reads books from dirty loan libraries, is rude to the lower
classes and slavishly servile to the higher, is innocent of the

slightest attempt at good form in society, considering it as his object in life to obey the policeman, to fill blanks with bureaucratic red tape, and to get a title in front of his name."

From the German side: —

"How does the Yankee look in the imagination of my countrymen? In the German language the adjective 'American' is usually connected with but three things. The Germans speak of American stoves and mean a kind of stove which I have never seen in this country; they speak of American duels, and mean an absurd sort of duel which was certainly never fought on this continent; and finally, they speak of American humbug, and mean by it that kind of humbug which flourishes in Berlin just as in Chicago. But the American man is of course very well known. He is a haggard creature, with vulgar tastes and brutal manners, who drinks whiskey and chews tobacco, spits, fights, puts his feet on the table, and habitually rushes along in wild haste, absorbed by a greedy desire for the dollars of his neighbors. He does not care for education or art, for the public welfare or for justice, except so far as they mean money to him." [1]

The American thinks the German "servile, reactionary, narrow minded," while the German believes the American to be "greedy, vulgar, brutal, and corrupt." The high task of the author is to make both peoples ashamed of this petty and philistine judgment. By patient instruction he tries to scatter these devils of misunderstanding by turning on the light.

His appreciation and praise of all that is best in our life and institutions is found in "The

[1] "American Traits," pp. 7, 8, and 9.

Americans." [1]   As it is addressed wholly to Germany, it lies largely outside the present purpose.   There are, however, few Americans who cannot find instruction in every chapter.   These contain some startling statements, the accuracy of which is very wide open to criticism.   They are often statements, however, flatteringly in our favor.   They are doubtless meant to be strong in order to reach the thick-skinned prepossessions against us in the Fatherland.   The author, moreover, frankly defends himself for touching lightly upon our faults and idealizing many of our virtues, because he addresses his message to Germany.   He admits that the larger book is a "study of the Americans *as the best of them are and as the others should wish to be.*"   This is, of course, only part of the picture, but it is for the author's purpose the truer and more essential part.   The man who uniformly takes his fellows at their best rather than at their worst is not only a wiser but a far more useful citizen.   The really great names on our roll of honor from Washington to Lincoln, with a kind of divine obstinacy, took their fellow-countrymen at their best.   The scamps and the half scamps, who have lowered life among us, as uniformly took men at their worst.   To lift the discussion and the estimate of foreign peoples so that they can be taken at their best would revolutionize for good every international relationship.   Nothing less than this is the spirit of this author's bulky volume.

[1] Published by McClure-Phillips, New York.

In the briefer study addressed to us, the working of our educational and democratic ideals is kept chiefly in mind. We have the educator in the critic's rôle. Before dwelling on strictures and warnings, let us note the full heartiness of his appreciation.

There is first the caution of the real critic in discrimination and avoiding that commonest pitfall — loose analogy, as when he deals with the press in both countries : —

"It is, for instance, not at all fair to compare the political German newspapers with those of America, and to consider them as mirrors of the nation. In Germany all the newspapers which have a political value are exclusively for the educated classes, while in America every paper, and especially those which are seen most, is written for the masses. Social economic conditions make that necessary; and it is, therefore, natural that the American paper makes concessions to vulgarity which would be impossible on the other side." [1]

Even our hateful gum chewing is "mere imperfection of the coördinating centres." Most foreigners have so misunderstood this domestic delight that they have invariably mocked at it and reviled it, but now our "motor restlessness" gets relief, as it does in the use of rocking-chairs, so that this traduced munching which an unscientific Englishman says "straightway transforms a pretty girl into a cow with her cud," becomes dignified as the proper care of one's health.

There is quite incandescent eulogy of the

[1] "American Traits," p. 27.

s

American girl which the most ardent of our early
French admirers did not surpass: —

"He [the foreigner] wanders in vain through the colleges
to find the repulsive creature he expected, and the funny picture of the German comic papers changes slowly into an
enchanting type by Gibson. And when he has made good
use of his letters of introduction, and has met these new creatures at closer range, has chatted with them before cosey open
fires, has danced and bicycled and golfed with them, has seen
their clubs and meetings and charities, — he finds himself
discouragingly word-poor when he endeavors to describe,
with his imperfect English, the impression that has been made
upon him; he feels that his vocabulary is not sufficiently pro-
vided with complimentary epithets. The American woman is
clever and ingenious and witty; she is brilliant and lively and
strong; she is charming and beautiful and noble; she is
generous and amiable and resolute; she is energetic and practical, and yet idealistic and enthusiastic — indeed, what is
she not?" [1]

[1] "American Traits," p. 130.

The fine glow of this tribute has scientific confirmation from a
source that ought to give Mr. Münsterberg a higher opinion of
Froebel. A child, still in the kindergarten age, wrote her first
essay on woman. Her father, a professor of natural science in an
Eastern university, had furnished the Darwinian atmosphere in
which the little girl grew up. She wrote, "Men and women
spring from monkeys. My father says so; but *I* says, women
sprung further *away* from monkeys than men did."

To be impartial one should also quote another qualifying
opinion about a great multitude of American women whom the
author thinks given to fads and intellectual hysterias. She
"cannot discriminate between the superficial and the profound,
and without the slightest hesitation she effuses, like a bit of gossip,
her views on Greek art or on Darwinism between two spoonsful
of ice cream."

Of things more serious than gum and gallantries, we have an honest attempt so to state the national traits which have excited most criticism, that they can be seen in their relations and with some qualification. Even of our begrimed politics he says: —

"The same complex historical reasons which have made the party spoils system and the boss system practically necessary forms of government have often brought representatives of very vulgar instincts into conspicuous political places; but that does not mean that the higher instincts are absent, still less that the alarming accusations which fill the press have more than a grain of truth in a bushel of denunciation." [1]

He then makes adroit distinction between policies that are directly under the heavy pressure of self-interest (tariffs, trusts, free silver, etc.) and those that represent the general political feeling and responsibility. It is in this more general sphere that —

". . . the American in politics proves himself the purest idealist, the best men come to the front, the most sentimental motives dominate, and almost no one dares to damage his cause by appealing to selfish instincts. Recent events have once more proved that beyond question. Whatever the senators and sugar men may have thought of it, the people wanted the Cuban war for sentimental reasons; and if the uninformed continental papers maintain that the desire for war had merely selfish reasons, they falsify history."

One other passage must be given: —

"The high spirit of the individual in politics repeats itself much more plainly in private life, where helpfulness and

[1] *Ibid.*, p. 28.

honesty seem to me the most essential characteristics of the American. Helpfulness shows itself in charity, in hospitality, in projects for education or for public improvements, or in the most trivial services of daily life; while silent confidence in the honesty of one's fellow-men controls practical relations here in a way which is not known in cautious Europe, and could not have been developed if that confidence were not justified. Add to it the American's gracefulness and generosity, his elasticity and his frankness, his cleanliness and his chastity, his humor and his fairness; consider the vividness of his religious emotion, his interest in religious and metaphysical science, — in short, look around everywhere without prejudice, and you cannot doubt that behind the terrifying mask of the selfish realist breathes the idealist, who is controlled by a belief in ethical values." [1]

After appreciation like this, it would be a poor return of courtesies not to heed the admonitions. They are not wanting either in number or in pungency. Even while he warns Europeans not to do us injustice or exaggerate our faults, he admits that we have still a good stock of the "more civilized forms of vulgarity."

"The result is not necessarily, as Europeans often wrongly imagine, a general moblike vulgarity: but a bumptious oratory, a flippant superficiality of style, a lack of æsthetic refinement, an underestimation of the serious specialist and an overestimation of the unproductive popularizer, a constant exploitation of immature young men with loud newspaper voices and complete inability to appreciate the services of older men, a triumph of gossip, and a crushing defeat of all aims that work against the lazy liking for money-making and comfort." [2]

[1] "American Traits," p. 29.   [2] *Ibid.*, p. 196.

Again, what is becoming of our fine hypocrisies about social equality? There is no need to refer to our behavior to the Chinese since the sand-lot orator, Denis Kearney, roused California masses against them, or the Indians, or the prevention of the negro vote. No reference is necessary to the open chase for foreign titles. The practical ignoring and even hatred of the equalities to which lip-service has been given, may be seen spreading like a contagion through our entire system. Quiet and ordinary Americans, whose means permit them to build a better house, as far as possible from the poorer neighbors, are quick to discover that they "really can't any longer send their darlings to the public school." The company is too common. Schools now numbering thousands, supported by millions of money, have sprung into existence and are fast increasing. These are frankly based on a principle of social selection that is the very breath of an imitated aristocracy. The public schools in which such brave hopes were placed as the bulwarks of democracy are now in a sinister sense *not good enough* for the well-to-do. Though the education and, above all, the most needed element of discipline may be better in the public school, it is not good enough *socially* for growing multitudes of Americans. We are very ingenious in the use of pretty sophistries to explain the reasons why children must go to "select" schools, but no one need be deceived. Dr. Münsterberg says: —

"Where is the equality in the inner life of America? Of course it is true that we have public schools where all are equal; the only difficulty is that they are not in use. Yes, there is no doubt that we are fast approaching a state where nobody in a city sends his children to the public schools when his means allow him to pay for the instruction of a private school." [1]

Or it is what the author calls "the pedigree spleen" which has now caught "the best material of the nation."

"If a single family of Connecticut needs three volumes of 2740 quarto pages to print its own history; if the Daughters of the Revolution have 27,000 members; if the genealogical societies like the Colonial Dames, the Daughters of the Holland Dames, the Mayflower Descendants, and so on, multiply with every year, — the aristocratic undercurrent cannot be doubted." [2]

The organized pilgrimages in search of proof that our family origins are in touch with the proud and the mighty now fill the land. A learned gentleman in charge of one of our genealogical societies tells me that to watch the good people who crowd his rooms seeking for aristocratic connections about which they can brag the rest of their lives, is to learn that human nature in this country is as full of toadyism as that of any people who ever lived. One industrious lady, after much expense and years of trouble, discovered a thread which connects her with an English yeoman. She hurried in agitation to the

[1] "American Traits," p. 227. [2] *Ibid.*, p. 228.

librarian to find out what a "yeoman" might be. The answer was a little disappointing. She said, "I suppose I've got to put up with him, but I did hope after all I paid out, I'd find an ancestor that wore armor and a helmet."

Another librarian tells me that it is one of his experiences to have these unsatisfied souls, after much seeking, come to him with the finger on some heraldic device that specially pleases them — they like its shape or colors — and say bluntly: "I've concluded to take that. How much is it?" When it is explained that coats of arms are not sold in that society, "I sometimes tell them there are plenty of places where they can buy them, and I have never known any persons to fail to make the aristocratic connection if they kept at it." To furnish very humble Americans with distinguished ancestry is an enormous business now in this country.

The *Boston Transcript* began some years ago very modestly; but now with rhythmic devotion several columns of fine print are given once a week to this cult. The urgency is such that the editor now appeals to contributors to have mercy. He has to print regularly this warning: —

"The pressure upon the genealogical department has become so great and matter has accumulated to such an extent that it is impossible to insert queries as soon as they are received."

Thus the "pedigree spleen" grows apace in the land where "all men are created equal."

Another graver fault in this author's eyes is the American superstition that "almost anybody can do almost anything." Any young girl is competent to teach a Sunday-school class or a country school. Any one who does service for the party in caucus or on the stump is fit to be consul, though totally ignorant of the language, customs, and commerce of the people to whom he is accredited. Everybody is fit to be a representative, on the school committee, or any kind of inspector. In discussing Winston Churchill's "Coniston" a politician of large experience in New Hampshire says: "The railroads have done much to corrupt the people, but there is a deeper evil. The common idea that everybody ought to go to the legislature and is fitted to go there, is what blocks the first necessary steps toward reform." According to Dr. Münsterberg, the greatness of Germany has been won by faith in the man of special training. We have practised this in all our most successful businesses, but it has been the bane of our political life to test fitness by a mere party fealty that bears no relation to the duties of the office sought. That we are now (as in the question of consuls) aroused to some sense of our long blundering, is to this critic bright with promise.

The name he gives to this superstition is "democratic dilettantism," which has smitten us with "an ineffective triviality which repels the best men and opens wide the doors of dishonesty." It is thought to be the crudest absurdity to ask any man to be the mayor of a German city, unless he has thorough administrative training in city business. To make this office, as it is made in this country, the helter-skelter prize of factional policies is properly described by a former German Minister, Schleiden, who wrote, "American municipal politics will remain corrupt and wasteful until the people learn that educated ability is the sole qualification for city offices." Professor Münsterberg attributes many phases of our weakness and troubles to this "chronic dilettantism." It works like a poison at the root of large parts of our educational system: —

"We have instead a misery which can be characterized by one statistical fact: only two per cent of the school-teachers possess any degree whatever. If the majority of college teachers are hardly prepared to teach in a secondary school, if the majority of high-school teachers are hardly fit to teach in a primary school, and if the majority of primary school-teachers are just enough educated to fill a salesgirl's place in a millinery store, then every other reform is self-deceit." [1]

This writer is saying only what other friendly and competent men have said of all but our exceptional education.

In a report of the Royal German Commission in 1904, Dr. Dunker writes of the average American school: —

"The difficulties are avoided, mistakes passed by; frequently the pupils are given great tasks whose performances would exceed their power, and the school is satisfied with a

[1] "American Traits," p. 76.

childish treatment of the subject and makes the impression
upon the children that the problem has been fully solved.
This results in quickness of judgment, self-confidence, superficiality, and dilettantism. . . .

"Everywhere there is credulous optimism coupled with
harmless dilettantism; everywhere high aim, liberal execution; but lack of solidity in matters of detail."

These observations are, of course, made daily by
our own abler educators, often in more uncompro-
mising terms. But the business now is not with
our own faultfinding. The essence of the criticism
is that we suffer grievously from lack of thoroughness
as compared to the German standard, and that, above
all, our general education fails in sustained *disciplinary* power. This lack of thoroughness and of
discipline leaves us with a thousand coddling private schools with no severity of standard whatsoever.
It gives the pretentious list of studies and the display
of pupils on show days when the public is admitted.
It tests education by its promise of immediate cash
returns. That the nobler and more disinterested
ideals of education thus lose honor, Dr. Münsterberg lets us see in a passage which will bear much
pondering: —

"A lack of reverence pervades the whole community and
controls the family, the school, the public life. The pert
American boy who does just what he pleases may thus get an
early training in democratic politics; but while he wastes
the best of the home and the class room, he gets at the same
time the worst possible training for the duties of life, all of
which demand that he do later quite other things than those
which he likes to do.

"He will learn too late that it is a great thing to command, but a greater thing to obey, and that no one can sign early enough the *declaration of dependence.*"

That it is greater to obey than to command is nobly true, and it has to be admitted that the ideals of obedience are less popular among our boys and girls than dreams of domination over others. Neither is it quite a fad among our youth to give their signatures to "the declaration of dependence." One of our teachers, into whose school came a small group of pupils from South Germany, said: "They seemed for one term to be a different species. They had not been cowed, but there was a charm of deference, a delicacy of consideration, and a capacity to blush which stood out in strange contrast to the mass of our pupils. Within a few months, I could see that these pretty ways could not be retained in the new atmosphere." For this loss do we get some compensation in greater "self-determination" which this critic notes as one of our traits?

The spirit of reverence as expressed in the docility of the German child we cannot have, any more than we can have the ruthless discipline of the German army. Since it is so hopelessly beyond our reach, let us believe that there are some compensations for its loss.

The final reproof of this author is graver still. If the American is sure of anything, it is that he enjoys an amount of freedom of which Old World societies know little. The possession of liberty is our strong point. But what does it signify to have liberty; really to be free in the large sense of that word? Is the South free to discuss the race problem strictly and fearlessly upon its merits? Hundreds of the best Southerners will tell you that the political and social spectre raised by that issue silences freedom of speech. Can their theological professors deal boldly with the accepted results of scientific and critical investigation? Can the Bible on one side, and Darwin on the other, have open and bold discussion? There are no better men in the South than those who say that this is impossible, and that many years must pass before anything like the German academic freedom will be attained. In scores of Northern colleges of sectarian tradition this is also true. This is what Professor Münsterberg has in mind when he points to the higher freedom in Germany. In this respect the Germans are our superiors. It is one of our humiliations that we still carry on the heresy hunt against men who merely try to interpret the elementary results of a scientific world scholarship.

The other sphere in which our moral liberty suffers is even more important. Intellectual slavery is nowhere so dangerous socially as in our politics. "To the independence of public men," he says, "and to their loyalty to the commonwealth, party bondage is fatal." Of certain legislative bills he is told in private how bad and mischievous they are; but when they come up, no one "dares to say a word."

The heresy for which men widely care is no longer theological, but economic, and even this word but half expresses the truth. The heresy for which blood money is now demanded is upon the surface political, but the unseen heart of it is business and property interests over which men are in conflict. It may be sugar on one side and Philippine tariff on the other, but the ordinary political contest is only an outer aspect of competitive struggles for desired properties. If people really value these more than they value other things, they will barter the spirit and the letter of the Great Declaration — all the stately syntax about equalities and rights — for the economic ends they have in sight. When that great dreamer and doer, Cecil Rhodes, said the English flag was a good business asset, he was putting in words, even if mockingly, what our most masterful business men systematically *act* upon. Politics is a pawn in the game of strategic business control. It is this, and this alone, which explains most of the lawlessness of "the great interests"; but also the other most serious criticism of four other of our fairest and ablest critics, namely, the "abdication of intellectual freedom" under the dictates of party politics — De Tocqueville, Chevalier, Bryce, and Ostrogorski.

They are also as a unit upon this other accusation: "The party ruler in America with his methods of nomination deprives the individual of his political powers more completely than any aristocratic system, and the despotism of the boss easily turns into the

tyranny of a group of capitalists." The paragraph
modernizes De Tocqueville's chief misgiving about
us. Ostrogorski,[1] who studied this feature of our
life with a fearless impartiality that won from Mr.
Bryce the highest praise, has drawn conclusions that
we have to face or become convicted of inexcusable
timidities. When he finds that the greater private
interests act so promptly upon Congress that the
freedom of individual members seems to be lost, we
think of a commanding state, the pivotal state, —
New York, — and her two present senators. Can
any one point to a solitary hint of constructive policy
that is traceable either to Mr. Platt or to Mr. Depew?
Are they free to act even for the *people* of their own
state? They are thought of as serving henchmen —
the one for a great railroad, the other for an express
company. What two men have had such chances
to know of the inner corruption of New York politics?
With all their knowledge of these things, has either
of them lifted a hand to disclose or check these evils?
One of our critics asks these perturbing questions,
speaking of one of our most famous senators, in whose
state party politics was managed by a boss of notorious venality: "How is it possible that this senator
should not know the practices of that boss? If he
knows them and willingly profits by them to keep his
place, in what is he better than the boss himself? If
he knows them, why is he not the first to cry out and

[1] "Democracy and the Organization of Political Parties,"
Macmillan, 1902.

appeal to the people against such corruption?" "The hardest thing to understand in the United States is that these political leaders in Eastern states like Pennsylvania, Rhode Island, Ohio, should consent to keep silent while a lot of journalists investigate and explain the evils to the public." Yes, this is hard to understand, and few of us ever heard the explanation. Our critics tell us that these men are in no sense free; that they are bound hand and foot so far as freedom to act and speak in the large public interest is concerned. Senator Quay could plead with a pathos of disinterestedness, for what? for the reforming at home of a systematized party corruption that has long been a by-word in the land? No, not for this, but for the Indians, in whom he had, I believe, a humane interest. But how safe and far away from home diseases these wards of the nation are!

The final Summary and Conclusion in the closing volume of Ostrogorski[1] should have a separate printing and be read by every American who knows the language. It is referred to here for its sturdy reënforcement of Münsterberg's gravest indictment.

We are familiar with *habeas corpus* and reckon it among the most precious of our political possessions. But this author asks us about *habeas animum*. We still deliver the body, but how next are we to deliver a *free mind* — how free the spirit from the dead body of party tyranny? This is the summons.

[1] Vol. II, pp. 336–741.

He says wisely that it is folly to throw the blame solely upon the party leaders. It is the whole mental attitude of the voters that needs to be unbound. It is this public, he says, that is now made to believe "that the citizen who follows his party blindly is a 'patriot,' and that the prostitution of power to a party is a pious action. These idols, as Bacon would say, must be destroyed. Men must be taught to use their judgment and to act independently. It is on the accomplishment of this work of liberation that the whole future of democracy depends.

"In the absence of this independence and this vigilance, demagogism and corruption have entered the house in broad day, as a thief enters in the night. Democracy thenceforth received a check, and not through an excess of liberty, as so many of its critics imagine, *but from a deficiency of it*, from a want of moral liberty in this government of free reason."[1]

Again and again we have passages like this: —

"And these men enter Congress as slaves of the Machine and the Boss, of sordid parochial considerations, or of powerful private interests, industrial or financial, which are so often in league with the machine. One or other of these servitudes of mind and conscience, or even of all combined, is what they have to pay for their seat. The House, therefore, is simply a diet of representatives of private or local interests, and it has been aptly remarked that every interest is represented in it except the public interest."[2]

[1] "Democracy," Vol. II, pp. 728, 729.
[2] Vol. II, p. 544.

We are not dealing here with irresponsible cranks or muck-rake journalists, but with friendly, impartial, and equipped scholars. Of the one now quoted Mr. Bryce could say that few men ever brought a more scientific spirit to his task.

Habeas animum; to get the really free mind in the realm of politics, to enlarge every fearless activity of political independence, is our supreme need. This warning is as if De Tocqueville spoke from the dead to say again what he wrote long since. Though in unsoftened phrases, it is the soul of Mr. Bryce's appeal for a manlier independence of party whips. Firm in his purpose to defend and to take us at our best, Dr. Münsterberg puts his finger on the same cancerous spot.

It is as if these well-wishers spoke with a single voice, "There is just as much safety for your Democracy as there is moral and mental independence of party tyranny in your citizens."

T

CHAPTER XV

A SOCIALIST CRITIC

SOME twenty years ago a scientific teacher in England, Dr. Aveling, the socialist, came to this country with his wife, the brilliant daughter of Karl Marx. I tried to interest them in some of the obvious prosperities in New England, but the task was without hope. That fortune had a smile for this trade-smitten country; that there was well-being anywhere among the workers, these visitors did not wish to hear. For the mishaps, calumnies, dishonors of our business and political life, they had the hungriest appetite. But that any good was to appear on the horizon of a country so given to business traffic, was not to be believed. Both had open-mouthed credulity for every evil report, and as gaping an incredulity about everything hopeful. In this spirit they took notes, which appeared later in a bitter and distorted book.

The veteran German Socialist and Parliamentarian, Liebknecht, was with them, but in far kindlier humor. He, too, thought we were going to the bow-wows, but were having a great deal of fun getting there. When he saw that the big stores were not swallowing up all the little ones, it did not make

H. G. WELLS
Author of "The Future in America"

him sulky. Thus Socialists, like other folk, come to us with different tempers. To those of more open mind it is an admirable discipline to visit this country and see it with some care.

A German professor (Katheder-Socialist) was here. He had taught for years that the state was a positive power that could be made to work productively in a thousand ways for man's welfare. To manage railroads, mines, slaughter-houses, telegraphs, was a small part of what it had yet to do. The state could be made creative. It could produce values and equalities. This has not been the American idea. We have been taught that the Government is a necessity, like the policeman, the tax-gatherer, and the court. These stand for order and justice among men, but they are luxuries that have to be paid for by the private industry and the thrift of the people. I do not know that this professor returned to his own country with any change of view about the German government, but he told me that he had never in the least realized what private and unaided effort could do in creating a stupendous material prosperity such as the world has not seen. "You think of your government," he said, "as if it were merely to be *supported* like a hospital; as if it were a negation, rather than a positive thing. Your people set to work as if they had never heard of it. Your achievements are so vast that they are a kind of final argument. Your way may be, after all, best, at least for you."

Another Socialist came, of extremer type. He had believed and taught that combinations were everywhere absorbing little industries. Our great primary industry of farming, to which he gave special attention, was very upsetting to him. He found many of the bonanza farms being cut up, because they did not pay or would pay better subdivided. He was told that the progressive up-to-date farming was steadily toward smaller areas. His chief amazement was the prosperity of the small farmer on good soils through the Middle West. "A more independent and thriving population than these tillers of the soil, I have not seen." America, he said, is "a great touchstone for social theories. No man should become *anything* until he has seen it well."

Mr. Upton Sinclair opens his new book [1] with the deliberate assertion that the great revolution is so close upon our heels that we shall be in the very throes of it within one year after the presidential election of 1912. He makes his prediction as "a Socialist and prophet." So soon will the touchstone of events be applied to *him!* Another precipitate Socialist signs his name in a Boston club, "Yours for the Revolution, Jack London." In the club was another Socialist who straightway followed with his signature, "There ain't going to be no revolution, H. G. Wells." So different in its effects is the great touchstone America!

I once heard a bumptious person criticising a por-

[1] "The Industrial Republic."

trait by a clever artist in his studio. When the critic
had gone, the artist made an unflattering speech,
which ended with these words, "What that booby
thinks of the portrait isn't interesting, but I should
pay well to know what the portrait thinks of him."
If it were articulate, what would the touchstone
America say of many of its critics?

I have sought diligently for American views of
Mr. Wells's book, " The Future in America." That
so many cordial opinions are expressed by those
who have experience enough to judge it largely, is
full of good omen. Very little criticism that cuts
deeper has been written about us. There are pages
(like some of those in the chapter on "State Blind-
ness") which most Americans would do well to
ponder long; passages, too, like this, after discovering the hideous fact that child labor is actually upon
the increase in the United States: —

"This is the bottomest end of the scale that at the top has
all the lavish spending of Fifth Avenue, the joyous wanton
giving of Mr. Andrew Carnegie. Equally with these things
it is an unpremeditated consequence of an inadequate theory
of freedom. The foolish extravagance of the rich, the archi-
tectural pathos of Newport, the dingy, noisy, economic jumble
of central and south Chicago, the Standard Oil offices in
Broadway, the darkened streets beneath the New York elevated railroad, the littered ugliness of Niagara's banks, and
the lowermost hell of child suffering are all so many accordant
aspects and inexorable consequences of the same undisciplined
way of living."

It is a book that many a reader will merrily skip
through, thinking its claims to serious attention are

very slight. This is an almost pitiful error. For a century, perhaps, several books a year have been written about us, but not a baker's dozen of them deserve more assiduous attention than this small volume. It is the charm of "The Future in America" that the author is just enough haunted by the magnitude of his task to be a little afraid of it. He does not take himself too seriously or fall into pedantries. He is very graceful in avoiding the hard realities that ask for too definite and cock-sure opinions. His polished gaieties serve him well in many a tight place, where a prosy literalism would leave him knee-deep in difficulties. It is a book full of imaginative insight, full of swift glimpses, as if the eye were aided by a powerful glass. Even when he looks upon a great question, like that of immigration, or of the negro, he throws more light into it and about it than many who have lived long in its presence. Let us first see his attitude toward these two issues. They, too, are touchstones.

The author has a keen and instructed interest in race problems. His eye, so quick to detect the inner taint in what seems flushed with health, is at once fixed upon the momentous inpouring of our immigration. It fills him with foreboding. He sees that the more disciplined peoples of North Europe have become a tiny stream as compared with the broadening flood from South and Eastern Europe. That Constantinople should soon be the geographic centre of these human tides opens a gloomy vista to his imagination, because we are so afraid of adequate state regulation. He sees us thrusting the vote upon these raw peasants, but "that does not free them, it only enslaves the country." He speaks as if he were watching a continent struggling with indigestion. ". . . the dark shadow of disastrous possibility remains. The immigrant comes in to weaken and confuse the counsels of labor, to serve the purpose of corruption, to complicate any economic and social development, above all to retard the development of that national consciousness and will on which the hope of the future depends." Very deftly he touches the points at which immigration adds to the weight of our burden. It does make the labor problem harder and political trickeries easier. It does complicate social development, and, most of all, it does retard the fusing of common social consciousness and will, that are indispensable to unified action in community life.

The deepest reason why employers and people of easy incomes generally want the immigrant does not escape him. He states it thus: ". . . that America, in the urgent process of individualistic industrial development, in its feverish haste to get through with its material possibilities, is importing a large portion of the peasantry of Central and Eastern Europe, and converting it into a practically illiterate industrial proletariat."

Again, with the same firm stroke, he traces two of the heaviest shadows that fall on this race move-

ment: first, the effect upon the child life born into
the poorer and most cramped quarters of our cities.
The parents come with the simple habits of country
ways.   They are diligent and of good behavior.   In
spite of some lying jugglery in statistical form, they
are very free from criminal propensities.   But their
offspring, thrust into city streets for their first habit-
making before the school begins! — here is an evil
sinister   enough.   The   second   is   the   inevitable
coarsening effect which the new liberties and freedom
from traditional restraints are likely to bring upon
hordes of the fresh comers to our shores.   This is
his estimate: —

"It seems to me that the immigrant arrives an artless, rather
uncivilized, pious, good-hearted peasant, with a disposition
toward submissive industry and rude effectual moral habits.
America, it is alleged, makes a man of him.   It seems to me
that all too often she makes an infuriated toiler of him, tempts
him with dollars and speeds him up with competition, hardens
him, coarsens his manners, and, worst crime of all, lures and
forces him to sell his children into toil.   The home of the immigrant in America looks to me worse than the home he came
from in Italy.   It is just as dirty, it is far less simple and beautiful, the food is no more wholesome, the moral atmosphere far
less wholesome; and, as a consequence, the child of the immigrant is a worse man than his father."

A young woman from a New York settlement
takes Mr. Wells to watch the patriotic exercises in the
school close by.   He listens, not without a thrill of
sympathy, to the clamorous adoration that lights a
hundred immigrant faces as the little flags go up.

"Do you know," he says, "I too have come near feeling that at times for America?" Then he goes out from this glad consecration into the dirty street, where he stumbles upon "a heap of decaying filth that some hawker had dumped in the gutter," and the fine spell is gone. The barbaric disorders disenchant him, and he sees in the murky perspective of some future near or far three words,

"LYNCHINGS! CHILD LABOR! GRAFT!"

Then comes the tragedy of another problem, that of color. He looks into the Southland at the negro and his destiny, close coupled with that of his white neighbors. Here he sees even less hope. As for immigration, he admits that America may suddenly rouse herself to heroic educational enterprises that may lift the peasant armies into disciplined efficiencies, that will make the vast invasion safe, but this riddle of the African so socially separated from the whites, with the coarse prejudices waxing rather than waning, what gleam of light is discernible here? From all sorts of Americans he seeks information, only to be staggered by utter failure. He cannot get even "the beginnings of an answer." He declares that "hardly any Americans at all seem to be in possession of the elementary facts in relation to this question."

In the mournful undertone of his speculation only one thing is clear to Mr. Wells, which is, that the

chief obstacle is not in the black man but in the white.
How shall this same proud white man educate himself to live in honor with the weaker people? These
weaker ones did not ask to come. Their fathers
and mothers were stolen on the African coast and
forced in terror and with immense atrocities to
come to this country. Their descendants are now
here with the blood of their masters flowing in their
veins. Only a freak here and there will talk of
deporting them. They are to remain in our midst.
How can we whites educate ourselves into that
larger tolerance that may make a common civilization possible? How can we use our superiorities so
that wisdom and statesmanship shall more and more
take the place of inherited bias and passion?

To Mr. Wells there is one unslain dragon. It is
the dragon of a Christless and religionless race
prejudice. He finds it as bullying and insolent in
the North as in the South. How are we whites to
rid ourselves of this great uncleanness? Nothing
less than this is the challenge.

Mr. Wells is not deluded about the black. He
does not see him as a white man who happens to
have a darkened skin. The indolence, thriftless-
ness, and gay unconcern of the negro are familiar to
him, and it is because he is aware of these that we
read with more interest the following tribute to the
best of the oncoming negroes.

"Whatever America has to show in heroic living to-day, I
doubt if she can show anything finer than the quality of the

resolve, the steadfast effort hundreds of black and colored men are making to-day to live blamelessly, honorably, and patiently, getting for themselves what scraps of refinement, learning, and beauty they may, keeping their hold on a civilization they are grudged and denied."

In this spirit he philosophizes, but always with the thought of how things are coming out. How do the negro and the immigrant bear upon the tasks of the next generation? He finds us wofully lacking in action that bears widely upon that future. We can dig ores and coal, fell trees, exhaust soils at a terrific rate, all of which we identify with "progress." But how is this frenzy related to the life ahead? Not one of his graceful pages will have its proper reading unless this future society is held in mind.

Mr. Wells is the man of letters and of science with a yearning for utopias. He has a fine disdain for the thing that is. What may *become* of the fact, what may be made out of it, that alone entrances him.[1] He is not to be persuaded to give an hour to the home of Emerson or to the resting-place of George Washington. Niagara bores him as much as the swift turbines enchant him. He is the first competent and unashamed Socialist to write a book about us. I say unashamed because he does not flinch

[1] Mr. Bryce in similar vein says of the House of Representatives: "Here, as so often in America, one thinks rather of the future than of the present. Of what tremendous struggles may not this Hall become the theatre in ages yet far distant, when the Parliaments of Europe have shrunk to insignificance?" — "American Commonwealth," Vol. I, p. 149.

from or shuffle with the logic of his faith. The whole conclave of our conventional idols — "business enterprise," "private initiative," "property," "trade," "freedom," "patriotism," bourgeois family and state — are to him half-amusing and half-mischievous superstitions. He is always the socialist with ample and generous tolerance for our illusions. There is no hysteria, no fuming, no frenzied invective after the manner of your ordinary Socialist, against the predatory culprits called Captains of Industry. If these masters of our commercial fate step with seven-league boots, if they move and act like a Colossus dividing the spoils after their own heart, Mr. Wells falls into line with the common army of admirers. He finds them diverting and full of instruction. How else can a people be taught the baleful logic of a consecrated capitalism? If huckstering and market-dicing with high finance are to be glorified until they absorb the best talent of the nation, how are the multitudinous victims to be disillusioned except they see stalking among them the embodied results of their system? These giant overlords, staggering under their incomes, are the best possible object lesson to an envious populace that meanly admires them. Let the comedy play itself out before all eyes.

He sees every one of our ills through the medium which the massed energies of the nation have created. This is business, everywhere business. Our ambitions and our achievements are scaled to this standpoint. We organize our dollar getting so that the general estimate of success is in terms of large ownership. This creates the atmosphere in which the very rich, simply *because* of riches, feel a prescriptive right, let us say, to a seat in the Senate. One of the most recent to enter this body is from a great state in the West, one of whose citizens says frankly, "Well, —— is our richest man; why shouldn't he go to the Senate?" It should be the one political body beyond taint of suspicion, yet some of its high places are bought as if it were a stock-exchange. Business masteries have so subdued our politics and our politicians that they are but the echo of what the stronger business men want.

What chance has socialism in such a community? Mr. Wells grows timid. Like a good *bourgeois*, he warns us against our own Socialistic preachers. It is his private faith that we are without hope until the world's chief business is taken from private hands and private profit makers. The community (town, city, government) must manage this wealth-making directly for the good of the people and for all the people. Yet when Mr. Wells looks into this same business in the United States, when he examines our politics and the spectre of corruption that is business on one side and politics on the other, he shrinks. Socialism is far too good for America. So busy have we been in gathering dollars that "nobody is left over to watch the politician." The boss, with his slavish army of heelers, has waxed great amidst the general laxity. We have allowed him to become the "professional," whose exclusive aim is personal profit. The pearl of socialism, says Mr. Wells, is not to be trusted to such as he. "Under socialism all business comes straight into politics and has to be managed by selected officials. Think of giving Standard Oil or railroad interests to politicians as they now are in the United States!" It strikes him as grotesque.

And here, to this author, is the essential tragedy, that we are so overpoweringly a trading people; that our distinctions, ambitions, energies, and education are so universally dedicated to the profit-making ends of trade. These habits are so nationalized, so all pervasive that *they cannot be kept out of any other part of our life.* It would still be well with us if we could keep the trader's instinct confined to its own field, but it is our tragedy that the trading ardor, with its sister propensity, gambling, invades all other fields. Gambling is the sport instinct exercising itself in rivalry against another, to get something for nothing. It is trade stripped of its decencies and restraints. Trade *plus* the license of the gamester thus takes possession of us. It first encroaches upon politics, filling the convention, caucus, and lobby with deals and bargainings. To counter and dicker with blocks of votes becomes identical with the chaffering of the market-place. The spoils system is merely systematized trading.

The church no more escapes than politics. It

has to be commercially organized with clerical salaries, pew-rents, and selected congregations that reflect to a letter the social standards which rest on a scaled material prosperity. The poor are no more wanted there than they are at a fashionable dinner. From the petty gambling at the church fair to the social consecration of bridge whist, the stamp of this prosperity is deep upon us. It materializes education, the theatre, and athletics.

Yet Mr. Wells feels no astonishment. We are cankered with "graft," but that is inevitable because we are a nation of traders, and trade is in essence overreaching. If you wish to see it as it is, watch the game of poker, — "a sort of expressionless lying called 'bluffing.'" In its essential quality, trading does not differ from cheating. ". . . the commercial ideal is to buy from the needy, sell to the urgent need, and get all that can possibly be got out of every transaction. To do anything else isn't business — it's some other sort of game. Let us look squarely into the pretences of trading. The plain fact of the case is that in trading for profit there is no natural line at which legitimate bargaining ends and cheating begins. The seller wants to get above the value and the buyer below it. The seller seeks to appreciate, the buyer to depreciate; and where is there room for truth in that contest?" [1]

"A very scrupulous man stops at one point, a less scrupulous man at another; an eager, ambitious man may find him-

[1] "The Future in America," p. 123.

self carried by his own impetus very far. Too often the least
scrupulous wins. In all ages, among all races, this taint in
trade has been felt. Modern Western Europe, led by England and America, has denied it stoutly, has glorified the trader,
called him a 'merchant prince,' wrapped him in the purple of
the word 'financier,' bowed down before him. The trader
remains a trader, a hand that clutches, an uncreative brain
that lays snares." [1]

We have been sufficiently taught that the sharp
higglings of the market, the calculating strife between
buyer and seller, were attended by incidental evils
that take on here and there vicious proportions. To
Mr. Wells these distinctions are the pious hypocrisies by which sharpers cloak their thieving. His
joyous tilting is not against the flagrance and abuses
of trade, but against all trade, and the very nature of
trade. It has been much and long believed that the
exchange function in trade — in spite of excesses —
carried with it immense common advantages. Mr.
Wells strives to free us from this illusion. The
trader, even the most enterprising and honest
one, has only "an uncreative brain." He merely
"clutches" and sucks like a parasite.

All these judgments Mr. Wells, of course, brought
with him. They are a part of his equipment as
Socialist critic, and their value is very great for him
and for us. They furnish him with a standard
which he is continually applying to our country.
He is not criticising us alone. To the Socialist,

[1] "The Future in America," p. 125.

England is as sick with graft as America. To him graft is an evil name for about all that England is, commercially. All her stately manors, all her parks and palaces, all her rent-bearing forms of property on which her great families fattened like parasites, are the quintessence of sponging and graft. The only difference to Mr. Wells, as he says plainly, is that Americans talk about their sins more openly and more vociferously. That we cry aloud, is our hope. If England should cry out about her own embedded graft, there would be more hope for her.

It is our peculiarity that we are so all-in-all given over to profit-mongering. We are accurately the counterpart of the great middle class trading and huckstering England. We differ only in this, that we can out-hustle England. We are friskier, and the dead hand of custom lies more lightly upon us. But we are the hammering, shopkeeping, middle class of his own countrymen set in freer and happier conditions for our work. Voltaire summarized England in these words, "The bottom, dregs; the top, the froth; and the middle, excellent." Wells agrees about the dregs and the froth, but the poor middle class has for him no excellences. Its shop-keeping prosperities are but organized vulgarity and overreaching of your neighbor. As for our-selves in America, we have the froth, but it is a pu-trid imitation, and the lees are ever thicker at the bottom, while the saving middle already becomes stale. We have nothing in common with the ele-

U

gances and responsibilities of upper class England, and so far, very little of the squalid deformity of her lowest classes.

"America is simply repeating the history of the Lancashire industrialism on a gigantic scale, and under an enormous variety of forms.

"But in England, as the modern rich rise up, they come into a world of gentry with a tradition of public service and authority; they learn one by one and assimilate themselves to the legend of the governing class with a sense of proprietorship, which is also, in its humanly limited way, a sense of duty to the state.

"America, on the other hand, had no effectual 'governing class'; there has been no such modification, no clouding of the issue. Its rich, to one's superficial inspection, do seem to lop out, swell up into an immense consumption and power and inanity, develop no sense of public duties, remain winners of a strange game they do not criticise, concerned now only to hold and intensify their winnings.

"This is the fact to which America is slowly awaking at the present time. The American community is discovering a secular extinction of opportunity, and the appearance of powers against which individual enterprise and competition are hopeless. Enormous sections of the American public are losing their faith in any personal chance of growing rich and truly free, and are developing the consciousness of an expropriated class." [1]

"A secular extinction of opportunity!" [2] This is one of his easy literary felicities to show us that the

[1] "The Future in America," p. 80.

[2] Matthew Arnold's statement is as follows: "England distributes itself into Barbarians, Philistines, and Populace. America is just ourselves, with the Barbarians quite left out, and the Popu-

froth at the top and the dregs at the bottom are already becoming indistinguishable from the middle.

If we reply that very many of our ultra-rich do develop a sense of public duty, that they dower education, art museums, hospitals, institutions for scientific research, on a scale unknown and unmatched among other people, our Socialist author has his answer, Yes, there never was such free-handed outpouring, but it is too unrelated, too indiscriminate, too pauperizing. One most princely gift bestower is thus described: —

"And through the multitude of lesser, though still mighty, givers, comes that colossus of property, Mr. Andrew Carnegie, the jubilee plunger of beneficence, that rosy, gray-haired, nimble little figure, going to and fro between two continents, scattering library buildings as if he sowed wild oats, buildings that may or may not have some educational value, if presently they are reorganized and properly stocked with books. Anon he appalls the thrifty burgesses of Dunfermline with vast and uncongenial responsibilities of expenditure; anon he precipitates the library of the late Lord Acton upon our embarrassed Mr. Morley; anon he pauperizes the students of Scotland. He diffuses his monument throughout the English-speaking lands, amid circumstances of the most flagrant publicity; the receptive learned, the philanthropic noble, bow in expectant swaths before him." [1]

lace nearly. This would leave the Philistines for the great bulk of the nation; a livelier sort of Philistines than our Philistine middle class which made and peopled the United States — a livelier sort of Philistine than ours, and with the pressure and the false ideal of our Barbarians taken away, but left all the more to himself and to have his full swing." — "Civilization in the United States," p. 79.

[1] "The Future in America," p. 94.

Thus one by one the pedestalled gods in our Valhalla are "called down." There is no billingsgate, no rough handling, but only a good-humored weighing and measuring of objects that are found wanting. They are not even cast aside, but put back in their places as if this kindly iconoclast said to us: "Let them remain until you yourselves find them out. Soon enough they must be replaced by quite other symbols."

The American reader who adds to "The Future in America" the later volume, "New Worlds for Old," will have a message as insinuating and persuasive as any that the literature of modern Socialism has to offer.

We watch his easy and sustained flight with more willing admiration because his truth-telling is as freely directed against collectivist frailties as it is against the present system. He is indeed rather the *enfant terrible* in the house of the Socialist.

Your revolutionist is in his eyes an undisciplined and half-baked person. Neither will Mr. Wells have any nonsense about a world sinking into deeper disorders and disgraces. Life, in spite of all drawbacks, is moving on and up. It grows sweeter as it lengthens.

This quick-witted observer sees more and sees better than scores of others who have stayed longer on our shores and travelled farther. His social and scientific interests furnish an equipment for observing society as it just now exists in the United States.

Our material strength and our political weakness are both phases of the capitalism which has been developed to its highest point. There is nothing that so fashions our entire life, religion, manners, morals, press, and education as this same capitalism, and it is precisely this central and determining force which the trained Socialist makes his study. The one needed lesson that modern socialism has for us is its criticism. The logic of its full and positive programme, we should do well to hold at arm's length, but its strictures upon the present business and social organization contain truths that only the very blind will ignore.

The most constructive statesmanship of our time has boldly taken its hints from the Socialist. He may mistake much, he may be wild in his exaggerations, he may draw crazy inferences even as other speculators, but he has this advantage — his specialty of thought and study is concentrated upon what has come to be overmastering in this country: our business methods, habits, and ambitions, and the devious ways through which these react upon our individual and collective life. Moulded after these material patterns are the prevailing ideals, the scrutiny of which are his main study.

Mr. Wells is one of the most luminous as he is one of the most fearless of these social arbiters. In "The Future in America" we meet the Socialist who knows a good deal about the dry economics of his subject, but knows it so well as to clothe it in the imagery and the imagination of the poet.

CHAPTER XVI

SIGNS OF PROGRESS

THAT our "progress" is manifest and assured is perhaps the most confident of American opinions. A French critic asks: "Why has the France of to-day such sickly doubts about herself, while America, in spite of her prolific sins, has the boisterous faith that does not really fear any danger or check upon her forward movement? Even if your American talks gloomily, it is all upon the surface. He is at heart a robust and reckless optimist."

This optimism, of which everybody is proud, gets sadly mixed up with most arguments for progress. It is the justification of optimism that has to be first shown. No one is quite equal to the task, because final proofs of progress cannot be given except in terms of character or of happiness and conscious well-being. But happiness! Who shall define it in its "higher" and "lower" scale? It has been the despair of dialecticians wherever this subject has been discussed.

I recall the sentence, "The age that has the most deserved and most diffused happiness is the age of highest progress." But who shall prove that the twentieth century is happier than the fifteenth?

or that the days of John Milton were happier than those of Socrates? The reign of the Borgias in Italy seems to us full of all sorts of terrors for average men, but the studies of Taine led him to believe it a happier age than ours. He believed this because the Italians showed at that time so much *vitality*. It was the age of "magnificent and daring action." On the other hand, we are told that India has lost her vitality, and with it the power of great activity. Yet a Hindoo scholar told an audience in Boston that the India he knew was far happier than we of the United States because she was uncursed by our feverish activity. Quietness and meditation, with the habit of not wanting too many things, were to him indispensable to happiness. We are likely to reject this Oriental test, but the reasons we should give would doubtless seem to this Eastern gentleman merely to beg the question.

We are thus driven to other and secondary tests of progress. This is here justified because it is with these that our critics are for the most part concerned. They have to do chiefly with the conditions of social growth upon which "deserved happiness" in part at least depends. The points raised by our critics enable us to discern changes in these conditions that have very vital connection with social growth.

I select first that part of the country about which the visitors were most in despair, the South. Nearly

thirty of them go there largely to study the institution of slavery and its social effects. They are
generally charmed by the manners and hospitality
which inspire many cordial pages. Progress or
the hope of it, few of them see. Mrs. Stowe never
wrote a line so withering against the results of
slavery as many of these foreign onlookers. That
the very roots of industrial and political society
under our form of government were already poisoned
by the reactions of slave labor, — giving the whites
contempt for honorable work, and turning to ridicule our whole theory of political equality, was the
theme on which much high-wrought feeling was
expressed.

That it would end all dreams of having one national life was believed by most of them. Then,
each after his own temperament speculates as to
the shapes the ruins will finally assume. A few
make good guesses, but the results, as we now see
them, would have amazed all these prophets. Social
destinies are still deep in the shadows, because the
"tragedy of color" has only changed its form.
Yet there is no misconception so fundamental as
to make this negro tradition in our day the determining or primary fact in the future of the South.
The essential evil of slavery was that the negro as
slave gave shape and direction to *the whole industrial life* and, therefore, largely to the political life.
Desperate as it now may be, the whole negro question has become secondary, while the entire new

Max O'Rell (Paul Blouet)
Author of " Brother Jonathan "

order of free industrial life is primary and creative. This seems to me the most impressive fact in the South.

Soon after the evils of "reconstruction," these changes in business structure and method began. Statistical measurements are at last accessible that are wholly trustworthy. From a date so recent as 1900, her products leap in value from less than one-half billion to nearly two and a half billions of dollars, cotton spindles from six to ten millions, her assessed property from 5266 millions to 8000 millions, her bank deposits from 87 millions in 1896 to 171 millions in 1906 — this is the material uprising of the South from the gaunt and awful poverty in which the war left her. But the growth of her educational purpose and achievement, her enlarged recognition of the unities of our national commonwealth, are still more impressive than all the climbing figures of her industrial prosperity. No one can travel there without seeing that the Southland tingles with new life which breaks through all crusts and all restraints. Her one grief is the lingering tradition of the slave. Yet, in the whole best side of that race, the progress as figured in property acquirement or by sacrifice for learning is as hopeful as any page of recent race history in the world.

Nor is it for a moment to be supposed that this special race burden is solitary or peculiar to the South. Largely a question of color and intermingling numbers, it faces and tests every civilized nation. It is the supreme lesson that all people have to learn together. Any one who reads Olmsted's masterly studies of the South before the war, together with the pages of that sagacious journalist, E. L. Godkin, a few years later, can test the strides the South has taken. Better than either of these writers, the Southerner Walter H. Page knows this subject. He knows it the better because he knows the North so well. Returning from a ten weeks' trip, he compares the gains made largely within a dozen years. Hear his judgment: —

"I doubt if anywhere in the world there has been so rapid a change in what may be called the fundamentals of good living and of sound thinking and of cheerful work, as the change that has taken place these ten years in many of these rural districts. Many a farmer who was in debt to his 'factor' now has money in the bank, a bank that itself did not exist ten years ago. The inherent good nature of the people approaches something like hilarity. If you direct the conversation toward prosperity, they will crack jokes with you about the needy condition of Wall Street, and remind you that their banks have money lent at interest in New York."

A dozen years ago, the talk of the Southerner was continually about the romance and drama of the past. To-day it is not tradition, not even the terrors of Reconstruction, that hold his attention. It is the present and the future. Mr. Page puts the spirit of the new change into this incident: —

"I asked a young man at one of the Southern schools of technology why he chose this training rather than training for one of the older professions. 'My grandfather,' said he, 'was a mighty man in theology in his day. He knocked out his opponents, and he battered the devil. My father was a lawyer and a soldier. He fought the United States by argument and in war. I notice that the devil and the United States are both doing business yet. I made up my mind, therefore, that I would change the family job and do what I can to build mills and roads in Georgia.'"

It should be added that Mr. Page sees even greater encouragement in the renaissance of education.

Since 1896, I have been nine times into the South, and I do not believe these words contain a single accent of exaggeration. With the skill of a good observer, Mr. Page does not take his reckoning chiefly from the favored border states, but rather from the lower South where the difficulties have been greatest. As one turns back to the gloomy conjuring of the older visitors; as one rereads the shadowed pages in Dickens and Abdy, one seems to ask for a stronger word than "progress" to tell the tale.[1]

We must of course be warned against the easy treachery of gauging real growth in material estimates. But these are not to be omitted if they are associated with other facts.

That the man who travelled yesterday in an easy

---

[1] In spite of much present opinion, the South was not happy under slavery. The most far-seeing of the critics constantly note the deep currents of unhappiness which that institution brought to the best men and, above all, to the best women of the South.

chair from New York to Philadelphia in an hour
and forty minutes was any happier than Mr. Jerrold
who bumped through, in a wagon with no springs,
in twenty-three hours, we cannot prove, because
we have no test for the sensations of either traveller.
That Mr. Jerrold had to get out frequently to
help boost the stage from the ruts; that he arrived
stiff and thick with mud, does not prove that he
was without enjoyment on that trip. The man in
the plush chair may have been more disturbed by
a delay of fifteen minutes than the earlier traveller
was by a delay of four hours. Yet the change
from twenty-three hours to two hours, from the
bumping cart to the plush chair, is an improvement which goes down on the side of progress.
The added comfort is no mean gain, but far more
are the economies in time and human strength.
When Madison was elected President in November,
1812, Kentucky heard the news in the following
February. This fact means much more than physical difficulties of transportation. It represents an
average of mental lethargy and indifference which
we have outgrown.

That a few years later than this, it should have
cost one hundred and twenty-five dollars to carry
a ton of coal from Pittsburg to Philadelphia, is
mainly a physical fact. It has quite other significance, that when our first critic was here, a Philadelphia publisher should be seriously advised
not to start a paper in that city, because *there was*

already one in Boston. There were those who gravely questioned whether the country could support two newspapers. It is in the same class with the latter fact that in a prominent college one professor could teach without protest botany, Latin, chemistry, mineralogy, midwifery, and surgery. At this time the clergy in Boston were thrown into a frenzy of moral revolt by the announcement that two of Shakespeare's greatest plays, "Hamlet" and "Othello," were to be presented on the stage.

Our study began with a whole order of social phenomena of this character. One of our critics at the beginning of the nineteenth century went from Baltimore to Philadelphia. He paid six cents per mile on the stage, two dollars and twenty-five cents per day at hotels, and was three days on the way. Another wished to go from New York to Albany. He watched the papers three days for a boat. When it was finally announced, there was a further delay of thirty-six hours because of the weather. He had besides to take his own bedding and food.

Here is a description of a trip from New York to Philadelphia: —

"We had about twenty miles down the Delaware to reach Philadelphia. The captain, who had a most provoking tongue, was a boy about eighteen years of age. He and a few companions despatched a dozen or eighteen bottles of porter. We ran three different times against other vessels that were coming up the stream. The women and children lay all night on the bare boards of the cabin floor. . . . We reached Arch Street wharf about eight o'clock on the Wednesday morning, having been about sixteen hours on a voyage of twenty miles."

The Scotch Wilson, who had been nearly as severe on New England hotels, thus describes those on a trip through the South.

"'The taverns are the most desolate and beggarly imaginable; bare, bleak, and dirty walls, one or two old broken chairs and a bench form all the furniture. The white females seldom make their appearance. At supper you sit down to a meal, the very sight of which is sufficient to deaden the most eager appetite, and you are surrounded by half a dozen dirty, half-naked blacks, male and female, whom any man of common scent might smell a quarter of a mile off. The house itself is raised upon props four or five feet, and the space below is left open for the hogs, with whose charming vocal performance the wearied traveller is serenaded the whole night long.'"

An Englishman with wife and child goes from Albany to Niagara Falls. The cheapest conveyance he could get cost him one hundred and fifteen dollars, and they arrived "half skinned" from the journey.

Yet it is neither the slowness, discomfort, or expense of this early travelling which tests most fully the improvement. It is rather *the safety*. Arfedson wrote in 1832:—

"A traveller intending to proceed thence (from Augusta, S.C.) by land to New Orleans is earnestly recommended to bid adieu to all comforts on leaving Augusta, and make the necessary preparations for a hard and rough campaign. If he has a wife and children unprovided for, and to whom he has not the means of leaving a suitable legacy, let him by all means be careful to insure his life to the highest amount the office will take."

In 1834–1835 Miss Martineau found steamboat travelling in the West extremely dangerous: —

"I was rather surprised at the cautions I received throughout the South about choosing wisely among the Mississippi steamboats; and at the question gravely asked, as I was going aboard, whether I had a life-preserver with me. I found that all my acquaintances on board had furnished themselves with life-preservers, and my surprise ceased when we passed boat after boat on the river delayed or deserted on account of some accident."

No man who ever came to us had more scientific caution in his statements than Sir Charles Lyell. As late as 1850, on his second journey of investigation, he said: —

"After comparing the risk it seems to be more dangerous to travel by land, in a new country, than by river steamers, and some who have survived repeated journeyings in stage-coaches show us many scars. The judge who escorted my wife to Natchez informed her that he had been upset no less than thirteen times."

I purposely select this test, because we are at last being shocked into some sense of social disgrace by the monthly horrors of our railway butcheries.

Our accident list is now as inexcusable as it is appalling, but man for man and mile for mile, travel is far safer than in the year 1800, and in the half century that followed. Until within a generation, there seems to have been no general public sensitiveness whatever as to these dangers. This growth of sensitiveness to what is cruel or socially harmful seems to me fundamental. But first let us select from the witnesses other hints of the conditions of a larger individual and social life.

There are many perfectly trustworthy comments to show us the rise of wages that lifts the whole standard of comfort in the community. The builders of the Chesapeake and Ohio Canal, in 1829, imported workmen for twelve dollars a month. The employers who paid the passage got in addition three months' labor for nothing. There are now classes of Italian workmen among us who earn enough in six months to make it worth while to pay their own passage twice across the Atlantic, and leave in their pockets more than these laborers of 1829 got in the whole year. In 1907 I found Italians in a California quarry earning $4.00 and $5.00 daily for less than nine hours' work.

At the present moment Italians are on strike in New York for more *per hour* than they got in South Italy *per day*, and for nearly three times as much as Chevalier found Irishmen at work for in 1834. This careful economist says he found a good deal of the hardest work done for sixty cents a day. At about this time women in the Lowell mills worked from five o'clock in the morning till seven at night for fifty cents a day. As compared with English wages, Godley finds even this surprisingly high.

In 1834 there was a strike among the men doing

the heavy work on Philadelphia wharves. They worked from six to six. I cannot learn what they asked, but when the employers met, they offered one dollar a day for work from sunrise to sunset. The men accepted it. Carpenters were paid there one dollar and a quarter for ten hours' work. In a small country town in New Hampshire I cannot now get a local carpenter for less than $2.50 for nine hours.

I have seen Slovak peasants doing work about our rolling-mills for $1.50 per day who never get beyond thirty cents in their own country and for nearly half the year received less than twenty-five cents.

From Seattle to Los Angeles one finds plenty of Orientals whose daily wage at home had been less than twelve cents. They land in Americanized Hawaii where they soon receive $18 a month. As they pass to Oregon and California, they are found working for $35, $40, and $50 a month.

Thirty years ago in the South, a Frenchman notes that negroes who can be said to be "emerging" are receiving forty cents a day. The larger constructive industry, like the railways, is now tempting them from the old agricultural standards with wages at least twice and often three times as high as in 1870. This higher wage is much more than a material thing. It is the open door to freedom from desperate and slavish indebtedness to the truck-store.

x

The year 1834 is, I think, the time when men agitating for ten hours in Boston were said to be "agitators." The city authorities refused to allow them to have a hall even to discuss the issue before the public. In 1835 the bakers in Philadelphia struck against working "more than eighteen hours a day." There was also a strike of sewing women against a wage scale of seventy-two cents at its lowest, and at its highest one dollar and twelve cents, *per week*.

Of the poorer workmen, McMaster says: —

"Their houses were meaner, their food coarser, their wages were, despite the depreciation that has gone on in the value of money, lower by one-half than at present. A man who performed what would now be called unskilled labor, who sawed wood, who dug ditches, who mended roads, who mixed mortar, who carried boards to the carpenter and bricks to the mason or helped to cut hay in harvest time, usually received as the fruit of his daily toil two shillings."

The man who "mixed mortar" and "carried bricks to the mason" is now called a hod-carrier. Within sight of where I am now writing a building is going up. Every hod-carrier gets daily three dollars and works but eight hours. In 1825 this class was getting seventy-five cents for a twelve-hour day.

The usual reply to this is, "But they could then buy so much more for their money!" The statement unqualified is not true. Rent and a very narrow range of foods were then, of course, far cheaper, but to-day the average workman demands and gets for his expenditure at least ten things where he then got two. Including these, he gets far more for his money. A large part of his house furnishings, as well as foods for the table, did not then exist. It is to this far better housing and improved variety of diet that another step in progress for the masses of the people is clearly seen in these critical records.

Among the few best tests of social bettering, what is fairer than the *health* of the community?

It would weary the reader if I were to put down a tithe of the opinions on health and its conditions in the United States during the first decades of the last century. It is only the recent critic who comments on the good health of the American woman. Until the present generation it was as common to discourse on our ill health (this chiefly of the women) as to note the use of the rocking-chair. The philosopher Volney is very curious about it and studies our diet and habits of eating, drinking, effects of climate, etc., to account for the phenomenon. He does not distinguish between the men and the women. His conclusion is in these words: "I will venture to say that if a prize were proposed for the scheme of a regimen most calculated to injure the stomach, the teeth, and the health in general, no better could be invented than that of the Americans." The acute Chastellux says that above all other people we "heap indigestions one on another," and "to the poor, relaxed, and wearied stomach, they add Madeira, rum, French brandy, gin, or malt spirits, which complete the ruin of the nervous system."

James Sterling reaches this conclusion as to the cause of such prevailing ill health as he found: "The deepest-rooted cause of American disease is the overworking of the brain and the overexcitement of the nervous system."

A Russian diplomatist, P. I. Poletika, here in 1810, 1811, 1812, and again in 1818, published an excellent book, "Aperçu." He has great admiration for the young American women, but says they are so delicate ("*si frêle et si passagère*") that they seem on the edge of invalidism. He attributes the lack of health to our climate.[1]

Alexander Mackay, in 1846, says of our women: "They are, in the majority of cases, overdelicate and languid; a defect chiefly superinduced by their want of exercise."

These among scores. Nor need we trust in this to foreign sightseers. There is plenty of undeniable testimony from our own authentic documents. Adams, in his first volume,[2] writes: "The misery of nervous prostration, which wore out generation after generation of women and children and left a tragedy in every log cabin."

Of our whole frontier life he says: "The chance of being shot or scalped by Indians was hardly worth considering when compared with the cer-

[1] p. 154. [2] Hist. of the U. S., p. 58.

tainty of malarial fever, or the strange disease called milk-sickness, or the still more depressing home-sickness." [1]

It was thought necessary by most of the early travellers to see life up and down the Mississippi, or through the thinly populated settlements. To find a healthy-looking woman was a surprise. It was usual to say that climate and "nervous strain" play their part, but it is also true that the meagre family income could not supply an adequate and varied diet. Ignorance about such diet, as about all sanitary measures, was no less a cause. That the standard of vigor has improved in the sixty years since Sir Charles Lyell's comments is about as certain as that our population has increased.

Inseparable from this health improvement of the women is the observed improvement in the speaking voice. One could easily collect a thick volume on the disagreeable quality of the American voice. Among all the earlier visitors, there is not the least disagreement on this point. There is much wonder as to the causes that can have brought this about. Climate is oftenest mentioned. Also "nervous strain and consequent depression." The necessity of straining the voice in "calling for men-folk to come to dinner." The women, it is said, thus get a harsh quality which was imitated by the children. "Incipient catarrh," "prevailing stomach trouble," "constant hurrying and anxiety," are

[1] Adams, Vol. I, p. 58.

other guesses. All the causes are beyond our knowledge, but it is, I believe, fairly clear that some generations of nervous ill health goes far to account for this lack of resonance and sweetness in "the American voice." Miss Martineau grieves much over this defect and is one of the few to trace it to ill health. She says:—

"A great unknown pleasure remains to be experienced by the Americans in the well-modulated, gentle, healthy, cheerful voices of women. It is incredible that there should not, in all the time to come, be any other alternative than that which now exists, between a whine and a twang. When the *health* of the American women improves, their voices will improve." [1]

Two recent critics express surprise that they find everywhere in the United States so many people with a speaking tone "as agreeable as anywhere in Europe." They speak of it as beginning and extending, not yet as commonly prevailing. It is very recent that we were conscious enough of the blemish to admit its existence. Foreign travel, the presence of certain nationalities among our immigrants, the teaching of singing and voice training in the schools, have so far aroused this recognition that the way to its healing slowly opens before us. We shall soon have sense enough to "standardize" voice quality: first of all for teachers. No teacher with a harsh, nasal, or "complaining" voice should be allowed to enter a schoolroom.[2]

[1] "Society in America," Vol. II, p. 200.
[2] I am told that this has already a definite beginning.

A little later we shall not allow boys with snarling or grating tones to shout their wares on the railroad train or to hawk papers in the streets.

There was much truth in a sentence just written in a London paper by an English teacher: "About one-half the Americans use tones that make you shiver. They will be shamed out of this only by hearing a pleasant voice long enough to feel the unpleasantness of their own."

Two college girls from New England lived a year in Spain. One of them says: "When I came home, at least one-half of my own friends spoke so that I wanted to put my hands to my ears. Yet I had never for an instant noticed this, until I had been surrounded by people for some months whose voice was a positive pleasure to the ear." This illustrates one precious lesson our critics have helped to teach us. We were "taking it in" even when we were hotly abusing our instructors. Dickens's brilliant caricature left its lesson for improved prison methods and for better manners. Even the saucy Mrs. Trollope, whose every page left a smart, actually modified some of our habits. Men who sprawled in their shirt-sleeves in a theatre box, or thrust a foot over the railing in the gallery, about 1840, often heard the word, "Trollope!" "Trollope!" shouted in the audience. All knew amidst the laughter what it meant. Much in these criticisms entered into our common thought and helped to form that self-criticism which makes the better possible.

Most of the hardest strictures concern frailties and imperfections that are easily accounted for by the newness, the narrowness, or the hard physical difficulties in the surrounding life. It was usually the point of the unsympathetic critic that our character and institutions were such that we could not free ourselves from the disorders.

It is a very different sign, but not less favorable, that so many of the early students of America believed that our democracy as a form of government chokes and hinders *opportunity* for the growth of higher, disinterested faculties. Science, art, letters, all the graces and real distinctions of civilization were, as they tell us, under baleful handicap, because we were committed to a democracy.

In nothing has the tone of the critic undergone profounder change than as regards this same word "opportunity," opportunity for the highest as well as for the commonest. St. Gaudens, the sculptor, has finished his work, and foreign artists are telling us that, with the exception of the French Rodin, the American had no superior in the world. Sir Robert Ball, the Astronomer-Royal of Ireland, recently left us. He is reported as saying that no higher astronomical work is done in Europe than here.

In 1830 it was written of us: "They have neither made any music nor do they show the slightest appreciation of it. Even their 'Yankee Doodle' and 'Hail Columbia' were not written by Yankees."

The French composer, Saint-Saens, was last year in this country. "Before I came here," he says, "people told me a great many unpleasant things about the New World. 'You won't like America,' they said. 'Everything over there will shock you and grate upon your artistic sensibilities.'" He now reports (not for the American interviewer, but in the Paris *Figaro*) his delight and surprise: "Everywhere I found excellent orchestras — everywhere excellent conductors."

Mr. Bryce's tribute to our higher education as on a level with the best that Europe offers is in the same key.

If opportunity, as an inspirer of faculty, be made the test of progress, we gladly accept it. The present-day voyager is indeed the first to use it in the larger sense, as characteristic of this country. "If you ask me," says one, "in what the United States differs from Europe, one word expresses it, 'Opportunity.'" One entitles a chapter "The Land of Opportunity." [1] A Socialist friend is very impatient with what he calls "all this fine talk about opportunity" in this country. Have we not sixty thousand tramps, grewsome poverty, and all the shame of the sweatshop and child labor? Yes, far too much of this shame is ours, but "opportunity" is a relative term. What land or people offers more to a larger part of its inhabitants? The

[1] The title of a German book is "The Land of Limitless Opportunity."

world's practical judgment about this has to be taken. Since our story began, some twenty-five millions of people at a good deal of risk and sacrifice have left their homes to come here. They came from all parts of the world and the pressure increases from year to year. It increases because those who have tried the country write back to their friends to follow them. The chief cause of immigration is the story which those continue to tell who have put the chances here to trial. No more final test is conceivable than this, that (as compared to other countries) the world's millions have found it, and still find it, the land of opportunity. An English consul, long in this country, says the charge of the English that the Irish are shiftless and ineffective at their tasks in Ireland has much truth, but he adds, "The moment the Irishman touches American soil, he works, and works with the best of them, because all sorts of chances open out to him and his children."

Now, what more than this same "opportunity" enters into and constitutes a people's hopefulness, courage, and happiness? If we are careful in our thought to add to the fact of economic opportunity the fact of the rapidly growing *educational* opportunity, hopeful chances never were greater in our history than now — I mean, for a larger proportion of the population.

Many who admit this are likely to add, "But this opportunity is closing up, it will soon be at an end."

No prophecy at the time it is spoken can be disproved, but the pages of our critics contain a great deal of testimony that bears directly on the point. Decade by decade through the century, our visitors are stoutly assured by the best-informed Americans, that the limit of assimilating immigrants has been reached. "It must be stopped or the Republic is at an end." This gloomy view held stiffly in 1825; it was rampant when De Tocqueville and Miss Martineau were here; it reached a crisis of alarm in 1840. "America," says one, "is always going to the devil, but never gets there." Yes, it has always been going to the devil, because of *something*. It is worth while to note some of these ever impending calamities.

Most of the first visitors heard from conservative and leading citizens that the President was to become a "despot" or "the slave of foreign potentates"; that the Senate was sure to become an oligarchy, because it sat six years and was not elected directly by the people; that the central government would swallow up the states or intimidate them by the army; even the House of Representatives would be made up of the rich and would tyrannize over the people; the small states would be at odds with the large states and lose their sovereign rights; Rhode Island could not maintain itself against New York. Bryce says of these dark misgivings, "Not one has proved true." There were many fears because of the size of our country. In a small democracy, it was said, you may extend power to the people, because the area of the problem is under control. With the vast domain of the United States, the interests will be so diverse and so conflicting that the factional spirit cannot be held in restraint. Bryce says very definitely that this factional unrest has, as a fact, "proved less intense over the large area of the Union than it did in the Greek republics of antiquity; to-day the demon of faction is less powerful in the parties than at any previous date since the so-called Era of Good Feeling in 1820."

Again, we were to be hopelessly vacillating in our foreign policy. Democracy, it was said, is "like a drunken man on horseback, falling now on this side, now on that." But Bryce will not even admit that, at our worst, we outdid most monarchies. "Royal caprice, or the influence of successive favorites, has proved more pernicious in absolute monarchies than popular fickleness in republics." With more conviction still, he says of our later years that "the foreign policy of the United States has been singularly consistent." This criticism, that we should be feeble and inadequate in foreign policy, was repeated and believed until the very close of the nineteenth century. But when commanding necessities came upon us, the man equipped for the new exigencies appeared in John Hay. We were told at his death by a foreign diplomat that in the whole field of world politics Mr. Hay had no superior. I heard it predicted that his successor

could not be found. Elihu Root did not have to
be found, he was at hand.

Another dire prediction was that with so many
states, dangerous and irresponsible experiments
would be tried. Especially would states here and
there legislate against private property, putting
the whole basis of society in peril. We now see
that this very experimental feature of state legislation has proved to be an advantage, and as for the
perils to private property, Bryce finds the prediction
wholly false.

Basil Hall was told that the rock on which we
were to split was the change in our inheritance laws
whereby all the children get their equal share, instead of the oldest son getting it all. This was to
destroy the saving social influence of the family and
property. This fear now sounds to us merely funny.

Giving equality of rights to women (first appearing in the youth of Lucy Stone) was also an in-
novation sure to introduce "a conflict of interests
— a lack of family unity — that no society could
stand." Woman has not won a right or an equality
that has not stood for progress.

That the church should be separated from the
state was another fatal step to bring in ruin. For
more than a generation our visitors were told that
the catastrophe always close at hand is the presence
of Roman Catholics.

I once had occasion to ask an aged man, whom
his fellow-citizens counted as one of their wisest,

some question about our social difficulties. When he had given his opinion, he added: "I suppose I am the more hopeful because my seventy years of pretty clear memory cover so many 'shipwrecks of the Republic.' My father was a hard-headed man, and nothing was more impressed upon my youth by him and his friends who came to us than the absolutely certain destruction of our government by the Catholics. I have lived to see that every one of their alarms was an entirely false one. As this has been true of a great many other scares, I have got into a pretty comfortable frame of mind about this country." He added, "Of course, something awful may happen to-morrow, but I am going to let the other man do the worrying." I use this because, better than any words of mine, it sums up the century of testimony on the approaching evils that were to overwhelm us.

De Tocqueville saw an impending peril from the growing "tyranny of the majority." How brilliantly he proved this! We now see that the proof had one defect — it wasn't true. How often it has been a glowering "Cæsarism" close at hand. Bryce notices this and thus writes, "Cæsarism is the last danger to menace America."

That before the death of George Washington, De Warville should see our doom in the "ravages of luxury" already rampant, sounds as droll to us as that a great number of enlightened people believed the Republic in immediate danger because

First Trip of Fulton's Steamboat to Albany, 1807

of that very innocent society of the Cincinnati, or as the fears expressed to Miss Martineau, because *young men were leaving the cities for the country districts.* The "decay of religion" was, of course, at all times working our early ruin.

Another form which the fear took was the certainty of "disrupting religious quarrels" because of the increase of Protestant sects. The Catholic Professor Klein comes here to find us so tolerant in this respect as to set a splendid example to the world. He wishes France could imitate us.

It should calm us a little that so many people in the first half of the last century were dejected about the "servant question." There has not been a decade since colonial times in which this frowning difficulty has not seemed to multitudes of home-keepers a despairing problem.[1] "The increase of intemperance" is another spectre constantly appearing in our story. A long chapter would be insufficient to show the clear and impressive evidence that, however intemperate we now are, the improvement in drinking habits is beyond a doubt.

There is one more shape which our early undoing takes on that is perhaps more instructive and more encouraging than any other. It is the agitated feel-

---

[1] The work of the servant a century ago is thus depicted: "She mended the clothes, she did up the ruffs, she ran errands from one end of the town to the other, she milked the cows, made the butter, walked ten blocks for a pail of water, spun flax for the family linen, and when the year was up received ten pounds (50 dollars) for her wages."

ing for more than a generation that we could not possibly survive the growth of "sectional hatreds." It is a feat of the "sympathetic imagination" quite beyond us of to-day, to appreciate what these sectional hatreds and jealousies were in the first forty years with which our criticisms deal. No opera bouffe could outdo many of these sober records of sectional spite. Trevelyan shows what this local prejudice meant among our soldiers in the Revolution. A military patriot from New Jersey gives his opinion of the corrupting influence of Pennsylvania soldiers. They would, he says, "be *pejorated* by having been fellow-soldiers with that discipline-hating, good-living-loving, to eternal fame damned, coxcombical crew we lately had from Philadelphia." This English historian adds that this amiable communication was from no less a man than General Livingston, and that it "was one among a hundred others which betoken a condition of feeling productive of endless scandal and immeasurable danger."

I had to look through a good many of our own history books in the effort to confirm the dire opinions which travellers record about these geographical animosities.[1] They record so many of them that only the briefest illustrations can here be given. One reports the president of Harvard College (the historian Sparks) as "much dispirited on account of California and her attitude." In a letter to De

[1] See, for example, "American Revolution," Vol. II, p. 196.

Tocqueville he writes, "Where will this end and how are such accessions and discordant materials to be held together in a confederated republic?" Marryat gives these "acrid jealousies" as a reason why a traveller cannot trust a bit of evidence that he gets in one part of the country about any other part of it. "The people of Connecticut will not allow that there is anything commendable or decent in New York." The German, F. J. Grund, is so impressed by this that he falls into a speculative nightmare. Through these prophetic mists he sees in the near future our collapse as a nation. He says: "I imagined myself somewhere near the Hudson or the Delaware in the midst of a large flourishing city, besieged, stormed, and finally carried by a victorious Western army." [1] It was against the playing upon these sectional discords that Webster spoke his great words, "There are no Alleghanies in my politics."

That we have grown in those integrities that constitute progress is not wholly proved by the kind of testimony just given. But it is a history of doubting and fearful opinions which we may read with a good deal of wholesome instruction and encouragement.

Such weight as this story of pessimistic apprehension possesses, we must take over into the final chapter. We shall see there the bearing of what our critics reveal on the gravest dangers to Democracy.

[1] "Aristocracy in America," Francis J. Grund, London, 1839.

Y

CHAPTER XVII

SIGNS OF PROGRESS — *Continued*

IN a lecture on this coy subject of Progress, I sat
beside an expectant stranger who listened with lessen-
ing attention for about twenty minutes. Then, with
visible irritation, he reached for his hat, saying,
"I'm too busy to listen any longer to this infernal
pig-iron theory of progress."

It was a true description of the discourse. It was
progress in terms of pig-iron and kindred material
products, and yet this waspish auditor was not altogether fair to the lecturer. His figures had a kind of
poetry of their own, as one watched the graphic tables
through which the story was told. It yet seemed to
me to stand for progress, that this impatient hearer
was unfed by all the dazzling accumulations. He
had heard the tale of our material greatness so often,
that he wanted other proofs. Is the time never to
come, he seemed to ask, when we can safely take
the pig-iron side of our civilization for granted?
We have heard the critics find a deal of fault with
our harping on all manner of bignesses and rapidities.
If social movement has a right direction in America,
if there is the movement of growth and improvement,

appeal has to be made to something besides bigness or swiftness. Questions mainly about the quality of things have to be asked, and not alone about the quality of *things*, but about the quality of whatever constitutes the moral and intellectual temper of our people and institutions. For example, is there among our citizens increase of public spirit as against sectional narrowness? Is there improvement in the public taste and manners? Is educational opportunity broadening, and the standard of education rising? Are we more ashamed of bluster and pretence? Is the public quicker to condemn the turpitude in business and public office? Is there a growing decency in our politics? Is the Press — "that test of democracy" — better or worse?

These are some of the hard questions that must be raised and in some way answered before the case for progress can be made out.

Several of these questions have already been hopefully answered by our critics. For more than half of the nineteenth century, the best of them are full of doubts about our future, so far as all ideals of mind and heart are concerned. Decade by decade the tone has changed until, toward the close of the century, we have from them ungrudging admission that the institutions and the people of the United States have far outstripped expectations, so far as education, science, and many of the arts are concerned. The last quarter of a century has revealed other hungers and other capacities that are classed

in every country among the things of the spirit.
In successive chapters, we have seen how ungrudgingly these higher attainments have been recognized
by the ablest men and women who have told their
story in all sorts of "Impressions of America."
About two things they hesitate, — our politics and
our press.

Let us look first at the press.   It would have disheartening significance if this were failing us; if it
were, as one often hears, becoming a meaner rather
than a nobler influence; if, taken as a whole, it were
on the devil's side.   For a hundred years it has been
singled out as an object of vituperation.   It was
"The Daily Bulletin from the sick-bed of civilization."   It has, says another, turned us into the
"Gehenna of the United States."   In 1898 a foreign
scholar wrote: "I ask but one proof that civilization
in the United States is a failure.   Her press alone
gives you more proof than you require."   Let us
accept the test, and allow the critics, with a little
nudging, to answer the question.

The above tone against the press continues until a
few exceptions begin to be noted near the middle of
the century.   But the press in general gets little
quarter until very recent times.   Even now, nothing
except our politics excites more critical condemnation.   The average visitor buys a batch of the more
notorious journals.   On the headlines and brawling
sensational features he makes up his little budget
of comments.   One of them writes, "If I wished to

convince any rational being that the ruin of democracy is certain, I should see that he spent a few evenings reading these sheets." This is as if one were to test the excellence of the Dresden Gallery by the dozen worst canvases on its walls, or a people's health by visiting the hospitals. Just above this type of observer is one who discriminates so far as to select in the East and West a group of papers that are admitted to be admirable, and to this extent the judgment is qualified. Matthew Arnold and Professor von Holst found certain journals in the United States as able as any printed in Europe, but scarcely before the twentieth century has any one attempted to study our press *as a whole*. A simple incident shows what this more careful and discriminating study produces in way of criticism.

Two years ago an author and editorial writer on one of the London papers came to investigate this subject. I begged him to include in his examination not alone the dailies, but the weekly, the fortnightly, and the monthly products, *The World's Work, McClure's, Review of Reviews, The Outlook, Collier's, The Ladies' Home Journal, The World To-day, The Youth's Companion, The Independent,* and a dozen others. Many of these summarize news and cope with every besetting problem as the older magazines that do us so much honor could not attempt. They are as integrally a part of our press as a sheet with five daily editions.

Some of these magazines are said to be given to muck-raking and to sensations. If the charge is true, it is a use of the rake that we need as sorely as the crippled or the sick need surgeons and doctors. The few have always known the existence and the nature of our real social perils, but methods of secrecy, created by the winners in our competitive system, have prevented the people as a whole from having the least intellectual grasp of ills from which they most suffer. One by one these eating sores, with the secrecy which sheltered them, are being laid bare to us all.

In this initial work of regeneration, the best of our dailies have had their influence immeasurably increased by periodicals of the type partially named. The cheap magazine is unhampered by local influence. It speaks to the nation. No one pretends that the magazines named are on sale to any capitalistic influence. If one were "bought," young fellows with ideals still burning in them would put another in its place. So incalculable has been their service in making the millions see the danger-spots in the Republic; seeing them so clearly as to bring the question of remedies within the region of practical politics, that they are already lively competitors in point of moral influence with the college and the church. Half playfully William James wonders if the future historian will not find young men turning from the university to the cheap magazine for help. This is already true. In every state and city where the fight for clean citizenship is really on, the achieving men get instruction and inspiration from these same sources, just as many an academic teacher goes to these same magazines to be trained for a part of his own proper work.

When the English author above mentioned had done his work upon this inclusive journalism, he told me, "No nation has a press that should excite more pride [1] and encouragement than yours. Nowhere is a part of it worse; nowhere is the other part so good. No other people *dare* to take the lid off as you do, and that is your safety."

Like every other issue with which we have dealt, the question of press influence is one of comparison and of tendency. Is the *collective* influence of the press greater for good in the twentieth century than it was in 1800 or in 1825? Any one who cares to spend two days upon the dingy files of those older organs, will see that they resemble the worst or the weakest of our present-day press, but bear little resemblance to the best of our press to-day. The temper of the time may be shown in a single incident in 1812. It concerns the *Federal Republican*,

[1] Another English editor, Mr. Stead, writes: "*The Century, Scribner's,* and *Harper's* are three periodicals the like of which we may search for in vain through the periodical literature of the world. The American *Review of Reviews* is much superior in price and general get-up and advertisements to the English *Review of Reviews* from which it sprang. We have no magazine comparable to the *World's Work*. Neither have we anything comparable to the *Youth's Companion, The Ladies' Home Journal,* or *Success.*"

published in Baltimore. For years it used against the Government and the democracy a personal bitterness so extreme that the building in which it was published was destroyed, together with the type and presses. Against all warnings, a plucky attempt was made by Editor Hanson to continue the publication. The author of "Home, Sweet Home" gave what proved to be most costly advice. A score of brave men promised to defend the new building from which the paper was to reappear. It was attacked with such fury that the public authorities were helpless. They got the men into jail to protect them, but this was attacked. Half the prisoners escaped, but nine were clubbed to death, after which their bodies were treated with insane brutality which only Indians on the war-path could have matched.

Our stomach is still strong for literary enormities in every variety, but the billingsgate and vituperation of a century ago we should not tolerate. It is only the "submerged tenth" of our press that equals it. It was not alone the famous Editor Duane of whom it was written : —

> "Law, order, talents, and civility,
>   Before your worshipful mobility,
>   Must bow, while you their thinking man,
>   Lead by the nose your kindred clan.
>   Thou art indeed a rogue as sly
>   As ever coined the ready lie
>   Amongst the Catilines of faction,
>   None calls more energies in action.

With impudence the most consummate,
You publish all that you can come at,
To make for discord's sake, a handle,
Of private anecdote, or scandal."

This editorial shyster is often singled out as an exception, but our ablest historian of that quarter of a century says he was but one among other "scurrilous libellers."

So too was

"William Coleman, who in 1801 became editor of the *New York Evening Post* under the eye of Alexander Hamilton; so was the refined Joseph Dennie, who in the same year established at Philadelphia the *Portfolio*, a weekly paper devoted to literature, in which for years to come he was to write literary essays, diversified by slander of Jefferson. Perhaps none of these habitual libellers deserved censure so much as Fisher Ames, the idol of respectability, who cheered on his party to vituperate his political opponents. He saw no harm in showing 'the knaves,' Jefferson and Gallatin, the cold-thinking villains who lead, 'whose black blood runs intemperately bad,' the motives of their own base hearts." [1]

But if democracy's chief educator — the Press — has improved; if the *totality* of press influence is now more effective for good; if the best of it is rousing the people first to a consciousness, and then to a new sensitiveness and shame about our national vices, can any comparable word of hope be spoken about our *Politics?* Very tardily we have learned that no answer can be given to this inquiry about

[1] Adams, Vol. I, p. 119.

politics unless we include in the question the chief
commercial activities, especially those that have a
monopoly character. Our more powerful business
interests give both shape and color to politics.
Politics does not improve unless business methods
also improve. Especially in a democracy, the
morals of business and of politics will rise or fall
together. If leading business enterprises are as
lax and reckless as they were after our Civil War,
nothing could prevent scandals as gross as those
in Grant's administration. Aaron Burr's sinister
political influence was neither greater nor less than
the corrupt business support that was behind him.
The politics of Pennsylvania and Rhode Island are
to-day largely what the chief local business methods
of monopoly character have made them. The task,
then, is no less formidable than this: to show that
standards have risen alike in business methods and
in political activity. The story of New York and
Chicago street railways, the story of St. Louis, Philadelphia, and San Francisco are fresh in our minds.
What at any time could have been worse than these
tabulated histories? The fleecing of the public in
these and a score of other industries is on a scale
so immense that the wiles of the older time seem in
comparison like the naughtiness of children. Yet
nothing stands out in our record with greater clear-
ness than the rise of business and political standards,
if the temper of the community is taken as a whole.
The only sure test of a rising standard must be in

the increased popular sensitiveness to social evils. If we are quicker to smart under them, if we are more ready and alert to oppose them, the spirit of improvement is astir among us. Whenever a community becomes conscious and sensitive about an evil, progress so far has begun. It may be cruelty to children or to animals. To get a new social feeling as to what this cruelty means; then to organize the feeling into a recognized standard, so that the cruelty may be penalized and put under ban, *is* progress.

This forward social movement may be seen in almost every phase of life noted by our critics. It is hard now to picture a community in the nineteenth century which tolerated a set of toughs who let their nails grow long in order to gouge out other men's eyes and to maim each other in ways still more hideous. Yet this was an amusement which never failed of an audience. As indications of callous inhumanity, those brutalities are little if any worse than the miscellaneous savagery against those who fell into debt, or than the prevailing treatment of the insane which few of us can now read without a physical shrinking. The prisons where these atrocities went on were openly accessible to public observation in the very pick of New England communities.

Here are examples vouched for by our historian McMaster:—

"The face of the land was dotted with prisons where deeds of cruelty were done in comparison with which the foulest acts committed in the hulks sink to a contemptible insignificance. For more than fifty years after the peace, there was in Connecticut an underground prison which surpassed in horrors the Black Hole of Calcutta. This den, known as the Newgate Prison, was in an old worked-out copper mine in the hills near Granby. The only entrance to it was by means of a ladder down a shaft which led to the caverns underground. There, in little pens of wood, from thirty to one hundred culprits were immured, their feet made fast to iron bars, and their necks chained to beams in the roof. The darkness was intense; the caves reeked with filth; vermin abounded; water trickled from the roof and oozed from the sides of the caverns; huge masses of earth were perpetually falling off. In the dampness and the filth the clothing of the prisoners grew mouldy and rotted away, and their limbs became stiff with rheumatism."

"At Northampton the cells were scarce four feet high, and filled with noxious gases of the privy vaults through which they were supposed to be ventilated. At the Worcester prison were a number of like cells, four feet high by eleven long, without a window or a chimney, or even a hole in the wall. Not a ray of light ever penetrated them."

"Modes of punishment long since driven from prisons with execrations as worthy of an African kraal were looked upon by society with a profound indifference. The treadmill was always going. The pillory and the stocks were never empty. The shears, the branding irons, and the lash were never idle for a day."

From a report of the committee of the Humane Society (New York, 1809) we get a glimpse of prisons that were in still more ghastly condition. In one, it was the occupation of a burly negro to strip and flog the inmates. The committee found those in chains who had been in these foul quarters so long that no one connected with the prison could throw the least light on the cause of imprisonment. One of these victims was found to be both insane and blind. He was in such tatters that the visitors, who called special attention to him, are told that it does no good to give him clothes because "*the rats will eat them off him.*"

That these abominations could exist; that they could be so widely known to the public, represents an indifference to suffering which we have put a good way behind us.

The atrocities committed against a large part of those who could not pay their debts may be seen in the fact that the Embargo of 1808 caused a business depression so sharp that thousands of hard-working and honest people could not meet their liabilities. They were not to blame for the panic, but in 1809 the prisons were choked with men and women who owed sums of less than ten dollars. For the very poorest of these there was in many instances actually no provision made by state or city even to feed them. There was no attempt made at ventilation, nor was there the slightest sanitary care. There seems never to have been room enough, so that damp cellars were usually crowded. Sickness and an appalling death-rate were, of course, inevitable.

In the United States of to-day those barbarities would excite a riot of moral revolt. We are still very dense in dealing with crime, but our advance in humaneness and in solicitude for suffering is so great that we seem to be in another world. But it is very evident that this improved feeling about *one* form of evil cannot long be confined to that alone. It will slowly assert itself in revolt against other forms of evil as their social harmfulness becomes clear.

This is what has happened also in the business and political world. We have at last begun to be sensitive about innumerable transactions that were accepted by our ancestors as they tolerated the atrocities of the prisons. When Marryat[1] reports the saucy unconcern with which an official tells him openly that his salary is so much and his "stealings" so much besides, it is not merely a facetious stroke, it represents a condition that we have outgrown to the extent that public opinion is now stung into criticism and into action.

The head of one of the best-known commission houses in New York City has in his library documents which record accurately the methods of his branch of business for two generations. He tells me that no one familiar with business can study that record without seeing that the "market tone"

[1] "I asked how much his office was worth, and his answer was six hundred dollars, besides *stealings*. This was, at all events, frank and honest; in England the word would have been softened down to perquisites. I afterwards found that it was a common expression in the States to say a place was worth so much besides *cheatage*." Marryat (I), p. 194.

has risen. It is not merely that a relatively larger and larger part of business is done on credit that *assumes* a prevailing trustworthiness in the trade, but he adds, "We are compelled to-day to be a great deal more solicitous about the entire moral side of our dealings."

As high a type of citizen and business man as New England has produced in our time — the late John M. Forbes — said openly that in his earlier business career "things were done by trustees that the public would not for an instant stand to-day, and they were done *without a thought of their being wrong.*"[1] As one moves from city to city toward the West, the same reply is almost invariably given. For a good many years I have sought evidence on this point. As older inhabitants will illustrate by their personal observation, the solid improvement in drinking habits; in social refinements; in more varied and wholesome pleasures; in all that touches public and private health; they will also tell you that the political and business trickeries, common in the older time, would to-day excite more instant criticism.

The sickening details of business and political corruption that followed our Civil War led the late Senator Hoar to examine the old records of our

[1] In speaking of the scandals after our Civil War, the historian Rhodes describes the popular feeling as severe against the bribe-taker but not against the bribe-giver. "In business ethic, the man who took a bribe was dishonorable, the man who gave it was not." Vol. VII, p. 11.

"idolized days" — the days of Washington, Adams, and Jefferson. The honest Massachusetts senator had been made half ill by the magnitude of revealed corruption during General Grant's administration (chiefly the whiskey frauds and those under Secretary Belknap). It was from this low ebb that he made his comparison. His judgment is unequivocally this, that the politics of those admired days were not only more corrupt than to-day, but more corrupt as compared to the worst of Grant's régime.[1]

In the chapter on "Our Greatest Critic" it was asked if there was anywhere in the pages of Mr. Bryce actual *evidence* for his sustained and buoyant spirit of hopefulness about this country. We may believe as a matter of faith, never so stoutly, that all is to come right, but Mr. Bryce's volumes scarcely contain the reasons for his optimism, apart from his faith and good-will. After he has disclosed some staggering political evil, we are often left speculating just why the flame of his good cheer loses neither light nor heat. It burns on undiminished, and we too feel that he is right. We too cling to our faith that all will turn out well with us and our institutions; but are there *proofs* that our movement and direction are right?

In the open record covered by our list of critics, there are substance and material in abundance to

---

[1] The reader who wishes to refresh his mind on the degree of corruption that came after our Civil War may find it in the calm, wise pages of Rhodes's " History of the United States," 7th volume.

answer the question. Bad as we now are and indefensible as our iniquities may be, our ancestors acted upon the whole with less political and business scruple than we now act. But a word of warning is necessary.

It would be most disreputable work to "show up" the infirmities of these ancestors, if it were to leave us with added self-complacency. Our sins are relatively and for our times as great as theirs, and we shall not wash them out except by suffering and by struggle. If this is our spirit, we do those ancestors no wrong in telling the truth of progress and of growth.

We have to go back hardly more than two generations before our first critic, to see many illustrious American families accepting undisturbed a goodly portion of their income from very murderous piracies on the high seas. They took the blood-money without a shiver. It was the wont and usage of the time. There was no conviction of sin about partnership in such robberies. This degree of callousness is left behind as we approach the nineteenth century. But in the year 1800, and long after it, there were business and political practices widely current that excited far less shame and protest than those practices now excite. This new sensitiveness, coupled with immense organized energies to curb the evils, is itself a definition of Progress. But are we making headway?

Let us look at the one state where we can best

z

see the interaction between politics and privileged
business early in the last century, the state of New
York. The work of transcribing events authenti-
cally from the journals of the Senate has been so far
done, that we know accurately what happened. It
was long thought that New York was the one unhappy exception. We now know that it stood fairly
for methods that were very general throughout the
country. In 1816 the aldermen were stealing the
city land by tricks inconceivable in that city to-day.
The great number of state licensed lotteries were
not alone a source of debauchery in themselves, they
had a political use which was even worse. The
history of favors secured by the Exchange Bank in
1818 was rank with venality. To buy legislative
aid with bank or insurance company stock was a
system. The frauds of the insurance companies
were far more openly gross than any we have known
in our day. From 1805 the relation of chartered
business to political scandals continued with regu-
larity and notoriety. In 1812 the Assembly compelled its members to pledge themselves not to sell
their votes, though this pledge was of short duration.
The story of the Brooklyn Ferry Monopoly, of the
Commercial Bank, of the Chemical Bank, of the
capitalization of the State Bank, and of the Man-
hattan Bank which the politicians controlled, are
one and all of the same character.[1] When the con-

---

[1] Let the reader turn to McMaster (Vol. VI, p. 405) and note
what banking methods were in use twenty-five years later.

test for full manhood suffrage came in 1820, the
richer class was shocked because "corruption would
come in *with the people*." It is true the people
were used to this end, but the essential evil in its
worse form was all there, and never more gluttonously
used than when the suffrage was confined to "the
safe property interests," to the genteel and the well-
nurtured. Why, then, should the blame have been
heaped alone upon the poor political goat, as if he
alone were the sinner? Why should the business
partner get off so easily? Not until within ten years
has this union between business and politics had a
popular and convincing explanation. We see at last
that if a great mining area like Montana develops
a fierce competitive and gambling spirit, the state
politics will merely reflect that spirit, and the richest
man who wants it will buy his place in the Senate.
If the chief industry is lumbering, and the competitive passion connives at the organized robbery of
public forests, the same type of man takes his seat
in that body. The cry was always heard, "Politics
must be reformed!" The cry should have been,
Those business methods which *create* politics must
be reformed! To have made this discovery; to
see what it means with the railroads, forests, grazing
lands, mines, and all forms of chartered privilege, is
more important than any mechanical discovery of
our age. To go straight on in the way we have at
last set out, to bring this whole group of privileges
under social control; to stop once for all private

persons from using these immense values as mere
dice in their game; to stop the interception of unearned wealth that has made our craziest inequalities,
is the kind of progress that puts\ justice and fair
dealing into our business and *therefore* into our
politics.[1] The whole renaissance of ardor and
interest in civic decency that is now alive in the
nation; that pulses in the best of our press; that
gives us a score of books each year and has created
hundreds of active organizations in the country,
is largely due to the new confidence that we see
what the evil is and how to measure our strength
against it.

Again and again, our best critics have noted a
sinister "fatalism" in our attitude toward these
evils. "You cannot get your American to kick
unless he is threatened by some dramatic disaster"
is said of us for a hundred years. The kicking has
set in, and the altered experience through which the
talent has developed is full of hope. Nearly three
generations ago Abdy was in despair about slavery
because "the people I meet will not admit it to be
evil." The second phase of this despair was that
"even if it is an evil, nothing can be done about it."
We have passed through both those phases as they
concern a great many social perils.

[1] We shall sometime wake out of our drugged condition to see
that the excesses of our tariff (as in Pennsylvania) have sunk
the political tone and method to depths from which it will require
the moral valor of a generation to lift and free us.

In 1830 a writer records this about tuberculosis:
"What they call 'consumption' kills the Americans
as if they were perpetually in battle; but they speak
of it as if it were in no way their concern, rather as
if God sent it for some reason of His own." We
are now assured that "simply to use the knowledge"
at our disposal is to check tuberculosis as effectively
as has been done in the case of smallpox.

But this new consciousness of power over evils
that had been accepted as fatal is no longer confined
to diseases of the body. We are learning that political and industrial diseases are no more a necessity
than yellow fever. A new shame has come to Americans throughout the land because they were so long
and so cheaply fooled by common rogues in the shape
of party bosses created and backed by privileged
interests. East and West so many of these creatures
have been put to rout and the tawdry tricks exposed,
that the question rises why we were so long lulled
into this fool's submission. It was largely because
we did not see straight. It was largely because the
deeper causes of bad politics were hidden from us.
To leave privileged monopoly in private hands, with
only a pretence of regulation, is an open and direct
premium upon organized bribe-giving and bribe-
taking. Every special vice was protected and en-
couraged by the methods of secrecy which these
favored monopolies were permitted to use. The
public gave outright every chartered condition on
which monopoly rests. These indispensable grants

gave rights to state and city which we forgot,
until the abuses became so topping and outrageous
that the close of the nineteenth century saw the beginning of a revolt which another generation will
count quite as revolutionary as the uprising against
slavery after 1830. If less desperate, the struggle
before us will be as long as that against the other
slavery. It will weigh men in the balance, even as
it did then. It will call forth noble heroism and,
alas! also the cringing cowardice which selfish
idolatries always engender. None of us will escape
the test. The Church, the College, the Press, will
no more avoid it than the politician or the man in
the street.

It is progress to be awakened to the facts. To
have begun the struggle is further progress. The
one hope of it all is to realize that the main work
has yet to be done. It lies there before us solely
as opportunity—opportunity for large and disinterested citizenship.

Not a tittle more democracy can be ours than that
which is measured by our freedom from the worst
of our business monopolies which we created by our
common negligence and our common ignorance, and
have so long permitted as to leave very few of us
without consenting guilt. As the mass and extent
of this lawlessness has been laid bare, so that the
people could see how deep and dangerous a pit we
have been digging for popular government, the
revolt has come. It has for the first time in our

history shown vigor enough to frighten the law-breakers. They are now crying for relief. In the words of another classic law-breaker, —

"I'm a quiet Old Cove," says he with a groan:
"All I axes is — Let me alone."

But why "let alone"?   "Because," says the Cove, "money incomes will be endangered. We have been corrupting and breaking the laws of the people. That is true of us; but to make us obey those laws will injure business and it will, moreover, hurt a great many innocent people."

This in its nakedness is the answer. The shabby excuse appears unashamed in scores of our papers. Yet, there is nothing less than the Nation's honor and health at stake. Will the people continue to tolerate the corruption and the lawlessness for the sake of these stock-exchange estimates? For the entire people and for a larger future even this cash-box reckoning is false. It is true, if at all, only for the few and for the immediate present. Political and business honesty must surely be best in the long run for the great body of our people. We shall go on struggling and caring for the money income, but we must learn also to care greatly and with some passion for business straightness and political cleanness. This nobler solicitude will prove the one unavoidable test of our democracy. We have begun now to compel our money kings to play a fair game and obey the law. This is well and necessary, because

many of them have so *conspicuously* disobeyed.
They have caused more havoc than lesser folk.
They have rifled the people's wealth. But most of
them have also organized, built up, and immensely
developed our national resources. This shall go
down to their credit. There is no unpleasanter
fact about "us common people" than the desire,
old as it is new, to have a scapegoat upon which
to pack our own sins. We are now forcing "the
rich" into this service. They must be made to
act legally; but so must all of us be made to act
legally.

To get this sense of law-abidingness into our minds
as a people is the duty above all others now before
us. To look the dishonors straight in the face; to
flay bribe-sanctioning at the top, as we flay bribe-
taking at the bottom; to see that the corrupting of
a legislature is a darker and a meaner sin than the
slugging of a scab; to ask for "law and order"
among the mighty as we ask it among the obscure;
to set ourselves grimly and a little sadly — as if
with a sense of common frailty — to the great task
of national house cleaning, is the solemn beginning
to which we are committed in these early days of
the twentieth century.

It will not pass as a spasm of moral irritation
because a deep and sustaining popular sentiment
has at last been aroused and instructed. Men with
stout hearts willing to fight on the outer lines may
now count on this support. It is a sentiment that

cannot lessen because the causes out of which it sprang are multiplying in the community. Where the people have suffered most, there the flame of the new feeling is at its height. From Oregon to Los Angeles the uprising is most clearly felt.

It was on that fateful Pacific coast that the people came first to see the farce of "representative government." Monopoly-made politics had there a stalking effrontery which was all the swifter to carry its convincing lessons to the people.

The ringing cry for direct primary, referendum, initiative, recall, and popular election of senators which fills that freer air is the challenge to monopoly privilege. It is the cry for that measure of economic and political equality which has long been our theory, but never our practice. It is the cry that democratic government shall now *begin* in the United States.

This hardier spirit is everywhere alive in the great West. It is alive in the East, but the sanctities of precedent and privilege lie heavier upon the older section. Yet the new moral reckoning is of no section; neither is it of any party, sect, or nationality.

In the long list of the century's critics there is scarcely a volume which does not directly or indirectly, willingly or unwillingly, bear witness to this slow rise in social sensitiveness, and in social purpose to free ourselves from industrial and political tyrannies. Twenty years ago, one of these censors used words with which I gladly close this study.

Though they apply quite as fitly to other nations, we can well afford to take the hint they offer.

"If the American should once become possessed of a little genuine humility, a humility without loss of courage or self-respect; if he lost a little hardness in his self-confidence and became more teachable, his mastery in the art of self-government would easily lead the world."

BIBLIOGRAPHY

BIBLIOGRAPHY

Abdy, E. S. Journal in the United States, 3 vols. London. 1835.

Arfwedson, C. D., Esq. The United States and Canada in 1832-3-4, 2 vols. London. 1834.

Arnold, Matthew. Civilization in the United States. Boston. 1888.

Archer, William. America To-day. New York, Scribners. 1899.

Ashe, Thomas. Travels in America. London. 1808.

Bradbury, John. Travels in 1809-10-11. Liverpool. 1817.

Bremer, Frederika. The Homes of the New World. New York. 1853.

Brothers, Thomas. The United States (A Cure for Radicalism). London. 1840.

Brown, William. America. Leeds, England. 1849.

Bryce, James. The American Commonwealth, 2 vols. Macmillan. 1888. (Later Edition.)

Buckingham, J. S. America (Eastern and Western States), 3 vols. London. 1842.

Burne-Jones, Sir Philip. Dollars and Democracy. Appleton. New York. 1904.

Butler, Mrs. Journal, 2 vols. Philadelphia. 1835. Plantation Journal. 1838-9. Harper. New York. 1836.

Cobbett, Wm. A Year's Residence in the United States, 3 Parts. New York. 1819.

Collyer, R. H., M.D. Lights and Shadows of American Life. 1836.

Combe, George. Notes on the United States, 2 vols. Philadelphia. 1841.

Cooper, J. F.   Notions of the Americans, 2 vols.   Philadelphia. 1832.

Dickens, Charles.   American Notes.

Duhring, Henry.   Remarks on the United States of America. London. 1833.

Duncan, John M., A.B.   Travels in 1818–19, 2 vols. Glasgow. 1823.

Faithful, Emily.   Three Visits to the United States.   Edinburgh. 1884.

Faux, W.   Memorable Days in America. London. 1823.

Fearon, H. B.   Sketches of America. London. 1818.

Fiddler, Rev. Isaac.   Observations, etc.   New York. 1833.

Freeman, E. A.   Some Impressions of the United States. London. 1883.

Godley, J. R.   Letters from America, 2 vols. London. 1844.

Griffin, Sir Lepel.   The Great Republic. London. 1884.

Grund, F. J.   The Americans. Boston. 1837.

Hall, Capt. Basil.   Travels in North America in 1827–8, 2 vols. Edinburgh. 1829.

Hamilton, Thomas.   Men and Manners in America, 2 vols. Philadelphia. 1833.

Hodgson, Adam.   Letters from North America, 2 vols. London. 1824.

Hole, Dean.   A Little Tour in America. London. 1895.

Kipling, Rudyard.   American Notes. Boston. 1899.

Lyell, Sir Charles.   Travels, 2 vols. London. 1845. Second Visit, 2 vols. London. 1849.

Mackay, Alex.   The Western World, 2 vols. Philadelphia. 1849.

Marryat, Capt.   Diary in America; also Part Second, 3 vols. London. 1839.

Martineau, Harriet.   Society in America, 3 vols. London. 1837.

Muirhead, J. F.   The Land of Contrasts. Boston. 1898.

Murray, Hon. C. A. Travels in North America. New York. 1839.

Playfair Papers, 3 vols. London. 1841.

, Power, Tyrone. Impressions of America, 2 vols. Philadelphia. 1836.

Priest, William. Travels, etc. London. 1802.

Shirreff, Patrick, Farmer. A Tour Through North America. Edinburgh. 1835.

Stead, W. T. The Americanization of the World. New York. 1902.

Sterling, James. Letters from the Slave States. London. 1857.

Steevens, G. W. The Land of the Dollar. New York. 1897.

Stuart, James. Three Years in North America, 2 vols. Edinburgh. 1833.

Sutcliff, Robert. Travels. York (Eng.). 1815.

Trollope, Anthony. North America. New York. 1862.

Trollope, Mrs. Domestic Manners of the Americans, 2 vols. London. 1832.

(See criticisms of this author in *American Quarterly*, September, 1832, and in *North American Review*, January, 1833.)

Vigne, G. T. Six Months in America. Philadelphia. 1833.

Weld, Isaac. Travels, etc., 2 vols. London. 1807.

Wells, H. G. The Future in America. Harpers. 1906.

Wortley, Lady. Travels in the United States. New York. 1851.

French Criticisms

Adam, Paul. Vues d'Amérique. Paris. 1906.

Ampère, J. J. Promenade in Amérique. Paris. 1855.

D'Almbert, Alfred. Flânerie Parisienne aux États Unis. Paris. 1856.

Bourget, Paul.   Outre-Mer, 2 vols.   Paris.   1895 (translated).

Brissot, J. P.   Nouveau Voyage dans les États Unis, 3 vols. Paris.   1791.

Chauteaubriand.   Travels in America and Italy, 2 vols. London.   1828.

Chevalier, Michael.   Society, Manners, and Politics in the United States.   Boston.   1837.

Crèvecœur, St. John.   Voyage, etc., 3 vols.   Paris.   1801.

De Bacourt.   Souvenirs d'un Diplomate.   Paris.   1882.

Dugard, Marie.   La Société Américaine.   Paris.   1896.

Gobat.   Croquis et Impressions d'Amérique.

Gohier, Urbain.   Le Peuple du XX Siècle.   Paris.   1896.

Huret, Jules.   En Amérique.   Paris.   1904.

—— De New York à la Nouvelle Orléans.   1905.

Klein, Abbé.   Au Pays de la Vie Intense (translated).   Paris. 1905.

Laboulaye, M.   Paris en Amérique.   Paris.   1870.

La Rochefoucauld-Liancourt.   Voyage dans Les États Unis. Paris.   1795-6-7.

Le Roux, H.   Business and Love.   Dodd Mead, New York. 1903.

Löwenstern, Isidore.   Le Éstats Unis et la Havane.   Paris. 1842.

Moreau, G.   L'Envers des États Unis.   Paris.   1903.

Murat, le Prince.   Letters sur Les États Unis.   Paris. 1830.   (Translation, New York, 1849.)

Nevers, Edmond de.   L'Âme Américaine.   Paris.   1900.

O'Rell, Max.   Jonathan and his Continent.   New York. Cassell.   1889.

Regnier.   Au Pays de l'Avenir.   1906.

Rousier, Paul de.   La Vie Américaine, 2 vols.   Paris.   1899 (translated).

Soissons, de S. C.   A Parisian in America.   Boston.   1896.

De Tocqueville.   Democracy in America, 2 vols.   (Bowen's translation.)   Cambridge, Mass.   1862.

Varigny, G. de. Six Months in America. 1833.

Wagner, Charles. My Impressions of America. McClure, Phillips & Co. New York. 1905.

German Criticisms

Altherr. Eine Amerikafahrt in Zwanzig Briefen. 1905.

Baumgartner, Professor A. Erinnerungen aus America. Zurich. 1906.

Boecklin, August. Wanderleben. Leipzig. 1902.

Bodenstadt, F. Vom Atlantischen zum Stillen Ocean. Leipzig. 1882.

Fulda, Ludwig. Amerikanische Eindrücke. Cotta. 1906.

Herter, A. Die Wahrheit über Amerika. Bern. 1886.

Hintrager, Dr. Wie lebt und arbeitet Man in den Vereinigten Staaten. Brentano. 1904.

Julius, Dr. N. H. Nordamerikas sittliche Zustände. Leipzig. 1839.

Knortz, Karl. Aus der Transatlantischen Gesellschaft. Leipzig. 1887.

Lamprecht, Professor Karl. Americana. Freiburg. 1906.

Münsterberg, Professor Hugo. American Traits. Houghton Mifflin. 1903.

Münsterberg, Professor Hugo. The Americans. McClure & Phillips. 1904.

Neve, I. L. Charakterzüge des Amerikanischen Volkes. Leipzig. 1903.

Ratzel, F. Die Vereinigten Staaten von Amerika, 2 vols. 1878.

Sievers, Wilhelm. Amerika. Leipzig. 1894.

Von Polenz, W. Das Land der Zukunft. Brentano. New York.

Von Raumer, Baron. America and the American People. New York. 1846. (Professor of History, Berlin.)

Zimmermann, Karl. Onkel Sam. Stuttgart. 1904.

2 λ

INDEX

The Social Unrest

STUDIES IN LABOR AND SOCIALIST MOVEMENTS

By JOHN GRAHAM BROOKS

Cloth   12mo   394 pages $1.50 net

"Mr. Brooks has given the name of 'Social Unrest' to his profound study, primarily of American conditions, but incidentally of conditions in all the civilized countries. The book is not easy reading, but it would be difficult to find a volume which would better repay thorough digestion than this. It expresses with absolute justice, I think, the conflicting interests. It shows the fallacies of many socialistic ideals. It admits the errors of the unions. It understands the prejudices of the rich and the nature of their fear when present arrangements are threatened. And the sole purpose of the author is to state the truth, without preference, without passion, as it appears to one who has seen much and who cares how his fellow-man enjoys and suffers.

"Mr. Brooks does not guess. He has been in the mines, in the factories, knowing the laborers, knowing the employers, through twenty years of investigation." — *Collier's Weekly.*

"The author, Mr. John Graham Brooks, takes up and discusses through nearly four hundred pages the economic significance of the social questions of the hour, the master passions at work among us, men *versus* machinery, and the solution of our present ills in a better concurrence than at present exists — an organization whereby every advantage of cheaper service and cheaper product shall go direct to the whole body of the people. . . . Nothing upon his subject so comprehensive and at the same time popular in treatment as this book has been issued in our country. It is a volume with live knowledge — not only for workman but for capitalist, and the student of the body politic — for every one who lives — and who does not ? — upon the product of labor." — *The Outlook.*

Mr. Bliss Perry, the editor of *The Atlantic Monthly,* says of it: "A fascinating book — to me the clearest, sanest, most helpful discussion of economic and human problems I have read for years."

Mr. Edward Cary, in *The New York Times' Saturday Review,* writes: "Hardly a page but bears evidence of his patience, industry, acuteness, and fair-mindedness. . . . We wish it were possible that his book could be very generally read on both sides. Its manifest fairness and sympathy as regards the workingmen will tend to the accomplishment of this result; its equal candor and intelligence with regard to the employers should have a like effect with them."

"The work is one of fine spirit, fully optimistic, and eminently sane. It does not deal with exploded theories where facts are at hand to give them the lie, contrary to the practice of the doctrinaire the world over. On the contrary, it is practically the first modern book to prove that all theories, whether of the individualist or the socialist, are powerless before the fact. Leaning rather to the point of view, so characteristically American, of the believer in no more government than is needful to secure individual freedom, it strongly advocates trades unionism as a bulwark against the legislative interference with natural laws which is being invoked with even more frequency by the employing class than by the laborer. It points out with a cogency startling at times the supreme fact that it is only when the laborer is denied the rights he is able to secure by organization that he turns to politics for a remedy." — *Independent.*

PUBLISHED BY

THE MACMILLAN COMPANY

64-66 FIFTH AVENUE, NEW YORK

Also by E. V. LUCAS

A Wanderer
in London

With sixteen illustrations in color by Mr. Nelson Dawson, and thirty-six reproductions of great pictures.

Cloth, 8vo, $1.75 net; by mail, $1.87

" Mr. Lucas describes London in a style that is always entertaining, surprisingly like Andrew Lang's, full of unexpected suggestions and points of view, so that one who knows London well will hereafter look on it with changed eyes, and one who has only a bowing acquaintance will feel that he has suddenly become intimate." — *The Nation.*

" Full of interest and sensitive appreciation of the most fascinating city in the world." — *Bulletin*, San Francisco.

" A suggestive, perhaps an inspiring record of rambles . . . a book as handsome in dress as it is entertaining and valuable." — *Argonaut.*

" One can hardly hope to find a better way of reviving impressions and seeing things in a new setting than through this cheerful and friendly volume." — *Outlook.*

" If you would know London as few of her own inhabitants know her — if you would read one of the best books of the current season, all that is necessary is a copy of *A Wanderer in London.*" — *Evening Post*, Chicago.

" In short, to read *A Wanderer in London* is like taking long tramps through all parts of the city with a companion who knows all the interesting things and places and people and has something wise or gay or genial to say about all of them."—*New York Times' Saturday Review.*

" Mr. Lucas is a competent and discriminating guide ; his interests are many-sided. He is connoiseur and raconteur as well as observer and chronicler ; and he knows and jots down just the sort of thing one would like to know about a house, or a park, or an institution, whether the association be personal or historical or critical." — *Herald.*

Races and Immigrants in America

By JOHN R. COMMONS

———

Cloth, 12mo, $1.25 net

———

Books upon the problems of immigration which have recently appeared have been of two kinds: one descriptive and narrative, graphic sketches of travel abroad in the sources of the flood, or scenic portraiture of the types coming to us; the other, books of statistics, data from the census and discussion of the political phases of the movement. What characterizes Mr. John R. Commons' *Races and Immigrants in America* is that while he keeps certain elements of the other types, he is chiefly interested in his problem as a student of sociology. He discusses Race philosophically. He analyzes democracy as a force bearing upon the social assimilation involved. He is not interested so much in the mere data of immigration in industry as he is in discovering what function industry forms in inducing immigration in the first place and moulding it later on. The same may be said about his careful discussion of the relation of immigration to crime and pauperism and politics. Just as Professor Steiner depicts the different races to us, so Professor Commons analyzes their traits and contributions to the body politic. The book is therefore not so much original in its data, as in the interpretation of the data. It is valuable largely because it is the last book, using a wide range of readings in other drier or more picturesque literature, and giving us, in addition to facts, his judgment as to their interpretation. Only a trained and versatile scholar could have given us what is, upon the whole, the most valuable and compendious book on this subject, up to date. The bibliography furnished is of especial value to the scholar.

———

PUBLISHED BY

THE MACMILLAN COMPANY

64-66 FIFTH AVENUE, NEW YORK

M

M